T0143595

Dashboard Design

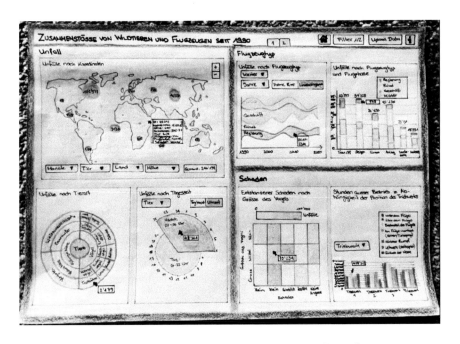

Michael Burch and Marco Schmid

RIVER PUBLISHERS SERIES IN COMPUTING AND INFORMATION SCIENCE AND TECHNOLOGY

Series Editors:

K.C. CHEN
National Taiwan University, Taipei, Taiwan
University of South Florida, USA

SANDEEP SHUKLA
Virginia Tech, USA
Indian Institute of Technology Kanpur, India

The "River Publishers Series in Computing and Information Science and Technology" covers research which ushers the 21st Century into an Internet and multimedia era. Networking suggests transportation of such multimedia contents among nodes in communication and/or computer networks, to facilitate the ultimate Internet.

Theory, technologies, protocols and standards, applications/services, practice and implementation of wired/wireless networking are all within the scope of this series. Based on network and communication science, we further extend the scope for 21st Century life through the knowledge in machine learning, embedded systems, cognitive science, pattern recognition, quantum/biological/molecular computation and information processing, user behaviors and interface, and applications across healthcare and society.

Books published in the series include research monographs, edited volumes, handbooks and textbooks. The books provide professionals, researchers, educators, and advanced students in the field with an invaluable insight into the latest research and developments.

Topics included in the series are as follows:-

- Artificial intelligence
- Cognitive Science and Brian Science
- Communication/Computer Networking Technologies and Applications
- Computation and Information Processing
- Computer Architectures
- Computer networks
- Computer Science
- Embedded Systems
- Evolutionary computation
- Information Modelling
- Information Theory
- Machine Intelligence
- Neural computing and machine learning
- Parallel and Distributed Systems
- Programming Languages
- Reconfigurable Computing
- Research Informatics
- Soft computing techniques
- Software Development
- Software Engineering
- Software Maintenance

For a list of other books in this series, visit www.riverpublishers.com

Dashboard Design

Michael Burch

Marco Schmid

Routledge
Taylor & Francis Group
NEW YORK AND LONDON

Published 2023 by River Publishers
River Publishers
Alsbjergvej 10, 9260 Gistrup, Denmark
www.riverpublishers.com

Distributed exclusively by Routledge
605 Third Avenue, New York, NY 10017, USA
4 Park Square, Milton Park, Abingdon, Oxon OX14 4RN

Dashboard Design/ADS Software / by Michael Burch, Marco Schmid.

Routledge is an imprint of the Taylor & Francis Group, an informa business

ISBN 978-87-7004-004-4 (hardback)
ISBN 978-87-7004-066-2 (paperback)
ISBN 978-10-0382-395-7 (online)
ISBN 978-10-3265-730-1 (master ebook)

While every effort is made to provide dependable information, the publisher, authors, and editors cannot be held responsible for any errors or omissions.

Contents

Preface

Teaching students in the field of visualization comes with a list of challenging tasks since most of them have neither an experience in computer and data science, data structures and algorithms, programming and web development, nor in visual and interface design, as well as many related disciplines such as user experience and usability, perception and cognition, or evaluation with and without eye tracking. However, all of those fields are required to design and implement a real-world visualization tool, maybe in the form of a dashboard, with the goal to support users with their tasks at hand. Leaving away one of the fields during education creates a gap in the entire data-to-visualization mapping process that it becomes hard to understand the field of visualization in its entirety. Consequently, it is important to work through all of those involved fields in a course, at least a bit of everything at the desire of and tailored to each student, to bring the students to an experience level from which they can understand the connections in the field of visualization. The biggest challenge in a visualization course is to take into account the students' different basic skills and experience levels to make the course interesting, motivating, and successful for everybody participating in it.

This book makes an attempt to bring together the many related fields in visualization, providing many examples that were taught over the years while giving courses in visualization, visual analytics, graphical user interface and dashboard design, user evaluation and eye tracking, or programming languages as well as web development. Visualization is that powerful so students can get inspired by many application scenarios that it can focus on, being it in fields like social networking, sports, software engineering, gaming, eye tracking, medicine, nature, or just looking at data from statistics or data science, to mention a few. Visual output can be interpreted, discussed, improved, disseminated, communicated to, or shared with others, and builds the basis for many further discussions among the students which provides a good way to give feedback, always targeting the goal of educating them and to make them learn about this interesting but challenging field. Visualization is some kind of practical discipline that allows to apply the theoretic concepts learned during the course, in order to solve a given realistic data science problem. Such problems can be manifold, stemming from various application domains, oftentimes with a link to a real-world data problem that students are aware of or even more actively involved in, for example, in the context of a company or industrial partner for which the students currently work or for which they have worked a while ago. Such a link can build a bridge between a theoretical course in visualization and a more realistic real-world data example, creating some kind of synergy effect.

The book is organized in a way to explain aspects from all of the involved fields, in a structured way, while at the same time giving plenty of real-world visual examples as well as runnable code snippets among discussions. Moreover, each section is concluded with exercises worth solving and thinking about, in order to learn the rules of designing and implementing dashboards for interactive data visualizations. As a benefit we also provide one possible solution, among many imaginable ones, to support the learning effect. We primarily focus on interactive dashboards, although many other solutions for a visualization problem exist and might solve the problem in a more efficient way. On the other hand, dashboards are easy to understand and to teach and quickly lead to a desired visualization tool solution equipped with various interaction techniques. This is also due to the limited amount of time planned for typical courses on visualization in universities that build a time frame in which a maximum must be learned with a minimum of effort. In many of the courses, it was an amazing experience to see the students' tool running in the end, either locally on our own computers or via a URL on the web, making it accessible for everybody who has an internet connection. This milestone was also reached for the weaker, less-experienced ones, even when they started with nearly no background knowledge about one or all of the involved fields in the beginning, again showing us that the content was successfully explained.

The remainder of the book is as follows: Chapter 1 starts with introducing the general problem and tries to show the bridges between all of the related fields. Chapter 2 makes an attempt to describe the data-to-visualization mapping with respect to dashboards, while also perceptual and cognitive issues related to visual and interface design are taken into account. In Chapter 3, we are going to explain the major programming ingredients to create dashboards for interactive visualization, while Chapter 4 builds the basis from an implementation perspective focusing on the programming language Python. Applications are provided in Chapter 5 coming with code examples as well as their visual outputs in the form of dashboards. The book is completed with many discussions on scalability issues and limitations which can be found in Chapter 6, before concluding the book in Chapter 7. A general remark on the book's reading strategy is that it can be studied in its entirety, starting from the beginning, page by page, or each chapter can be read individually since it builds its own learning unit. This means that an experienced reader in programming might skip the chapter on programming and might focus on chapters including visualization, interaction, or design aspects.

List of Figures

List of Tables

xxi

List of Abbreviations/Acronyms

1D	one-dimensional
2D	two-dimensional
3D	three-dimensional
AOI	area of interest
ASCII	American standard code for information interchange
AWT	abstract window toolkit
C	programming language
C++	programming language
CSS	cascading style sheets
CSV	comma-separated values
D3	graph gallery
DNA	deoxyribonucleic acid
EEG	electroencephalography
GUI	graphical user interface
HTML	hypertext markup language
IDE	integrated development environment
NCBI	National Center for Biotechnology Information
NP	nondeterministic polynomial time
PCP	parallel coordinates plot
PX	pixels
R	programming language
SPLOM	scatter plot matrix
UI	user interface
URL	uniform resource locator
XAI	explainable artificial intelligence

1

Introduction

Making data available in a visual form is of great interest in these days since the visual output generates a method to find patterns, correlations, and anomalies in a dataset [178]. The main benefit of visualization comes from the perceptual strengths of the visual observers [115, 245, 246], allowing to rapidly detect hidden data patterns that help to find hints or solutions to the data analysts' tasks at hand. Although there are various visualization techniques, diagrams, charts, and plots available today, and many more will be developed in the future, it has become a tedious task from a design and implementation perspective to put all of the needed ingredients together in order to create a runnable, user-friendly, efficient and effective, aesthetic, and responsive solution for a specific data science task at hand, which is the general goal to find insights and knowledge in data. However, data comes in a variety of forms, consisting of individual and primitive or combined and complex data types, stored in different data formats, on local files or databases, accessible via a URL from the web, being static, dynamic, or even evolving in real-time at frequent update rates. All of these data issues already span a rich space of possible solutions, but the human users are finally the deciding factor in figuring out if the implemented data visualization solutions meet their needs and help them to solve their tasks at hand.

In this book, we are going to describe this interesting topic with various Python code [149] examples. We briefly introduce the visualization pipeline [177] combined with interaction techniques [258] before we step into the ingredients required to develop dashboards [13]. For the unfamiliar ones, we are going to introduce the programming language Python with the major concepts to build running programs with already quite a lot of functionality. The Python code is needed to allow some kind of variability in a dashboard, starting from data reading, parsing, and transformations, finally, leading to preprocessed data that builds the core ingredient for interactive and scalable visualizations placed in a user interface, in our case, coming in the form of a dashboard. Application examples round up the book by showcasing larger running examples that can be tried out by the readers, even be manipulated or modified to get the code running for one's own application examples. Finally, the experiences of the human observers play a crucial role in the entire development process. Since we do not know such prior knowledge of our readers, we try to describe all of the required concepts from the perspective of nonexperts in computer science, data science, programming, visualization, and user evaluation.

1.1 A Visualization Pipeline

The general idea behind data visualization is a mapping that describes how data is transformed from original data sources into something visual, something with which users can interact, following the common goal of detecting insights and knowledge in a known or unknown dataset. This whole process can be illustrated in a visualization pipeline [177] (see Figure 1.1) starting with raw data, bringing it into a preprocessed form, transforming it into structured information while finally, presenting those structures in a visual depiction in one or several types of diagrams, charts, plots, or visualizations, each depicting a certain kind of data feature, hence providing a visual perspective on the data under exploration. Human users are, thanks to the invention of the computer, in the great role of interacting with all of the views, adapting and modifying them, changing parameters, asking for new layouts, and all of this in a fast response time to make the visual exploration a user-friendly experience. The ultimate goal, however, is to get some user feedback to detect design flaws and, based on that, improve the visual as well as the interface, that is, dashboard and design.

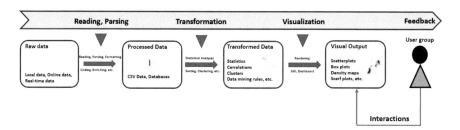

Figure 1.1   A visualization pipeline: Starting with raw data, processing it, transforming it, building visual structures, and finally visualizing it in a dashboard.

The data-to-visualization mapping is a complex one, consisting of a multi-stage model with crucial stages and transformations (see Figure 1.1). All of the involved stages will be described in the book, also taking into account aspects like visual perception [115] and cognition, to create powerful visual depictions of data that are not cluttered [202], that do not lie, and that are free of chart junk [232]. Moreover, we also take into account design principles for the visual depictions but also for the visual interface and take a critical look at visual variables [180] that occur in a variety of forms:

- Stages:
  - Raw data: This brings the questions into play how the data is structured, how large it is, if it consists of several data sources, or if it contains missing or error-prone values. Moreover, the data might be stored locally on a computer or might be accessible via a URL from the web. The data could even be static data or dynamic, in the most complicated way existing in a real-time form.
  - Processed data: In many cases, we can find the raw data in a strange format or even consisting of several unlinked data sources for which a common key exists to link them into one dataset. One good idea would be to put all of the data under exploration into a common data file (maybe in a comma-separated values (csv) format) or to put it into a database. The general idea behind this stage is to make the data available for a data analysis or visualization tool in one data source and avoid looking it up at several locations which might cause challenging issues due to bad performance during runtime.
  - Transformed data: To really get more structured information from the preprocessed data, we need some user-defined algorithmic approaches that put the data into statistical outputs, correlations, clusters, or even results that are based on data mining extracting association or sequence rules, just to mention a few of the transformations.
  - Visual output: Finding insights in any kind of data, either in a raw, processed, or transformed form, might be supported by visualizations that make use of the humans' abilities to rapidly detect patterns due to their perceptual strengths [115]. Various visualization techniques exist, each focusing on certain data types and users' tasks at hand [245, 246].

- Manipulations:
  - Reading/parsing: Some steps have to be taken into account to bring the raw data into a processed data form, for example, during the reading and parsing process, the data can already be partially cleaned or annotated with extra information. However, most of the advanced enrichments can only be done after a more thorough data transformation process.
  - Transformation: The processed and partially cleaned data can further be analyzed for common patterns, correlations, outliers and anomalies, as well as certain sequential behavior in case the data has a sequential or time-dynamic property.
  - Visualization: The visual depiction of the data is of importance, however, the rendering process has various options to use visual variables, to use different display technologies, as well as interface styles and designs, which is particularly important for dashboards.
- Users-in-the-Loop:
  - Feedback: The user group is able to interact with all of the aforementioned stages (however, in Figure 1.1, we only show the interaction with the last stage). While interacting and trying to visually explore a dataset, users typically form some kind of confidence level that describes how well the interactive visualization supports them in solving tasks at hand. This is typically evaluated in a complex user study, giving concrete tasks based on formerly stated hypotheses, by measuring dependent variables like error rates and completion times. Modern evaluations even incorporate eye tracking and further physiological measures to get even more hints about visual attention behavior, visual task solution strategies [46], or body-related issues such as blood pressure, EEG, or stress levels. However, the analysis of such data is typically very challenging and demands for further advanced visual analytics systems, meaning statistical evaluation alone is not enough to find insights.

Furthermore, if users interact with the visualizations, those get transformed as well into different perspectives, layouts, filtered views, and so on. Hence, those operations are another kind of modification, but typically work on the visual level, not on the data level. However, mostly the interactions require further algorithms to be applied which are running in the background and which might cause longer waiting times depending on the algorithms' performances and/or the dataset sizes in use.

Exercises

- Exercise 1.1.1: Imagine you have found a certain dataset on the web and are interested in the patterns, correlations, and anomalies hidden in it. Describe the ingredients you need to solve this problem by taking into account the stages of the visualization pipeline illustrated in Figure 1.1.
- Exercise 1.1.2: How can the users be integrated into the design and implementation process of a visualization tool or dashboard? What are typical challenges when asking real users to apply a visualization tool to a given dataset?

1.2 Human Users and Tasks

Visualization is not good per se, the human users with their perceptual abilities [245] decide if a certain task or task group can be solved reliably, or if at least some hints about the data patterns to be searched for can be provided by an interactive visualization tool. However, not every user behaves in the same way. All of them have varying properties, are members of different property groups like layman versus domain expert, young versus old, nonexperienced versus experienced, disabled vs. non-disabled, and many more. It is very important during the design process of a visualization tool or a dashboard in general to take into account those user properties, otherwise, we might run into problems that are hard to fix later on, once the tool is designed and implemented. The design process is typically guided by formerly built hypotheses or research questions about a given dataset. The goal of the visualization tool is to provide answers to the hypotheses and research questions, either trying to confirm or reject them, in many cases, refining them or leading to new hypotheses and research questions. However, all of them require tasks to be solved, either completely or at least partially.

The biggest issue here is that real users can be included in the design process right from the beginning, in subsequent development stages, however, such a strategy is time-consuming and expensive. But the human users with their research questions are required to make a tool powerful and applicable to real-world problems. In many visualization designs, we can find the users' feedback in the end, that is, after the implementation phase has ended, but at the cost of getting a lot of feedback worth incorporating. The value of the feedback also strongly depends on the users' experience levels with both, visualization as a research discipline as well as the application domain where the data stems from. For example, building an interactive dashboard for visual analytics in medicine demands a user who is able to read and interpret visualizations and diagrams while at the same time having some profound knowledge in medicine. Such a combination of expertise makes the development of a visualization tool quite challenging, time-consuming, and cost-intensive [33].

The value and effectiveness of visualizations [95, 237] are also dependent on the tasks that have to be solved by using them. Each visualization technique typically only follows a certain number of specific tasks for which it is designed and for which the human users perform best. There is an endless list of typical data exploration tasks that can be supported by visualization techniques, however, some of the tasks might be solved just by applying an algorithm that can be given some parameter values, and then the desired task solution is delivered after some time. But in cases in which there is no clear definition of such input parameters, that is, in cases in which an algorithm cannot be specified clearly enough to produce a solution, we might wish to look at a diagram to let the human users judge and evaluate the visual patterns. This brings us to a situation where a certain freedom of decision making is allowed, in the best case leading to the fact that an algorithm is known or can be created to faster find a task solution.

Figure 1.2   Searching for a visual object in a visual scene is denoted by the term search task that typically requires focused visual attention and a visiting and checking strategy to identify the visual object-of-interest. The observer might search for a set of neighbored dots visually encoded in a certain color pattern.

Well-known and often occurring tasks from a much longer list are for example:

- **Search task:** One of the most time-consuming task comes in the form of a visual search, for which the entire display has to be visually inspected in the worst case, to identify the visual object-of-interest (see Figure 1.2). The search can be more efficient if a certain visual feature of the object-of-interest is known beforehand, for example, a certain color or color pattern, hence leading to some kind of visual pre-filtering of the display.

- **Counting task:** In cases in which only a few objects are visually represented, we might start inspecting them one-by-one and count the visited objects, for example, to get an idea about how much information is presented visually. The number of objects to be counted should not be too large; otherwise, a counting task would become a tedious procedure that one would probably not like to solve.

- **Estimation task:** If too many visual objects are depicted, we typically do not count them one after the other. In such a scenario, we would switch into some kind of estimation task that gives an approximate number of visible objects. In most cases, groups of visual objects are estimated based on the number of objects and those are later compared, for example, after having applied a clustering algorithm, for which a visual output is displayed.

- **Correlation task:** If two or more variables are under exploration we are typically interested in a certain correlation behavior, asking whether those variables behave in a similar way or show some kind of contradicting, opposite effect, for example, the values of one variable show an increasing behavior while those of the other variables are decreasing in the same time period.

- **Pattern identification task:** A very general task comes in the form of pattern detection, which requires to understand what a pattern is. This can actually be a problem for algorithmic solutions, which do not know exactly which kind of pattern we are looking for. The pattern identification task might be supported by visual outputs which make use of the perceptual and cognitive strengths of the humans' visual systems [246].

There are many more tasks that are imaginable, too many to mention all of them here, but typically tasks are based on a sequence of much simpler tasks. The general question in usability is how users solve tasks step-by-step. This sequential visual attention process can give useful insights in the fact if a user interface, dashboard, or visualization tool has been designed and developed by following the rules that make it a powerful tool for data exploration and analysis. Eye tracking [44, 87, 123] is a modern technology applied to interactive visualizations [8] with the goal to record visual attention behavior but, on the challenging side, to also visually and algorithmically explore the eye movement data.

Exercises

- Exercise 1.2.1: Imagine you have a dataset about a social network, for example, people from a certain region who are related or not. Which hypotheses or research questions might be interesting to ask, given the fact that we have a social network dataset?
- Exercise 1.2.2: Which kind of tasks do we need to solve, to find solutions to the formerly stated hypotheses about the social network dataset?

1.3 Programming Directions and Solutions

There are various programming solutions for this kind of problem. On the one hand, we can decide to use a certain programming language like Python, Java, JavaScript, C, C++, R, and the many options we have these days [37]. On the other hand those programming languages typically support visualization libraries or frameworks from which we can choose. Such libraries are, for example, matplotlib, Bokeh, Plotly, Swing, D3, CUDA, and R Shiny, just to mention a few from a really long list (see Table 1.1 for a longer, structured, and temporally ordered list). Which ones are finally chosen depends on the developers' decisions and on which tasks the designed and developed tool should be created in particular. However, not only the programming language and visualization libraries are important, we also have to know about the design issues that have to be taken into account in order to create a usable visualization tool. For example, the visual design and the interface design play a crucial role for usability, that is, if such rules are not followed properly we might run into a situation in which the tasks at hand are not solvable or in which the tool suffers from a degradation of performance at some tasks [202]. The visual design typically depends on the visualization library (see Figure 1.3 for some visual examples created with different visualization libraries) while the interface design is typically guided by given or self-created layouts combined with additional component properties like margins, distances, borders, sizes, fonts, and many more.

Table 1.1 Examples for programming languages, visualization libraries, the year of first development, and additional special properties.

Programming language	Visualization library	Year	Special properties
Java	AWT	1995	Graphical user interfaces (GUIs)
Java	Swing	1996	GUI widget toolkit
Python	Matplotlib	2003	Interactive visualizations
R	ggplot2	2005	Lattice graphics
Javascript	D3	2011	Web standards
R	Leaflet	2011	Spatial data visualization
R	Shiny	2012	Interactive web applications
Python	Bokeh	2012	Modern web browsers
Python	Seaborn	2012	Statistical graphics
Javascript	Plotly	2012	Web-based
Javascript	Chart	2013	Open-source library
Python	Geoplotlib	2016	Hardware-accelerated
Python	Chartify	2017	Open source library
R	Esquisse	2018	Drag and drop interface

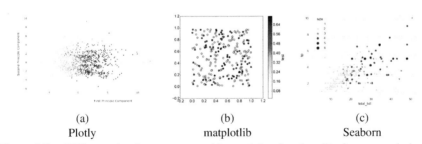

| (a) | (b) | (c) |
| Plotly | matplotlib | Seaborn |

Figure 1.3   Different visual outputs created by applying functionality from several visualization libraries: (a) Plotly. (b) matplotlib. (c) Seaborn.

The biggest challenge from a programming perspective is to choose and to connect the right components in order to create a successfully running, efficient, and effective visualization tool. However, this is actually a big issue and requires profound knowledge about a multitude of scientific disciplines, with visual design and programming among them. To summarize this problem, we have to know how to build a visualization tool, starting from raw data and ending with an interactively running visual output, possibly be accessible online via a URL that has to be typed into the URL field of a web browser. Such a web-based tool is easiest to start from users' perspectives since it just requires to simply write or copy and paste the correct URL into the web browser, no extra installations are needed. Actually, a dashboard can be built in exactly this way, keeping the burden for the users quite low and hence, with such web-based visualization tools, we can quickly distribute it among a large community, for example, to disseminate some valuable results based on visual analyses of data. One big issue can still occur. We need a stable internet connection to access the implemented visualization tool successfully; otherwise, a locally stored version of the tool would also be an option, but negatively, the users have to understand how to get it running on their computers.

If a dashboard is running, it cannot only be used for data exploration but even for services, for example, a company might need it to sell products or request customer reactions and the like. There is an endless list of application scenarios in which dashboards are worth designing and implementing. However, more and more dashboards are created to make data visually observable, for example, by showing the relations in a social network, informing about weather trends, showcasing the international flight behavior, or illustrating earthquakes happening on earth every day, from a daily, monthly, or yearly perspective, provided by multiple coordinated views [200] and the integration of various interaction techniques [258]. The data scientists are much more experienced to use algorithms and visual outputs since it belongs to their daily jobs to deal with data of different kinds; however, the biggest issue here is to make the data understandable to the laymen, the nonexperts in data science and data visualization, hence a dashboard that runs online can be of great help, also for people who do not regularly work in the field of data science. The goal of this book is to involve interested people in this domain, that is, nonexperts, to make them aware of the technologies and processes to build such tools by themselves one day. This has a positive benefit that they are not dependent on the work of others anymore, but can create their own independent solutions to their tasks at hand.

Before starting to create one's own dashboard, we have to understand the aspects surrounding this whole process. Visualizations have to be understood and which purpose they have for a certain data type. For example, prominent visualization techniques like histograms, bar charts, pie charts, scatter plots, star plots, scarf plots, dendrograms, or geographic maps with additionally overplotted information (maybe population densities) are a first step but also the various interactions they support and how they can be linked for creating a more flexible and complex visualization tool with much more functionality can be of great interest. Even animated diagrams might be interesting; for example, if some kind of dynamic story has to be told with data which is oftentimes preferred in the industrial environment to show processes to customers. It may be noted that even if all of the involved technologies to build a dashboard are understood and can be applied, a big issue still comes from the computer science side which also deals with algorithms and their runtime complexities [102]. If a dashboard does not only show data visually, but the data have to be transformed in an earlier stage or even in real-time, the implementors might get confronted by several more hard-to-tackle issues, also including the data handling and efficient access to the data, for example, stored in a database or in a text file. In general, creating powerful visualization tools, maybe in form of a dashboard, include many hidden bottlenecks and drawbacks. However, we try our best to explain those step-by-step in a tutorial-like book with many examples and exercises with solutions.

Exercises

- Exercise 1.3.1: Search for programming languages and visualization libraries and describe their benefits and drawbacks for the task of creating visualization tools and dashboards.
- Exercise 1.3.2: What are the positive and negative aspects when using web-based solutions for visualization tools?

2

Creating Powerful Dashboards

A dashboard can be regarded as some kind of user interface that 'lives' in a certain display with a certain horizontal and vertical extent [161]. These dimensions can be made use of to place the required interface components and visualizations, diagrams, plots, or charts. But also, the interaction techniques [258] are dependent on the display, the visualizations-in-use, how they are coordinated [200], and which tasks the users plan to solve. Dashboards are not static, but they are interactive, dynamic, and hence, they are full of life with a lot of functionality. They are a quite easy-to-implement way to create a visual output to illustrate data, in particular, to show the patterns, correlations, and anomalies contained in data. Apart from just showing data, we might also be interested in analyzing data, for example, by applying several algorithms that transform the data to get what we are looking for. In many cases, the results of such algorithmic approaches are that complex that a visual depiction is needed to understand the outputs of an algorithm, either after it has terminated or during its runtime [59, 62]. A dashboard offers a powerful method to let users play around and experiment with the data in a visual form, either with the raw data or with processed data. Moreover, if a dashboard is available online it can be used to disseminate the found insights, for example, to present them to a larger audience, either in a talk or by sending around the dashboards' URLs that interested experts or nonexperts can easily get started to see the results.

The topic of creating dashboards for data analysis is getting more and more interesting for many research communities, in particular, if they deal with datasets that need to be explored for patterns and outliers or anomalies. Since the programming experience of many researchers might be limited because they rely on existing tools and techniques to build a dashboard or they have to use an already implemented dashboard that might be expensive and that might not contain all the desired features. However, although any of the aforementioned approaches might be useful to get some good results, it

13

is not easily possible to be flexible in the sense of being able to decide which functionality, which visualization, and which interaction to offer at what place and at what time in a dashboard, that is, creating one's own solution might still be the better option. There is a lot of support for building dashboards like Microsoft Power BI, QlikSense, Tableau, or Grafana, just to mention a few. Those consist of a lot of functionality and negatively, as also in the case of a purely programmed solution, they have to be learned to efficiently work with them. Once they are understood, the dashboard creators are missing functionality and control that is needed to build dashboards designed for their tasks at hand and to easily extend them with new functionality. Programming a dashboard from scratch, on the other side, can be a longer-duration solution, but these kinds of dashboards can be designed for nearly any kind of task [255] that has to be solved in data analytics, flexibly equipped with interaction techniques. However, a profound knowledge about Python, for example, is required to equip the dashboard with all of the features that are needed.

Not only the programming side is problematic, but also questions about data handling, visual and interface design, including HTML and CSS to guide the layout, appearance, and aesthetic appeal of a dashboard, human–computer interaction, as well as user evaluation might be worth studying, in order to really get the most powerful solution we are waiting for, to dig deeper in our own or other people's data, to explore it for patterns, correlations, rules, outliers, and anomalies. Moreover, linking all views and perspectives on the data, storing snapshots of the current state of the visual and algorithmic output, uploading data, sharing, and disseminating the results in the form of URLs, visualizations, or parts of a dataset that contain valuable information, are powerful, and can only tap the full potential if most of the techniques in this interdisciplinary field of designing and implementing dashboards are understood. No matter which kind of dashboard is created, the human users, with their tasks at hand should definitely be consulted, maybe in a controlled or uncontrolled user study, with the intention to get valuable feedback about the design flaws in an interactive dashboard. Such design flaws could be based on the visualization techniques in use or on the visual interface given by the dashboard with its visual components like sliders, buttons, text fields, and the like as well as their layout and interactive response. Moreover, from an algorithmic perspective, it might be worth studying how the data gets processed to understand the runtime complexities and bottlenecks in the form of poorly running algorithms that finally, also impact the interactivity of such a dashboard. Nobody wants to wait for a long time until the next interaction can be applied.

Actually, building a dashboard can be based on many programming languages. For example, the language R with its visualization library Shiny has shown to be a good solution, but for the newcomer in programming and in dashboard design, we recommend the programming language Python with either its powerful frameworks like Bokeh or Dash by Plotly. There is some tendency to use Dash since many users report on the fact that it is easy to learn while already quite powerful simple dashboards and web apps can be built with basic programming skills. However, if more advanced dashboards have to be created, much more profound knowledge about Dash, Plotly, and Python is needed. Dash itself is JavaScript-based to some extent since it makes use of React, a popular web framework based on JavaScript and Flask which is a prominent web server based on the programming language Python. Dash does not only support Python but programming languages like R or Julia as well. Deploying the first dashboard results and testing them online, might be done by using Heroku or pythonanywhere, but for larger results in the sense of using big data and more advanced functionality in the form of powerful algorithms we recommend an own virtual machine, in order to let it run on a server to make it accessible for anybody on earth who owns a computer with a stable internet connection.

In this chapter we explain which typical ingredients are needed to build a dashboard, starting from the perspective on the data that can come in a variety of forms (Section 2.1). We will also take a detailed look on aspects related to visualization and algorithmic approaches (Section 2.2), also including the human users with their tasks at hand to be solved. To include the aforementioned visual aspects in a broader context, we will describe typical visualization examples and applications (Section 2.3). The various rules for visual and interface design with good practice and no-goes will also be taken into account (Section 2.4). Finally, we look at interaction concepts, modalities, and displays (Section 2.5).

2.1 Data Handling

Data is actually the starting point of the design and also the development process of an interactive dashboard for data analysis and visualization [187]. There are typically lots of patterns, correlations, and anomalies in a dataset, but those are hidden somewhere in the flood of data, which makes data analysis and visualization a powerful concept to detect them. However, the detection is in most cases more difficult than expected since we typically do not know what to look for, where to find it, and which tool, that is, analysis technique and visualization [245, 246], to apply. For this reason, we either know the structure of a dataset and can use well-known and well-researched techniques, or we have to deal with a totally unfamiliar dataset, making us rely on hypotheses and research questions that come up with tasks at hand to be solved. These tasks and hypotheses guide the design and implementation of a visualization tool, for example, a dashboard. A dashboard might be improved in an iterative way until the given tasks are solved and the hypotheses are finally either confirmed, rejected, or refined [141]. However, in many cases, after having used a dashboard for data analysis and visualization we get even more hypotheses. The reason for this is that the tool with all of its functionality is that powerful that it provides more insights than we would have expected in the beginning, before getting an algorithmically processed and visualized dataset. On the negative end, it is impossible to create a dashboard that is able to provide answers to all tasks, hypotheses, and research questions at the same time. Before we start designing and implementing such a tool we have to carefully look at our data and the users' tasks at hand to come up with a list of useful features worth implementing. Moreover, we have to understand how those features are linked, for example, by interaction techniques [258]. The challenging problem with such a first design phase is that there are various data types that a dataset can consist of. Those typically build the starting point for further steps and stages.

2.1.1 Data types

The data to be analyzed and visualized plays a crucial role in the design and implementation phases of an interactive dashboard for data exploration [13]. We cannot just start creating a dashboard without knowing about the data in use. This process might be comparable to building a house without knowing the environment and the ground it should be built on. The data can come in a variety of forms, being primitive or complex, static or dynamic, univariate, bivariate, trivariate, or even multivariate, being stored in a text file or in a database, being homogeneous or heterogeneous, and even more distinguishing features we might find when we are talking about data [216]. However, no matter which kind of data a dashboard is based on it can typically be split into its basic forms while those basics are important to understand to start with appropriate design decisions right from the beginning, no matter if the visual or interface design is taken into account. There are some kind of pre-defined and well-established algorithmic approaches and visualization techniques for each data type, and we recommend, to use them whenever possible since they have shown to be powerful for certain tasks at hand that are solved based on them [44]. Hence, the approaches and techniques are not only based on the data types but even more on the users' tasks. It is recommended to take into account both sides of the story, the data and the users who are trying to find insights in the data, but actually, getting the feedback of users is a challenging task, and in the best case, it should even be considered in any design and implementation phase, not only after the final product is created [220].

From the perspective of data type structures, we might distinguish between primitive data and complex data, that is, typically composed of two or more primitive data types or even more complex data types, although there is actually no limit about what to combine and to what extent. For example, a network of objects consists of the objects themselves with relations among them and the object properties which could be given as multivariate data, and this might even be time-varying. Primitive data can occur as quantitative, ordinal, or categorical data.

- Quantitative data: This kind of data exists in the form of numerical values and meaningful arithmetic operations can be applied on it. For example, a certain number of cars has to be transported by a car truck. Each car has a weight, that is, a quantitative value. Summing up all car weights makes sense, for example, if all of them have to be placed on the car truck and we are interested in the total weight to avoid overloading the truck. Hence, this kind of data can be regarded as a quantitative data type.
- Ordinal data: This data typically also exists in the form of numerical values, but it can also exist in any kind of form for which an inherent absolute order among the elements is given. Arithmetic operations do not make sense but all elements in the dataset can be ordered in a certain well-defined way. An example might be given by show sizes in a department store. Those are represented by numerical values. However, summing up shoe sizes does not make sense; ordering them makes sense; otherwise, a customer would hardly find the right shoes in the department store.
- Categorical data: This kind of data puts elements into categories, as the name already suggests. It can also exist as numerical values, those cannot be transformed by arithmetic rules nor can they be ordered, they are just categories. For example, bus lines could be identified by

numerical values, but it does not make sense to add bus line 5 to bus line 8, for example, nor makes it sense to order the bus lines by their numbers. The lines are just representatives for certain routes a bus is taking in a city.

Apart from primitive data, we typically meet much more challenging data types, challenging in a way that it is more difficult to apply algorithms and visualizations to detect insights in them. Those complex data types could be classified as relational, hierarchical, multivariate, textual, spatiotemporal, or trajectorial data, just to mention a few from a much longer list.

- Relational data: Data objects can be related to some extent. These relations are expressed in relational data which can consist of binary or multiple relations between two objects. The data structure we are talking about in such a case is a graph [248] which can be undirected, in case the direction of a relation is irrelevant, or directed, in case the direction is relevant. If weights of the relations are of particular interest and the relations are directed, we call such a graph a network. For example, a social network, as the name suggests, contains data of a relational data type. The people are the data objects while the network itself, with all its connections, is given by the (weighted) relations between all those people.
- Hierarchical data: If data objects are superior to some others causing some kind of parent–child relationship we consider this kind of data structure a hierarchy [196]. It consists of a root node (the topmost object), inner nodes (objects in-between), and leaf nodes (objects on the lowest hierarchy level). An example for such a hierarchy data type might be a file system on a computer which starts with a directory that contains other directories (subdirectories), again some other directories, and on the lowest level there are the files. There are two types of hierarchy data types which are containment hierarchies and subordination hierarchies. The file system is a containment hierarchy, while a company, a family, or a sports league hierarchy is based on the principle of subordination, not containment.
- Multivariate data: Data that has the form of rows and columns with numerical values is denoted by the term multivariate data [116, 117]. Each row, that is, case or observation, contains values for each column under a certain condition, that is, a variable or an attribute. The value can exist between the minimum and maximum of a given scale while the scale can vary from column to column. An example for such a data

type would be an Excel table full of values representing the COVID-19 attributes for each of the countries in the world. Each row would be a country and each column would refer to a value under a certain condition, that is, an attribute like the number of infected people, the number of vaccinations, the percentage of men/women, or the number of people currently in hospital due to COVID-19, just to mention a few.

- Textual data: Such data might be interpreted as a sequence of characters, each having a meaning. The sequence has a well-defined order to make it interpretable. However, text can only form a semantic meaning if it is interpreted as a whole and not by inspecting its parts, letter by letter. Textual data could be interesting as an augmentation for visualization, for example, as labels, in cases in which a pure visual depiction is not enough or in cases in which the visual representation should be emphasized by additional textual information, such as in geographic or public transport maps. Textual data can occur in small pieces or even in larger ones, for example, including textbooks or source code of a software system that is typically hierarchically structured as well which shows us a classical example for the fact that data types can be composed of several other types like textual and hierarchical ones as in this scenario.

- Spatiotemporal data: Two aspects might occur together in data, for example, space and time, making it of a spatiotemporal data type. This means that the data might be recorded in a spatial dimension like one-dimensional (1D), two-dimensional (2D), or three-dimensional (3D), and the data might even change over time in those dimensions. An example would be eye movement data that is typically recorded during visually attending a 2D or 3D static or dynamic stimulus over time [152]. Also, traffic data could be considered as being of a spatiotemporal nature since traffic happens in certain geographic regions and typically varies from hour to hour, or day to day, depending on the temporal granularity and temporal effects like rush hours or anomalies like car accidents causing road blockages [111].

- Trajectorial data: Movements in a spatial region from location to location, forming a sequence of spatial positions are creating data of a trajectorial data type. This data type is related to spatiotemporal data, but the spatial aspect might not consider 2D or 3D, it is more based on 1D curves in space. For example, a mathematical function might produce a trajectory since it describes a mapping from one dimension to another one, typically time to locations in a map or on a 1D scale. The stock market over time could be interpreted as a trajectory, but for example, throwing a stone might be considered much more as a trajectory if we are interested in it in a physical experiment. Also vehicles and the human eye typically form trajectories over space and time, with the extension that they might stop for a while at certain locations.

As already seen in the spatiotemporal data type, data are in many cases not static but are changing over time [4], making it a dynamic data type. The dynamics of the data bring into play new challenges since the dynamics of the data might be explorable after a certain time, making it some kind of offline data analysis problem, or the data might be explorable during the dynamics, making it an online, real-time data analysis problem [84]. The offline problem might be easier to solve since from an analysis perspective, we have more time to react on the data, meaning the analysis works as a post process. In the online, real-time scenario, the analysis techniques must keep pace with the incoming data chunks, transform and process them quickly, and provide real-time rapid solutions. This can actually become the bottleneck of a data analysis point of view, hence in typical situations not all data chunks are processed, just a representative one at a certain well-defined periodically occurring point in time. Defining these representatives can also be a challenging problem. The biggest problem is to not lose any important information from the original data. We actually do not know beforehand what the important information is and might make a lot of mistakes here in one of the earliest stages of the data analysis and visualization process.

Exercises

- Exercise 2.1.1.1: Imagine you have an Excel table full of values. Which kind of data type would this scenario refer to? Which kind of data type do the individual entries refer to?
- Exercise 2.1.1.2: People in a social network know each other, are sending messages to each other, but might even be related by other attributes, for example, in a family hierarchy. Which kind of data types can you find in such a scenario?

2.1.2 Data reading and parsing

The data to be analyzed and visualized can occur in several forms. It might be existing in a data file or in a database for example. Those could be a local file or database, or it could be accessed remotely via an internet connection, for example, by just making use of a URL to access the data. This might be the best option for real-time data that cannot be stored in typical scenarios due to its immense growth and change over time. Only the latest snapshots of the data or the data in a certain temporal distance to the current version of the data are still available. The remote access is beneficial if the data is huge [140], hence being stored on a server that is capable of keeping much more data than a standard personal computer, laptop, or notebook. On the negative side, we actually see the challenging problem of keeping the internet connection alive, stable, and able to access large amounts of data in real-time; otherwise, the application, that is, the data analysis and visualization tool, would suffer from various limitations and restrictions or it would not start at all. This is an important aspect for presentations in which the latest results have to be shown. If the internet connection is a problematic issue in a conference or meeting room, we might work with a local tool version, for the analysis and visualization itself, but even more for the data. However, if the data is too big to be stored locally, we should be aware of the fact that only the most important data pieces can be mirrored on the local machine and the interactive results can only be based on these data portions. The data might be pre-aggregated by summing up, averaging, classing, or finding a representative data element from a list of data elements.

If the data is stored in a database we must take into account that there must be a library supporting the access of such a database, that is, the reading and writing of data entities. On the other hand, if the data is stored in a data file we must be aware that there are several data formats that the analysis and visualization tool must be prepared for. For example, a multivariate dataset might be stored in a comma-separated values (csv) file that could be opened by using a Pandas Dataframe [169], a Python concept with which it is possible to actually read such data with only a few lines of code. If the data is a hierarchical dataset, consisting of parent-child relationships like a file system or an NCBI taxonomy, we might be confronted by a Newick file format for which there are also libraries available that can read such a data type. In the most general data type scenario, we must define our own data reading functionality that parses the data, that is, each data entity, in corresponding data objects that are internally processed and stored to make them usable for the tool, maybe to analyze and visualize the data in the form of an interactive dashboard.

Exercises

- Exercise 2.1.2.1: In many scenarios in the field of data science, we find the data to be analyzed in several nonlinked data files. How would you design a data reading and parsing functionality to get all the information you need from all of the data sources?
- Exercise 2.1.2.2: How should a data parser be designed and implemented to be able to react on different data formats or even on changes in a given data format?

2.1.3 Data storage

Not only reading and parsing the data can be a major issue when designing and implementing dashboards for data analysis and visualization. Also storing might already be difficult, although storing just means placing the data somewhere on a big heap to read, parse, transform, and process it later on. Storing data is still important since users of a data analysis and visualization tool can decide to reduce the original dataset by applying filter techniques based on certain features and insights that have been found by applying such a tool. Not even the original data format has to be kept, but the tool might offer functionality that can transform the data into a better more tool-specific data format with which we can work much easier at later stages. For example, the stored data snippet might be loaded later again to show the found patterns and anomalies to an audience which has the benefit of not managing the whole big dataset again and again, which would lead to a waste of time. If the data is located on several data sources the tool might already link those datasets and puts them together in a linked data source that is then stored in an individual file in a certain format. Hence, the formerly heterogeneous data gets combined into a common data source that might be easier to reload in the tool again and again.

Soon we are in a situation in which we have to deal with big data [140] for which profound knowledge about data handling aspects is required in order to achieve an interactively responsive dashboard. Many of the bottlenecks, from a usability perspective, are caused by a poorly running data handling, for example, a slow access to the data or performance issues when transforming the data, from one dataset to another one, in a different data format, maybe based on the input–output mechanisms of certain algorithmic concepts. However, most of the aforementioned problems come from the size and complexity of the original data, how it is stored in a data file or database, and how it is further modeled internally in tool-specific data structures. Big data brings into play the five big V's that are volume, variety, velocity, validity, and value [206]. Volume stands for the sheer size of data, for example produced by sensors, the internet, or the behavior of users who order articles, pay with credit cards, or travel around the globe. The data can even be so big that they cannot be stored anymore on traditional computers, hence they must be moved to special servers or even be split into different data sources at the cost of maybe reuniting them again for certain data analysis. Variety expresses that data can come in many forms, which can be structured or unstructured, hence creating an understandable data format from which the data can be accessed quickly and effortlessly is a major challenge. Velocity describes how fast we have to access the data, for example, if an algorithm must generate real-time analyses we only have fractions of milliseconds to respond to requests and the algorithms themselves have to operate very quickly. Validity focuses on the quality of data, for example, freeing the data from noise or add missing data entities that would hide certain patterns, and that might increase the runtime of algorithms. The value of the data is important to express which impact the results from the big data can have, that is, which value they produce for the academic or industrial community.

Exercises

- Exercise 2.1.3.1: What is the biggest dataset that you can store on your computer? How could you reduce the size and the complexity of the original dataset so that it fits again on your computer for a locally running tool?
- Exercise 2.1.3.2: If we are talking about big data, we come across the five big V's standing for volume, variety, velocity, validity, and value. Discuss which of the V's is problematic for the implementation of a dashboard and which solutions exist to mitigate this situation?

2.1.4 Data preprocessing

One goal of data preprocessing is to get rid of many negative issues and problems in the original data, for example, removing irrelevant information that is not needed. Such data-cleaning processes can reduce the size and complexity of a dataset before it gets passed through more advanced algorithmic analyses. Moreover, noise in the data typically leads to an unwanted size of the dataset. Hence, it would be beneficial to get rid of data noise, that is, data in data that has no meaning for data analysis. In contrast, there might even be not enough information in the data. In such cases, the goal of a preprocessing step might be to close certain data gaps, for example, by interpolation, even measurement errors, or uncertainty effects whenever this is possible. In many situations, data preprocessing tries to improve or augment original data, but as a negative consequence, there could be the negative effect of removing relevant data elements unintentionally. Consequently, the preprocessing step must be taken with care to not lead to misinterpretations later on. The positive side effect of a data preprocessing can be that the interactive responsiveness of a data analysis and visualization tool gets much faster due to the fact that irrelevant information is removed or in the opposite effect, relevant but missing information is already added and reduces the runtime complexities of algorithms in the data transformation step.

The data preprocessing typically happens before the algorithmic analyses and visualizations as the term pre already suggests. However, in some situations, the preprocessing cannot work properly without the interventions of human users. For example, it might be a good idea to show the data in its original form and let the users decide which algorithm to apply to remove noise in the data. In some situations, it might actually be the noise or a gap pattern that we are looking for, which is important for detecting insights in data or to confirm or reject hypotheses. Consequently, it would be a bad idea to automatically remove those patterns in a preprocessing stage leading to the effect that we would never see what we are actually interested in. A visualization tool should support both options, that is, showing the data in its original or preprocessed form. Even a difference between both forms might be useful to explicitly point at data elements that are not needed or that are missing on the other hand.

Exercises

- Exercise 2.1.4.1: What could be the reasons for erroneous data, missing data, or uncertain data?
- Exercise 2.1.4.2: What are typical solutions to handle missing data elements in a given dataset?

2.1.5 Data transformation

In rare cases, we can start right away with original data that is read by the tool and parsed into tool-specific data structures. The more general situation is that we can read the data and know which data types it is composed of and which

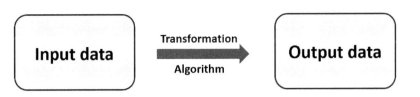

Figure 2.1   Algorithms transform input data to output data. How this is done exactly depends on user tasks, that is, under which perspectives data will be explored.

attributes it contains; however, this raw information is not useful to guide a data analyst to data patterns like correlations, trends, or anomalies. To reach the ultimate goal of a data analysis and visualization tool, maybe given as a dashboard, we have to transform the data into other formats that are typically stored internally. Such formats might uncover special relationships among the data elements, that is, formerly unrelated items when scrolling through the data, get internally linked by advanced algorithmic concepts. In most cases, the applied algorithms transform a given dataset into a different kind of data only carrying the required information, the one that supports data analysts to solve given tasks in order to confirm, reject, or refine given hypotheses about the original dataset. For example, a dataset consisting of a list of people with ages, genders, interests, and messages sent around might be transformed into a matrix of weighted relations telling to what extent certain person pairs are related. In the original list of people, it would be hard to identify any groups of related people; however, after applying an algorithm that takes the crucial information from the list and that transforms it into pairwise relations of people, we can solve tasks answering such person relation questions much easier.

There are many examples from a long list of data transformations. All of them might be described by starting with an input dataset and modifying the input to an output that shows the original input data under a different perspective (see Figure 2.1). A few prominent examples are data aggregation, ordering and sorting, clustering, data mining, dimensionality reduction, or even deep learning approaches that try to train a model by making use of neural networks with the goal to learn certain patterns on which the algorithm can react in case new data entities come into play. There are various advanced algorithms that transform data, some are very fast, others might have a high runtime complexity for which profound knowledge is required to find heuristic approaches that quickly compute solutions that are not optimal but still acceptable in the sense that they create a local minimum. Examples for such problems are the optimal linear arrangement problem [74] (also sometimes called MinLA problem for the minimum linear arrangement). It is challenging and very time-consuming to compute the optimal arrangement for a matrix of pairwise relations but a local minimum might be sufficient to detect clusters among the pairwise relations. Such NP-hard problems [102] are known to create challenges for a visualization tool, in particular, if the focus is on fast interactions.

Exercises

- Exercise 2.1.5.1: What are the benefits and drawbacks when transforming data from its original form to a transformed one?
- Exercise 2.1.5.2: Aggregation can be a form of data transformation that has the benefit of reducing the dataset size. How can a new data element stemming from an aggregation of several original data elements be computed?

2.2 Visualization and Visual Analytics

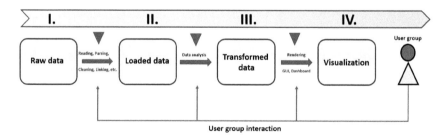

Figure 2.2   The visualization pipeline [177] illustrates how raw data gets transformed step-by-step into a visual output. The user group can interact in any of the intermediate stages and can intervene to guide the whole algorithmic and visual exploration process.

Data alone in all its varieties and data types with all data preprocessing steps and algorithmic transformations can only tell us half of the truth about certain phenomena from the real world. We can store any kind of data with incredible sizes and complexities but without seeing a visual output in the form of graphics, we, the human users, are not really able to derive insights, to see patterns, correlations, or anomalies [245]. Interactive visualizations [258] are powerful tools with their expressiveness and information communication, making use of the perceptual abilities of the humans [115, 246] to rapidly detect visual patterns (see Section 2.2.2). Those visual patterns alone are not the final solution, they need to be interpreted by remapping them to data patterns, with the goal to confirm, reject, or refine formerly stated hypotheses, or to build new hypotheses about the data that we would never think of without having seen the data in a visual form [139, 141, 143]. Such hypotheses are typically involving user tasks that guide the whole data exploration process (see Figure 2.2 for an entire visualization pipeline). For example, if we are interested in a maximum value in a dataset and we are trying to solve this visually, we have to solve a comparison task that tells us that a certain value is the largest one among all visually displayed values.

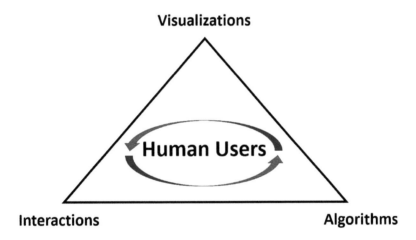

Figure 2.3   Visualizations, interactions, algorithms, and the human users with their perceptual abilities build the major ingredients in the field of visual analytics.

Visualization is powerful for problems for which we are not able to specify an algorithm with parameters [179]. The maximum search described above, on the other hand, can be solved by a pure algorithmic solution, by using a maximum finding algorithm. This is possible since we know the input and output parameters as well as the computation routine that computes a maximum from a given list of input values. In some situations, visualization alone and algorithms alone do not provide a solution to a given task. In those situations, we have to combine both powerful concepts described in a famous quote by Leo Cherne or Albert Einstein [92] as "the computer being fast, accurate, but stupid while the human users with their perceptual abilities being slow, inaccurate, but intelligent. Together they are even more powerful." Such a synergy effect is reflected in the research field of visual analytics [139, 141, 143] that includes the human users with their tasks at hand, algorithmic concepts, visualizations, human–computer interaction, perception, cognitive science, data science, and many more to make it an interdisciplinary approach. The interdisciplinarity makes the field applicable to many real-world examples, typically involving big data [205]. Figure 2.3 shows some of the most important fields that are included in the interdisciplinary field of visual analytics [252, 251].

2.2.1 Visual variables

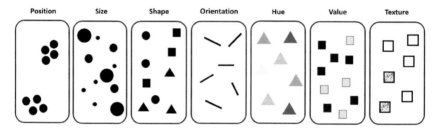

Figure 2.4   Visual variables [180] describe from which core ingredients a visualization is built: Position, size, shape, orientation, hue, value, or texture are just the major ones from a longer list.

If we talk about visualization we have to consider visual variables [21, 22, 23]. Those are the fundamental ingredients of each visualization. They describe how the data is mapped to visual encodings, for example, color, size, position, shape, thickness, area, volume, angle, and many more [180] (see Figure 2.4). Using a different repertoire of visual variables for the same dataset can affect human perception and power when solving tasks at hand tremendously. The reason for this phenomenon is that some visual variables can be easier interpreted than others for a certain well-defined task, but again, this effect depends on many factors, with the perceptual abilities of the human users as one of the most important ones. For example, quantities can be best compared visually when they are mapped to positions in a common scale [73], better than when mapped to angles [122]. Figure 2.5 illustrates this issue with the example of bar charts and pie charts for the same set of quantitative values. In bar charts, the observers can solve the task of ordering the quantities

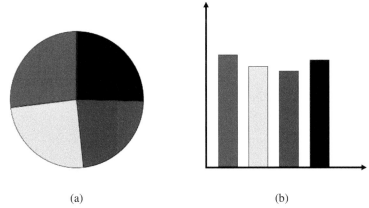

Figure 2.5   Pie charts are based on the visual variable "angle" or "area" while bar charts are based on "position" or "length" in a common scale [73] which seems to be better for solving comparison tasks for quantities.

much faster and more accurate than in pie charts. One reason for this effect comes from the fact that humans can judge quantities shown with the visual variable position in a common scale, as used in bar charts much better than using angles as in pie charts for the same task. There are various such experiments investigating the task of which visual variable is best for a certain situation, that is, for a task at hand for a given dataset based on one or several data types.

Such user experiments are important to figure out if a designed and implemented visualization or visualization tool, for example, a dashboard, can be used reliably by a user group. For this reason, we can find many comparative user evaluations taking into account the visual variables as independent variables and measuring the response time and accuracy as dependent variables while confronting the users with typical tasks that have to be solved by using the corresponding visualizations as stimuli in the user experiment. Even interaction techniques [258] (see Section 2.5) integrated in the visualization tool are typically evaluated although those user studies are much more complicated due to the dynamic stimuli, that is, changing representations of the visualizations and the typically more complicated and time-consuming tasks to be answered. Also, eye tracking [44, 123] is a powerful technology to find out where and when visual attention is paid to a visual stimulus, be it static or dynamic. However, the dependent variables that come in the form of spatiotemporal eye movement data and extra physiological measures are much more challenging to analyze, hence visual analytics with a combination of algorithmic approaches, interactive visualizations, and the human users with their perceptual abilities (see Figure 2.3) and their decision makings plays a crucial role here to identify patterns, correlations, and anomalies in the visual attention behavior. This again can help to identify design flaws in the visual design, consequently, it also explores the combination of visual variables and their strength as a tool to analyze data.

Exercises

- Exercise 2.2.1.1: Histograms typically show the distribution of quantitative values on a (numeric) y-axis. Whereas the (numeric) x-axis stands for a scale on which the data is measured. An example would be the number of people with a certain income in dollars. Which visual variables can you generally identify in histograms?
- Exercise 2.2.1.2: What are the benefits and drawbacks when using either bar charts or pie charts for visually representing a dataset with 5/10/20/50/100 quantities?

2.2.2 Perception and cognition

Even if we followed most of the design rules to create interactive visualizations in a graphical user interface, we can never be absolutely sure if the designed visualization tool is useful in order to analyze and explore data. Most problematic from a visualization perspective are perceptual and cognitive issues, that is, those that come from the users' side of view. Perception is a powerful field of research that can be referred to the process of attaining awareness or understanding of sensory information [244]. In the field of visualization, this process is responsible for how well a human user can derive visual patterns from a visual stimulus that is composed of a multitude of visual variables like color, size, length, shape, position, area, volume, texture, and many more [115]. The combinations of those visual variables are responsible for creating a powerful visualization technique, one that encodes data in a visual form, interpretable by human users to remap the visual patterns to data patterns and, consequently, to knowledge and insights extracted from the given data. Color perception [198], as an example, can have a huge impact on how people extract information from a visual field. This research field has been studied for years, with the results of the research also being applicable to information visualization, that is, for perceptually better designed graphical user interfaces linking visualization techniques in multiple coordinated views [200].

Cognition, on the other hand, describes how we process information in our brains, that is, how we think about the processes to react on certain patterns [31]. It is some kind of knowledge acquisition and thinking process but also using experience to understand while the senses play a crucial role to get the information we need [245, 246]. This mental action includes a variety of aspects and functions, combined in a clever way to derive knowledge and insights from a visual scene in a rapid manner, incorporating not only the powerful perception again but also attention has a big impact on how we find visual patterns and anomalies in a visual scene. By deriving those patterns and combining them, we use the brain, our short-term [183] and long-term memory [168], to react on the visual scene, for example, to judge about visual effects, to reason about what we see, to solve problems, to make decisions, or to just comprehend the visual scene and its linked aspects, for example, to present them and to explain them to a larger audience. Hence, without cognition, the humans were not able to extract new knowledge and insights partially based on old knowledge, that is, experience that we got over the years in maybe different living environments.

In particular, visualizing outliers and anomalies hidden in a dataset can be effectively done by making use of the mighty principle of pre-attentive processing [115, 229]. By using this visual pop-out effect it is guaranteed that visual elements can be detected in a fraction of a second, the users pay visual attention to them quickly, that is, in case the task is to rapidly identify outliers that should be visually encoded in a much different way than the rest of the visual objects, that is, in a pre-attentively processable way. There are various such examples from the field of information visualization. The most obvious one might be a red-colored circle in a sea of blue-colored circles (see Figure 2.6) while the blue-colored ones are called distractors since they distract from solving a given (search) task which is the identification of the red target circle. In summary, one rule to create effective visualization tools is to include pre-attentive features when the task is to quickly and effortlessly spot the outlier(s) in a dataset that is visually represented in a certain visual way. There are various pre-attentive features [115, 229] like color, size, shape, hue, movement, and many more from a longer list.

Also, visual memory [115] plays a crucial role in solving tasks by using visualization techniques. For example, for solving a comparison task, we might first look at a visual scene, store this scene or parts of it in our visual memory, and try to compare the stored scene with a new one. Without the

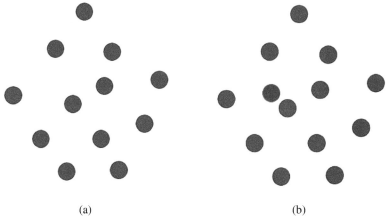

(a)   (b)

Figure 2.6   Visual objects can be observed while trying to solve a search task: (a) Only blue circles. (b) Blue circles with one red circle which is called the target object, whereas the blue ones are the distractors.

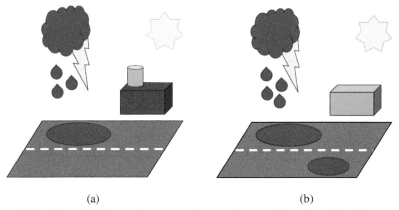

(a)   (b)

Figure 2.7   Change blindness when comparing two images: From the original image in (a) there are several differences compared to the image shown in (b).

power of the visual memory such comparison tasks could not be solved efficiently. Change blindness [181] is a concept that describes the challenge of detecting visual elements in one scene that are not present in another one, also illustrated in the famous error search images (see Figure 2.7). If the reason for not seeing the change is caused by the viewers' missing attention, we call this inattentional blindness [203]. For information visualization, this is a mighty concept since we are comparing visual scenes all the time, be it for comparing two static pictures or to identify changes in a dynamic scene that is composed of a sequence of static scenes, like in an animation or a video stripe. In a visualization tool, we might be looking for visual patterns, and we are typically trying to compare the observed patterns with patterns that we have seen a long time ago, that is, we learned visual patterns and got some experience with them. Hence, we actually build a growing repertoire of visual patterns mapped to some meaning which are requested all the time when we see new visual scenes. For comparing two visual scenes, we typically use short-term memory. When we make use of experience, that is, visual experience, we look up those patterns in long-term memory.

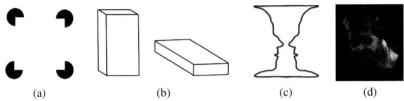

(a) (b) (c) (d)

Figure 2.8 Some of the popular Gestalt principles: (a) Reification: An incomplete visual object can be completed. (b) Invariance: A deformation of a visual pattern still allows to recognize the original object. (c) Multistability: A visual object might be interpreted in various ways (at least two ways). (d) Emergence: A visual object or a person can be detected from a noisy background.

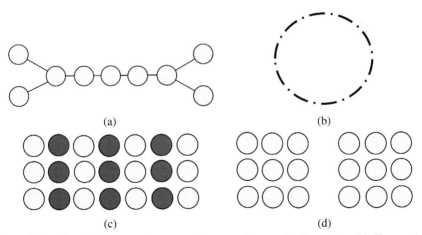

Figure 2.9 Visual objects can be grouped in several ways: (a) Symmetry. (b) Closure. (c) Similarity. (d) Proximity. There are even further laws like the law of good form, common fate, or continuity.

In Gestalt theory, we follow the principle of "the whole is greater than the sum of its parts" [114, 147]. This means that our brain is not trying to see visual scenes as composed of many small pieces, but it more or less tries to derive complete visual patterns immediately. This powerful strategy happens effortlessly and helps us to rapidly derive patterns. Moreover, experience also plays a central role in Gestalt theory since already-known patterns are found much easier and faster than patterns with which we do not have much experience. Figure 2.8 illustrates several of the Gestalt principles like emergence, reification, multistability, invariance, or grouping which can be categorized into the laws of proximity, similarity, closure, symmetry, common fate, continuity, and good form (see Figure 2.9). Most of them are really obvious, but their impact on information visualizations and how we detect visual patterns to explore data has a tremendous impact on the usefulness of the visualizations. This again also shows that experience plays a crucial role in the field of visualization.

Figure 2.10   The Hermann grid illusion demonstrates how "visual objects" in the form of gray dots can pop out although there are no such gray dots included in the image.

Also, optical illusions might occur in a visualization. For example, a color might be interpreted as a wrong color, and hence, a data value might be misinterpreted, like in the famous Rubik cube illusion [209]. Moreover, visual objects might occur where actually no objects are, like in the popular Hermann grid illusion (see Figure 2.10), in which gray dots might pop out at the intersection points of the white gaps between the black-colored squares. Optical illusions should be avoided whenever possible; however, in some situations, we are not aware that they might occur. They can cause misinterpretation issues when trying to derive visual patterns from a visualization. There are various prominent optical illusions that can also accidentally be incorporated into an information visualization tool, for example, in a dashboard. Those can cause problems when judging visual elements for parallelism, length, color coding, movement and speed, and many more [85].

Exercises

- Exercise 2.2.2.1: Find an example of error search images (Google image search can help). Look at them and try to find the differences between the original and the manipulated image. What is your search strategy, that is, how do you strategically solve this task (e.g., based on your eye movements)?
- Exercise 2.2.2.2: Draw a Hermann grid (Figure 2.10) and check the impact of different colors, can you observe any difference depending on the color effect? Describe your findings!

2.2.3 The role of the human users

To check if visualization tools are really useful for tasks at hand, it is best to confront real users with such tools and measure how fast and how accurate they are. Moreover, additionally, we could record the humans' eye movements [44] to get hints about visual attention that is paid to the dynamic and interactive visual scene [151]. User studies [93, 214] in visualization have been conducted a lot in the past, and many more will follow in the future. The biggest issue with such user studies comes from the fact that only a few parameters can be checked, which serve as the independent variables in the study. The recorded user behavior, be it as response times, error rates, or eye movements (or further physiological measures [25]), are the dependent variables and describe which impacts a change to the independent variables has on the dependent ones. Given a certain task to be answered by observing an interactive visualization, the independent-dependent correlation can consequently provide insights about certain drawbacks, or design flaws in a visualization tool. The developers of such tools try to get rid of the drawbacks, or at least a certain improvement to this situation might be achieved based on the users' feedback. Apart from the independent and dependent variables, there are plenty of confounding variables that should be controlled as good as possible to avoid misleading or erroneous study results.

The human users typically have different experience levels which make a general claim about the usability of a visualization tool a difficult endeavor. We might have experts or nonexperts, young or old people, visually disabled people, and more groups of study participants with certain properties might occur. All those factors must be checked beforehand to understand what caused certain issues when trying to solve tasks and to make decisions, for example, when interacting with a dashboard. In visual analytics, this situation and the role of the human users get even more complicated since such systems are most powerful if an interplay between humans and machines is guaranteed, however, the decision-making is still partially on the humans' side. The big challenge when using visual analytics is to build, confirm, reject, or refine hypotheses [139] that focus on answering one or several research questions by means of visually and algorithmically exploring data of any data type, homogeneous or heterogeneous data, structured or unstructured data, small or big data, and the like. Such user studies might run over several weeks of time, as some kind of longitudinal study, maybe splitting the visual analytics tool into several components that can or must be researched separately to avoid blowing up the study design due to an otherwise huge parameter space demanding for many study setup variations and hence, a really large number of study participants to cover all possible setup possibilities. From a study type perspective, there are various options, typically depending on the research questions under investigation, for example, controlled versus uncontrolled studies, small population versus crowdsourcing studies, field versus lab studies, standard versus eye-tracking studies, expert versus nonexpert studies, and many more.

Exercises

- Exercise 2.2.3.1: What are typical challenges for the task of recruiting people for a user study? How can we tackle those challenges to get as many study participants as possible?
- Exercise 2.2.3.2: Describe the benefits and drawbacks of controlled versus uncontrolled user studies.

2.2.4 Algorithmic concepts

Algorithms are as important as visual representations for understanding data, based on certain user tasks like finding patterns, correlations, and/or anomalies. If the data are shown visually, we rely on the perceptual strength of the human's visual system [115, 245] to detect visual patterns that can be mapped to hidden data patterns [65]. But in many cases, the data cannot just be visualized. It has to be transformed and processed by efficient algorithms (see Section 2.1) to bring it into a format that can be graphically represented to reflect those patterns. For example, if we are interested in temporally aggregated data, we might first compute the daily values from the hourly values, and then, as a second step, we visualize those aggregation results [4]. Without the aggregation step, it is difficult or impossible to visually solve the task of identifying a daily evolution pattern in the data. Also, the task of finding group structures in a dataset, for example, in a relational dataset like a graph or a network [194], is typically not solvable by visualizing the data in its raw form. A clever clustering algorithm [3] might compute such group and cluster structures beforehand and then, as a second step, visualize the clustering results [238]. However, no matter how powerful an algorithm is, it mostly produces another kind of dataset, from a given input dataset, that is too complex to understand it without a visual depiction of it. For a dashboard, it can become a problem if certain inefficient algorithms are included in the data analysis and visualization process, since they can cause some kind of delay in the data exploration. In some cases, the reason is just a wrong implementation of such algorithms, but in many cases, it could also be the case that the algorithm itself falls into a class of algorithms that has a high runtime complexity per se. Such NP-hard problems create algorithms that are not able to rapidly find an optimal solution to a data problem at hand. We need a heuristic approach to the algorithm that does not compute the optimum but a local minimum or maximum instead. Examples of such NP-hard problems are the subset sum problem [148] or the traveling salesman problem [204] among many others.

Applying algorithms in visualization typically means waiting for the results of an algorithm, starting with inputs and producing outputs that are then visualized. Another challenge is to explore the algorithm during its runtime [62], maybe to understand why it caused a wrong result or why it is not well performing. The algorithm itself is then of interest as a dataset. It is not treated anymore as a black box but we more or less open this black box to look inside, to understand what is going on, step-by-step. This can be as simple as understanding how a sorting algorithm works [35] or how a shortest path is found in a network [62], for example, how a Dijkstra algorithm is walking from node to node via edge to edge in a network. The steps taken produce a complex dynamic dataset, typically focusing on a basic dataset like a graph/network (Dijkstra algorithm) or a list of quantities (sorting algorithms). If the basic dataset is even more complex, for example, a neural network for which we are interested in how the weight function is modified to find a suitable model in the network we run into a challenging visualization problem due to the sheer size of modifiable parameters in such a network. This example brings into play a relatively new field of research denoted by explainable artificial intelligence (XAI) [164]. From a visual depiction of such dynamic processes, we have two major concepts which are animation or static representations of the dynamic data [233].

Exercises

- Exercise 2.2.4.1: Imagine you have 5 (not sorted) natural numbers. Find a visual representation of those numbers and present the intermediate steps of a sorting algorithm applied to those 5 numbers.
- Exercise 2.2.4.2: What is better for visualizing a running algorithm? Animation or a static representation of the intermediate steps. Discuss the benefits and drawbacks of each concept.

2.3 Examples of Visualization Techniques

Each dataset requires one or several visualization techniques to make it visually exploratory by the human observers [44]. There might be a multitude of visualization candidates for the same dataset, but finally, the human observers with their tasks at hand decide if the chosen visualization candidate is powerful enough to support them in solving those tasks. For example, a quantitative dataset might be visually encoded into a bar chart if the task is to compare the quantitative values by means of the visual variables height or positions in a common scale [73]. If we have to deal with relational data, we might choose a node-link diagram [106] consisting of circular shapes for the objects and of straight lines for the relations between objects. This visual metaphor is much more complex than the bar chart metaphor due to the fact that the data type is much more complex than the quantitative data type. Moreover, due to this complexity, there are many more options for the encodings of the objects and the relations. For example, the objects might be encoded in circular, rectangular, or triangular shape with different colors, even indicating another categorical attribute on top of the objects, while the relations can be shown as straight, curved, orthogonal, tapered, or animated links [125] to mention a few. Even partially drawn links [60] might be an option to avoid link crossings that cause visual clutter [202] if too many of them occur. This example shows that there is a multitude of combinations of visual variables, all focusing on providing a visual encoding of the given dataset that is powerful to support tasks at hand.

Not only quantitative or relational data provide a basis for visualization candidates. Also hierarchical, multivariate, textual, and many more data types exist, even in combination, making the choice of suitable visualization techniques limited, but also offering the opportunity to combine and link various visual variables to the visual output that someone desires. An even more challenging aspect of data visualization comes from the fact that nearly any part of a dataset might have an inherent temporal behavior [4]. This means that the data is not stable or static, but it is dynamically changing over time. This dynamics in the data brings into play comparison tasks, that is, data analysts are typically interested in exploring if there is some kind of trend in the data like a growing or decreasing behavior. In many cases, it is not a good idea to just use the visualization candidate for the static data and put it next to each other, one for each time step, to show the dynamics in the data. Such a small multiples representation [64] is easy to implement but suffers from visual scalability issues, and even more, the visual comparisons can become tricky because the visual observer has to move from one snapshot to the next one to spot the differences over time. However, still, many time steps can be seen in one view, which is much different from an animation of the time-dependent data [233]. In many scenarios, the visual metaphor for the dynamic case is completely different from the one used for the static case of the same data type.

In this section, we are going to explain various visualization techniques, each falling into a certain category that is given by the data to be visualized. Simple data types are discussed in Section 2.3.1 while graphs and networks are the topic in Section 2.3.2 followed by a section on hierarchies (Section 2.3.3). Visualizations for data that exist in a tabular form, that is, multivariate or hypervariate data, are described in Section 2.3.4. Trajectories and possible visualizations for them are explained in Section 2.3.5, while textual data and its visual encodings are described in Section 2.3.6.

2.3.1 Visualizing simple data types

Even for simple data types, we can make a lot of mistakes during the decision for a suitable visualization candidate that shows the data in a visually understandable way. The tasks at hand are some guidelines for choosing the right visual metaphor with the right visual variables. For example, if a dataset consists of five quantitative values and we want to compare those visually, we might choose a so-called pie chart that encodes each value proportional to an angle that spans a certain circle sector with an inscribed area. This visual variable is actually the problem here with this radial kind of visual metaphor [83]. Another visual variable, for example, the length or the position is much better for visualizing quantitative values if the task is to visually compare those values [73]. This aspect has been known for a long time already, but still we can find pie charts in newspapers and magazines for illustrating the results of an election for example. In most cases, the designer of such a pie chart typically starts adding the percentage values as textual labels to each of the circle sectors. This additional information should mitigate the challenging situation of judging the values by areas of circle sectors but why is visualization required at all if we start reading the labels instead of looking at the visual variables that should help us rapidly finding patterns. Actually, the only task that pie charts might support is the so-called part-to-whole relationship, that is, showing how much each value adds to 100%. In scenarios in which we have, let's say, more than five quantities, we might also run into problems when judging the small values but even more, if the pie chart is rotated we might get problems for judging how large a value is added to the 100% even if only a few values exist in a dataset.

Looking at the example visualization in Figure 2.11, we can see that four quantities are visually represented as circle sectors with different areas (and angles). Additionally, the textual labels representing the percentage values help to solve a comparison task, but what would happen if we let away those labels? For the light red sectors it might be easy to judge and compare their sizes reliably but the darker red sectors differ in size only a little bit (just 1.8% difference), making it perceptually hard to explore them for their size difference with a pie chart. On the other hand, visualizing the same dataset as bar charts make a big difference in the response time and accuracy for the task of comparing the values for their sizes, in case we conducted a comparative user study. The difference comes from the visual variables in use. In the pie chart, the visual variables angle and circle sector area are used, which make it perceptually more difficult to solve this comparison task than the visual variables used in the bar chart which are bar length or even just the position of the tallest point of each bar. The phenomenon of having various options for visualizing data can be found in nearly any visual encoding of a dataset. Finding out which visualization is best for the task at

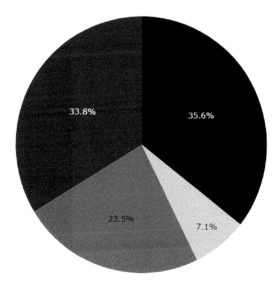

Figure 2.11 A pie chart is one way to visualize quantities, but a bar chart makes it easier to compare the values due to the fact that it encodes the quantities in the bar lengths instead of the circle sector angles [73].

hand can be done by conducting a user study, varying the visual variables as independent variables and measuring the response time, accuracy, or even eye movements [44] as dependent variables. However, this generates another kind of dataset, in the case of eye movements, a spatiotemporal dataset for which advanced visualization techniques and algorithmic concepts are required to identify patterns [8].

Apart from quantitative data, we can also look at ordinal data for which an order of the individual data elements is required. Such an order is typically visually encoded by the position on the display, for example, showing the bigger ones on top and the smaller ones at the bottom of the display. Categorical data describes the fact that data elements might belong to one or several categories or classes. In a visual encoding, such categories are typically shown by a grouping effect using the Gestalt law of proximity or similarity, sometimes even visually drawing borders around visual elements, for example, when applying a clustering algorithm that does not create clear group structures but produces some group overlaps. Hence, another visual variable has to be used to indicate the groups and subgroups.

Exercises

- Exercise 2.3.1.1: Imagine you have counted the number of cars and their brands crossing a certain measurement station at a motorway. Design a bar chart that shows the number of cars per brand.
- Exercise 2.3.1.2: If you have additional time information, for example, hourly, daily, or weekly measurements. How would you design a diagram that lets you compare trends of such numbers over time?

2.3.2 Graph/network visualization

Relational data exist in many forms but always have one aspect in common. The idea behind such data is that it connects objects or people, that is, if those stand in some kind of relation, we speak of relational data, or a graph to express it in another way [18, 47]. For example, people might communicate via a social network or they might write emails to exchange information with each other. This scenario makes the people to the vertices of a graph and the number of messages or the extent of the messages to weighted relations, also called edges in the terminology of graph theory [84]. There are lots of options to visually encode such vertices and edges [47], typically focusing on identifying paths in a graph or exploring certain structures [106], so-called clusters. However, to reach the goal of a good visualization of a graph, or also called network if the edges are directed and weighted, one has to follow aesthetic graph drawing criteria [190, 191, 192] that describe how nice a graph looks like or even more, how well a graph can be read for paths and clusters, hence aesthetics is understood in the sense of readability instead of pure beauty and aesthetics [38]. Prominent aesthetic criteria in graph drawing and graph visualization are the minimization of link crossings, the minimization of link lengths, the minimization of node-link, link-link, and node-node overlaps, the maximization of symmetries in a graph, the maximization of orthogonality (i.e., size of angles at link intersections), or the minimization of link bends (if those are used) which is just a short list of such criteria [192].

Visualization techniques for graphs exist in two major forms: node-link diagrams and adjacency matrices (see Figure 2.12). Node-link diagrams model the vertices as visual representatives of certain shapes like circles, triangles, or squares [47], while the edges are encoded as straight lines (with or without arrowheads for indicating the direction (see Figure 2.12(a))) of a certain thickness, tapered, partial, curved, or orthogonal links, just to mention

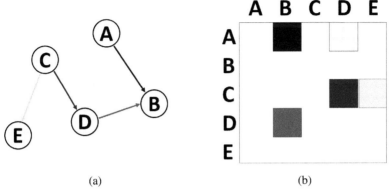

(a)   (b)

Figure 2.12 Two different ways to visually encode relational data while the edges of the graph have directions and weights, also known as a network [106]: (a) A node-link diagram. (b) An adjacency matrix.

a few [125]. Adjacency matrices, on the other hand, represent each vertex twice in a row and column of a matrix while the weighted edge is visually encoded as color-coded cell at the intersection point of the corresponding matrix row and column (see Figure 2.12(b)). The benefit of such matrices is that they scale to millions of vertices and edges since they do not produce link crossings and can even be drawn in pixel size; however, reading paths from such a representation is challenging, even impossible [106]. But identifying clusters can be done easily, in case a matrix reordering algorithm has brought the matrix into a good structure beforehand [20], typically requiring advanced algorithms with high runtime complexities. Node-link diagrams are good at showing paths in a network but, on the other hand, they suffer from visual clutter [202] if too many links are crossing each other. There are even further visualization techniques for graphs, for example, adjacency lists [121], but also combinations from node-link diagrams and adjacency matrices are imaginable and might have their benefits for certain user tasks. Famous examples of such hybrids are MatLink [118] or NodeTrix [119].

Exercises

- Exercise 2.3.2.1: Think about your own social network, for example, Facebook, Twitter, or LinkedIn. How can you visually represent with whom you and the others from your network are connected/connected most?

- Exercise 2.3.2.2: How do you represent different kinds of relations between you and your friends, for example, knowing each other, sending emails, calling, family relationships, and so on?

2.3.3 Hierarchy visualization

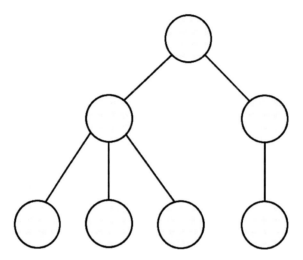

Figure 2.13   A hierarchy can be visualized as a node-link tree with a root node, parent nodes, child nodes, and the nodes on the deepest level being, the leaf nodes.

Hierarchies [211, 212] can come in two general forms, either as some kind of containment hierarchy or based on the principle of subordination. A containment hierarchy leads, as the name expresses, to containing elements. The most popular example of this is probably a file system in which files are contained in subdirectories and again contained in other subdirectories, actually everything is contained in a root directory. Also, geographic regions might be considered as some kind of containment hierarchy. Regions are contained in countries, countries in continents, and all continents belong to the earth. On the other hand, if we look at family hierarchies [63] composed of grandparents, parents, and children, we are confronted by the principle of subordination which also exists in a company structure or a league system, for example, the football leagues which consist of several levels depending on the professionality and strength of the teams.

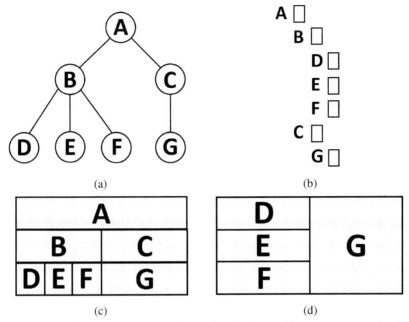

(a)   (b)

(c)   (d)

Figure 2.14   At least four major visual metaphors for hierarchical data exist coming in the form of: (a) A node-link diagram. (b) An indented plot. (c) A stacking approach. (d) A nested representation (in which only the leaf nodes are shown).

Hierarchical data can be stored in a so-called Newick format, which is some kind of nested parentheses format with semicolons separating the elements on the same hierarchy level. Each hierarchy has in common that it has a root node, parent nodes, and child nodes which stand in a parent-child relationship. Nodes on the same hierarchy level with the same parent are called sibling nodes, while nodes on the deepest level in the hierarchy are called leaf nodes or leaves for short. Nodes that are neither a root node nor a leaf node are called inner nodes. Each inner node has a number of children which is expressed by the so-called branching factor. Actually, a hierarchy can be infinitely deep, but for reasons of simplicity, we only look at finite hierarchies, in this book, this is, they consist of a finite number of nodes (see Figure 2.13 for a node-link diagram of a hierarchy).

For the visualization of hierarchies, there actually exist four major metaphors which are following the principles of indentation, nesting, stacking, or linking (see Figure 2.14). Actually, also hybrid forms are imaginable, which combine two or more of those hierarchy visualization metaphors.

Typical tasks in hierarchy visualization [224] are to visually explore if a hierarchy is balanced, how deep it is, how the branching factor is, or which subhierarchies look similar or dissimilar. Also data attachments can be explored in different hierarchical granularities, for example, water levels in a river system (which is hierarchical by nature) [65] or software metrics in a software system (in which the hierarchy is defined by the developers) [39, 54].

Exercises

- Exercise 2.3.3.1: Create a family tree of all the people from your own family like father, mother, grandfathers, grandmothers, sisters, brothers, and so on.
- Exercise 2.3.3.2: Design a good visualization for the hierarchical file system on your computer. How do you show the file sizes and the file type in the hierarchy at the same time?

2.3.4 Multivariate data visualization

Multivariate data typically occurs if we have to deal with tables [116], for example, given as an Excel table. Such tabular data consists of rows and columns while the rows are so-called observations or cases, and the columns contain the attributes or variables. At the intersection cells of each row with a column, we can find entries that can come in numerical, categorical, or textual form, to mention the most important ones. The form actually gives a hint about the data type each column attribute is based on. We talk about univariate data if just one column exists, bivariate data if two columns exist, trivariate data if three columns exist, and multivariate data if more than three columns exist.

The most important task to be solved when we work with multivariate data is a correlation task. This means we are asking the question whether two or more of the attributes stand in a correlation behavior, that is, for example, the values under one attribute are behaving in a similar or dissimilar way to the values of another attribute. If the values under one attribute are increasing while those of another attribute are decreasing, we speak of a negative correlation, if both behave in the same or similar way we denote this behavior by a positive correlation. There are even finer differences in the correlation behavior such as exact linear, strong linear, homoscedastic, or heteroscedastic behavior [249], just to mention a few.

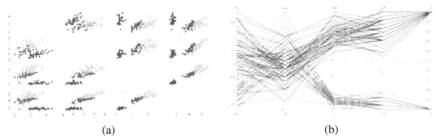

(a)   (b)

Figure 2.15   Visualizations for multivariate data: (a) A scatter plot matrix (SPLOM). (b) A parallel coordinate plot (PCP).

Visualizing such data is challenging, but there are some prominent visual encodings like histograms [185] (for univariate data), scatter plots [157] (for bivariate data), scatter plot matrices (SPLOMs) [78], parallel coordinate plots [130], or glyph-based representations [138] (for tri- and multivariate data) (see Figure 2.15). Scatter plot matrices are based on simple scatter plots and allow comparisons between all pairs of attributes as long as there is enough display space to show all the individual scatter plots of the scatter plot matrix. Parallel coordinate plots use parallel vertical axes to show the attribute values and polylines in-between. Those plots only show subsequent axis comparisons and typically suffer from visual clutter [202] caused by line crossings. Finally, glyph-based representations only show one glyph per case and make comparisons impossible; hence, correlation tasks are more difficult to solve than in scatter plot matrices or parallel coordinate plots in which the individual lines are integrated into the same diagram, and this is not the case in classical glyph-based visualizations like Chernoff faces [72], leaf glyphs [99], or software feathers [17].

Exercises

- Exercise 2.3.4.1: Compare typical visualizations for multivariate data like parallel coordinates, scatter plot matrices, and glyph-based representations like Chernoff faces, software feathers, or star plots.
- Exercise 2.3.4.2: Imagine you have an Excel table with multivariate data that is changing from day to day. Develop a visualization technique with which we can visually explore changes and trends in the correlation patterns.

2.3.5 Trajectory visualization

Moving objects, people, animals, or humans' eyes create some kind of trajectory [107]. That means they can rest for a while at a certain point in space, and then they slowly or rapidly move to the next position at which they might rest again for another while of another temporal extent. The challenging issue with trajectories is that a visual depiction can generate occlusion effects and visual clutter [202] very soon, in case one trajectory is quite long, and the same spatial regions are visited from time to time, or we have to deal with various trajectories that follow similar paths in space, leading to problems to take one for the other due to many crossings and overlaps of the line segments when visualized as a line-based representation. Modifying the shape of the trajectories to reduce clutter or to show similar movement behavior, for example, by edge bundling [124, 126], can be a powerful idea, but the original data is spatially changed, and hence, there is some kind of lie factor in the data-to-visualization mapping.

Figure 2.16   A static stimulus overplotted with a scanpath, that is, a sequence of fixation points. The sizes of the circles typically visually encode the fixation duration, that is, how long the eye fixated on a certain point in the visual stimulus.

One prominent application field for trajectory data comes from the research in eye tracking [87, 123]. An eye tracker [256] is a device that records fixations of people's visual attention and saccades between two consecutive fixations [56], that is, rapid eye movements. Each fixation can have a certain fixation duration while the saccades in-between more or less rapidly move between those fixations without acquiring any meaningful information from the visual stimulus (see Figure 2.16). Also, bird or general animal movements [146] are of particular interest for trajectory visualizations since birds might travel far distances from one continent to another one due to changing seasons, weather conditions, and the modifications in food offered by mother nature. Biologists are interested in the birds' traveling strategy to understand how they generally behave, for example, whether they are exposed to anomalies due to changes in their natural environments. The bird behavior might give insights into effects that are hardly recognizable without such trajectory data. There are various application examples in which trajectories play a crucial role, however, visually exploring such spatiotemporal data over space, time, and the objects, people, or animals involved in is a really challenging task.

Exercises

- Exercise 2.3.5.1: Take into account your own moving strategy over one day from starting the day until going to bed in the evening. Design a trajectory visualization of such a dataset and add your own data to a geographic map.
- Exercise 2.3.5.2: Why is it difficult to visually compare thousands of trajectories over space and time? Can you imagine algorithmic solutions for this problem that support the visualization?

2.3.6 Text visualization

Text is probably occurring most frequently in our everyday data lives. We would not consider text as data, and it is more used to communicate, to exchange information among people. But text can also be taken into account from the data perspective, for example, trying to find patterns in it like word frequencies which is a simple task, to explore semantic meanings of text fragments which turn out to be much more challenging. Hence, modern neural networks are powerful techniques to support data analysts in such semantic-finding tasks. From a visualization perspective, there exists various text representations, with a word or tag cloud [51, 133] as one way to show frequent words in a text corpus (see Figure 2.17). More complex ones use pixel-based representations [142] to show the distribution of special text fragments in a larger text corpus. For example, in source code of a larger software project, one might be interested in the occurrences of special programming language-specific keywords, for example, indicated by color coding as in the SeeSoft tool [91] or in a triangular shape for code similarities [58].

Figure 2.17   A text corpus can also be split into words and their occurrence frequencies while the common prefixes can be used to reduce the display space in use for showing a word cloud, known as a prefix word cloud [51].

If we consider DNA sequences as textual data, one task might be to identify similar subsequences in several of those DNA sequences. This can hardly be done purely visually. We need algorithms that are able to rapidly compare several such sequences and maybe align them in a way that similar subsequences are placed on top of each other in a so-called consensus matrix [71]. These multiple sequence alignment algorithms [137] can work on any kind of text fragments, for example, as a naive way to detect plagiarism in two or more texts. However, the pure algorithmic solution is only half as valuable if it is not supported by extra visual encodings applied to the alignments. For this reason, color coding can be of great support to quickly recognize similar subsequences and also anomalies, that is, subsequences that are not fitting in the text structure.

In general, all of the data we described in this section can have a time-varying, that is, dynamic nature. Visualizing the dynamics in the data is of particular interest for researchers, for example, to set the current state in context to the past, but also to learn from the past to predict the future. The last idea could involve deep learning and neural networks to solve such classification or prediction tasks reliably and efficiently. However, visual depictions of the time-varying data [4] are still important, even if algorithms have to process the data to generate structures and insights in it, maybe on several temporal granularities.

Exercises

- Exercise 2.3.6.1: Imagine you have two different texts of a certain length. How could you design a visualization that shows similar text passages?
- Exercise 2.3.6.2: Could a matrix visualization be useful to compare two or more text fragments? How can the matrix be extended to compare more than two text fragments?

2.4 Design and Prototyping

Apart from the visualization techniques for the individual data types we should take into account the visual and interface design rules to create a user-friendly and powerful visualization tool equipped with various interaction techniques [258] (see Figure 2.18 for an example of a hand-drawn user interface). The design is typically guided by user tasks, that is, hypotheses about the data that have to be confirmed, rejected, or refined [139, 178]. To find answers to these hypotheses, the users of such a tool have to solve tasks from a certain task group, for example, search tasks, counting tasks, estimation tasks, comparison tasks, correlation tasks, and many more, typically depending on the application field the data stems from and the users in the form of experts or nonexperts who are trying to find hints about their data problems at hand. The design of a visualization tool or dashboard is not just, including the user interface with buttons, sliders, text fields, and so on, but also the visual design that is required to create powerful and perceptually useful visualizations for the tasks at hand. Those user interface components as well as the visualizations have to be arranged in a user-friendly and well-designed layout, in the best case a dynamic one, allowing the users to adapt the layout on their demands. Moreover, interaction techniques have to be taken into account that connect and link the individual components. This means the interface components must be connected in a meaningful way but even the interface components with the visualization techniques, as well as the visualizations themselves in case they are shown as multiple coordinated views [200] to provide insights on the visually encoded data from several perspectives.

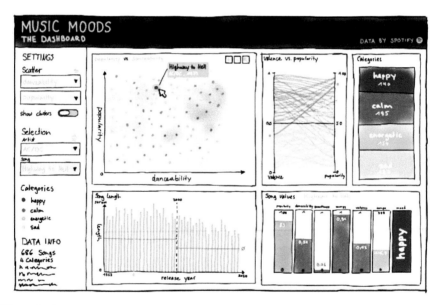

Figure 2.18   A hand-drawn graphical user interface composed of several views and perspectives on a dataset (permission to use this figure given by Sarah Clavadetscher).

Creating such a user interface with all of its ingredients at the right places requires in understanding some rules about prototyping, meaning either drawing the dashboard by hand, as some kind of sketch or mockup, or if the designer is familiar with external tools, the dashboard might even be designed in a computer-supported style. However, drawing it by hand typically means more flexibility for the designer than using a computer program (see Figure 2.18 for an example of a hand-drawn graphical user interface). This section is organized as follows: In Section 2.4.1, we describe visual design rules and which aspects are important when creating a dashboard from the visual perspective. Section 2.4.2 illustrates some no-goes in visualization and which concepts exist to get rid of them or at least improve the situation. The interface design rules are explained in Section 2.4.3 while we describe how a user interface can be created step-by-step in Section 2.4.4, also looking into mockups, hand drawings, sketches, wireframes, and prototypes.

2.4.1 Visual design rules

Creating visualization techniques for a given dataset can be a simple but even a challenging task, depending on how the dataset is structured, which data types it is composed of, and which role the tasks at hand will play. No matter how complicated the creation task gets, we should definitely follow some predefined visual design rules to avoid creating diagrams that become useless or lead to difficulties when interpreting the visually encoded data [232]. Some of the visual design rules only occur in very specific situations, but we should be aware of them during the creation process already and not afterward to guarantee a more efficient design process. One general problem comes from the fact that we have to design a visualization that allows us to rapidly detect visual patterns [245] that gives us a chance to explore the visually encoded data. Hence, the visual design should follow a rule that data interpretation gets supported in a visual way. The second but less prioritized aspect during the visual design phase is aesthetics. A diagram should look aesthetically pleasing [38] because that it is attractive to the eye and people like to watch it. This might help us to remember a specific diagram much better, that is, to build some kind of mental map. The challenge with data interpretation and aesthetics [38] comes from the fact that these criteria stand in a so-called trade-off behavior. The better we can interpret the data visually, the less aesthetics is involved, and vice versa. Therefore, the best strategy is to first focus on data interpretation before we try to make it nicer.

It is important to let the data speak [34], that is, support storytelling [186]. This also means that we should not immediately start with summaries and aggregations, a typical scenario for statistics focusing on deriving aggregated values from a dataset like a median, a variance, or a standard deviation for example. Showing the data in its complete nonaggregated form can help to identify data gaps, without guiding the observer in a wrong direction, causing misinterpretations of the data. A person inspecting a diagram can hence interpret the data in its raw form and try to interpret the data gaps, asking questions about why the data elements are missing and in the best case allowing to even fill the gaps with missing values. A picture of the data is of great support to solve those tasks since a picture can say more than a thousand words [88], in case it is designed in a proper and accurate way. Hence, it is a good advice to use graphics whenever possible, be it for data exploration or for presenting and disseminating the obtained results. Pictures can even visually encode many aspects about data, like numerical values from several attributes, in a very small display region, making it a visually scalable approach.

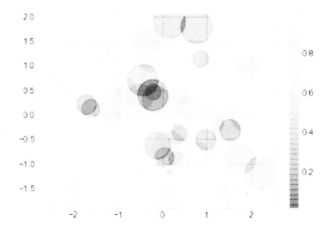

Figure 2.19   A diagram that includes axis labels, scales, guiding lines, and a legend.

Even if we created a good diagram to show the data, there are very important ingredients that one should never forget. For example, adding labels at axes if there are some. Hence, this is important to set the data into some general context. Such labels could express meta data like physical units for example, or even numerical values for the scale in use, or even several scales in use. It makes a difference if we inspect the diagram focusing on meters or kilometers. Moreover, the scale should be including guiding lines that do not occlude or clutter [202] the rest of the diagram. Such guiding lines help the eye to solve comparison tasks, for example, when reading several values in a diagram (see Figure 2.19 for a simple diagram following the visual design rules). In general, diagrams need words to make them even more understandable, but if too many words are used, this might again be counterproductive. Such words or labels should be distinguishable and they should be readable, meaning choosing a good size and font style. If too many visual variables are integrated into a diagram, and they might be unclear when just looking at the diagram, legends should be placed next to the diagram to explain the data-to-visualization mapping, for example for the values and categories in use and which sizes, lengths, or colors are encoding the data values. Color is one of the most applied visual variable in a visualization, but picking the wrong color scales can lead to misinterpretations when trying to interpret the data by looking at a visual depiction, for example, the often cited rainbow colormap [32] could cause problems or colors that are problematic for people who have color vision deficiencies or who are color blind [174]. Color perception [260] is a research field on its own. Similar rules hold for scale granularities meaning values for minimum and maximum should be derivable from the legend. All in all, the storytelling is one of the most important issues when designing a good visualization. A diagram should be readable just like a good book, following a red line, chapter by chapter, with a final Aha effect.

Exercises

- Exercise 2.4.1.1: Create a scatterplot for bivariate data with labels, axis descriptions, and scales, together with guiding lines for the scales.
- Exercise 2.4.1.2: Can you create a diagram that includes more than one scale on one axis but that is still usable and readable?

2.4.2 No-goes and bad smells

There are lots of design aspects that have a negative impact on data interpretation. Such no-goes have to be avoided whenever possible, in cases, we are aware of them. Hence, it is of interest to study this section since it describes some of the major problems, we can be confronted with when designing a visualization. Increasing the aesthetics and beauty of a visualization does not necessarily mean that it also gets more effective from the data interpretation side, meaning with such a nice visualization it might still be difficult to understand the visualization and to find visual patterns that can be remapped to the data patterns, with the goal to explore the underlying data. When possible, we should avoid the three major problems that we identify as visual clutter, the lie factor, and chart junk (see Figure 2.21) [202, 232]; however, in some cases it is hard to completely mitigate such a situation, for example, if too many visual elements are present, and we have to show all of them to

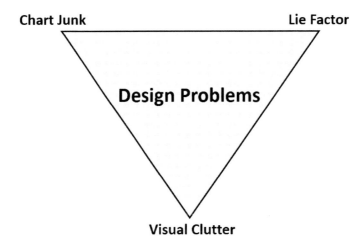

Figure 2.20   Three of the major design problems come in the form of chart junk, the lie factor, and visual clutter.

understand the data or if the data values do not allow to encode them in a visual variable in a proportional data-to-visualization manner, maybe due to the lack of display space.

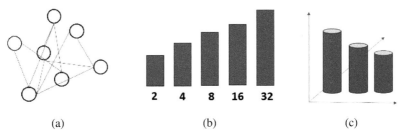

(a)   (b)   (c)

Figure 2.21   Design problems can occur in several ways: (a) Visual clutter. (b) A lie factor. (c) Chart junk.

Visual clutter is "the state in which excess items or their disorganization lead to a degradation of performance at some task" [202]. As the definition says, there could be too many visual objects or a certain number of them might not be well organized, that is, visually structured to derive some meaning and knowledge from them. This effect typically occurs in line-based diagrams containing many line crossings and overlaps. The lie factor describes the situation that the effect in the data is not the same as in the corresponding visualization, leading to visual distortions and hence, to

misinterpretations of the data. The following formula expresses the general
lie factor l for a sequence of values $v_{i,\,1\leq i\leq n}, v_i \in \mathbb{R}, n \in \mathbb{N}$

$$l : G \times D, (g, d) \mapsto \frac{g}{d}$$

while g is the size of the effect in the graphics and d is the size of the effect
in the data. Moreover, the size of an effect is given by the ratio $\frac{v_i - v_{i-1}}{v_{i-1}}$ while
v_i is always the second value and v_{i-1} is the first value in the ordered values.
The lie factor should be between 0.95 and 1.05 to avoid distortions. Chart junk
describes the effect of having "overdesigned" a diagram, meaning the same
data variable is visually represented in several visual variables. This issue can
cause misinterpretations, mostly if 3D is used for an originally well-designed
2D diagram. One of the rules here could be: "Less is more," a fact that might
refer to Tufte's principle of minimalism or minimalistic design, also bringing
into play the so-called data-to-ink ratio explaining the idea of using as less ink
as possible for visually encoding data elements, or the concept of maximizing
the data-to-ink ratio. Ink should not be wasted for visual objects that we do
not associate with data elements, and there should also not be any redundant
elements, maybe leading to visual ambiguities. The chart junk and data-to-ink
problems are oftentimes found in so-called infographics that try to include
specific application domain aspects into a diagram, trying to put the diagram
into a certain application context, but in most cases, decreasing the visual
usefulness of such a diagram by reducing the data interpretability aspect, for
example, perspective distortions.

Some further design aspects are to keep the visual design consistent and
to not include unnecessary modifications of the visual scale, for example
by using several scales in several diagrams depicting the same dataset. For
dynamic, that is, time-varying data, we should be careful with animated
diagrams [233] since those create a challenge for comparison tasks. Nonan-
imated, that is, static, diagrams show most of the dynamic data in one view
and give an observer time to inspect all shown time steps while reducing
the cognitive effort when comparing the data elements over time. This refers
somehow to the visual information-seeking mantra: Overview first, zoom and
filter, then details-on-demand [216]. In an animation the overview about the
data is completely lost. It is also important to inspect the data from different
granularity levels, bringing into play issues like overview-and-detail [100] or
focus-and-context [128].

Exercises

- Exercise 2.4.2.1: Find a visualization or a diagram on the web that suffers from visual clutter, chart junk, and/or the lie factor. Describe in which form the visual design problems can be found in the visualization or diagram.
- Exercise 2.4.2.2: Given a sequence of natural numbers $v_1, \ldots, v_n$. Design a diagram that visually encodes such values with and without an explicit lie factor.

2.4.3 Interface design rules

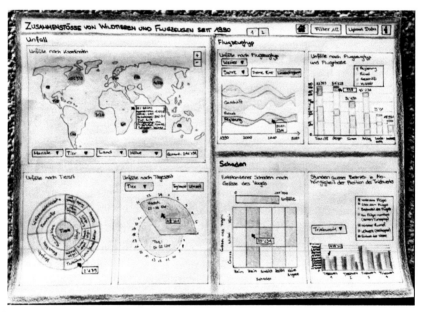

Figure 2.22   A hand-drawn mockup of a graphical user interface (permission to use this figure by Sarah Last).

Not only do the visualizations have to be taken into account when designing and implementing a dashboard for interactive data visualization, but even more the user interface [109] in which the visualization techniques are integrated as well as additional user interface components for applying interactions, starting algorithms, or just adapting parameters (see Figure 2.22 for a hand-drawn mockup of a graphical user interface). A user interface is a complex playground that has to follow a certain layout, to help preserving the mental map when finding user interface components easily and rapidly, to reduce the cognitive efforts in case we have to start searching for the important things all the time. The eight golden rules of user interface design [217] describe a good way to follow the most important principles, just like a checklist, when thinking about a user interface, even in the phase of creating a sketch or a mockup already. The challenging issue with a user interface for visualization comes from the fact that it is not only dependent on those eight rules, but even more on the design and interactive functionality of the integrated visualizations. It may be noted that there are various design rules when it comes to designing user interfaces, in particular, graphical user interfaces (GUIs) but many of those rules are also dependent on the application scenario. For example, designing a user interface for medical applications [75, 76] is much different from one for fraud or malware detection [67], but there is some kind of common design rule set that holds for any kind of user interface. Finally, a user evaluation with or without eye tracking [8, 152, 153] is required to find hints about usefulness, user-friendliness, and performances in terms of response times, error rates, or even eye movements [26] with additional physiological measures [25]. Also, the qualitative feedback from the users in form of verbal interviews, think-aloud, or talk-aloud, even gestures, can be of great support for the designers, in particular for visual analytics tools [27].

One of the first criteria is to keep the design consistent. This holds for the color coding, for the shapes, for the presentation speed when using animations [233], actually for any kind of visual component that includes some kind of visual feature. Also certain actions and interactions should be consistent for similar scenarios, for example selecting a visual element should always work in the same way, no matter which kind of visual component the selection interaction actually is applied on. Consistency is important since it reduces the cognitive efforts [231], that is, users do not have to rethink again and again for the same or similar processes, meaning the mental map is somehow preserved [9, 10] during a visual exploration strategy. An identical terminology should also be chosen for labels or textual output that is produced in the interface, but not too much text should be shown to avoid an information overload. Menus, descriptions, error messages, and the like should follow the same rules, for example font sizes, font faces, font types, and the like. Also the layout in the components and subcomponents should be the same, even the borders or distances of the components to each other, exploiting the Gestalt laws of proximity and similarity [147]. The universal usability is also of interest, for example, a user interface can be used by Europeans, Asians, or Americans, but all having different backgrounds, experiences, languages, signage, symbols, and the like [156]. The design must include a dynamic nature of a user interface, for example, adapting the labels and textual information in a user-defined language. Apart from the regional differences, there might even be differences between experts and nonexperts, young and old users, even visually impaired or physically disabled people should be taken into account during the design phase [89]. Since a user interface is interactive, it reacts with feedback to actions. This also holds for a progress bar that shows, as the name says, the progress of a process that runs in the background telling users how long they should be waiting for a result. Such feedback should also be given for buttons, for example, indicating a reaction by showing a different color of the button or showing it as "pressed". Longer dialogues should be split into dialogue groups to create some kind of confidence after the completion of each dialogue group.

Even if we integrated any kind of feature into a user interface we should avoid impossible actions by graying them out in the menu already. This strategy leads to the positive effect that users are not able to make errors that easily. The user interface reduces the chance to allow errors by removing impossible actions. Related to error prevention is the guidance to certain features by useful hints. Just in case an action was wrongly done, there should be an option to undo this action [258]. In any case, the users should keep the control over the user interface, however in some situations it is good if the machine takes over and at least suggests some useful next steps [171]. This could be more important for nonexperts than for experts. Finally, the number of things to be remembered should be reduced due to our bad short-term memory [245]. We have a very limited capacity to store and process information, also in the field of visualization in which we can see the objects visually in front of our eyes. All of the aforementioned rules are useful for UI design, but they are dependent on the application scenario as well as the display space differing between mobile phones, laptops, and powerwalls [210]. Moreover, if web-based applications are in focus, keep in mind that the users can vary a lot, and they might have various experience levels, requirements, and demands.

Exercises

- Exercise 2.4.3.1: In a user interface we oftentimes find so-called progress bars to show us how long we must wait until a process is completed. Describe typical challenges when including a progress bar in a user interface.

- Exercise 2.4.3.2: What are additional challenges when sharing a user interface online, that is, making it accessible to all people in the world?

2.4.4 Creating a graphical user interface

A graphical user interface is something like the playground for any visualization or visual analytics tool, but also a dashboard "lives" in there. This means the playground builds something like the limited environment in which we can find functions, tools, and algorithms to explore data. To keep the data exploration tool running in a reliable way, the components have to be chosen carefully as well as their layout [217]. The designer has to come up with a list of features that are absolutely necessary to solve the tasks at hand and places them somewhere in the user interface. Moreover, such features, in the form of interface components and visualizations, have to be linked in a clever way, by interaction techniques that the users can apply depending on their tasks-of-interest. Although this sounds like a simple idea it can become quite challenging, in particular, if a dashboard contains various features that have to be placed into the limited display region in a meaningful and user-friendly way. Before starting the implementation phase we should be able to provide some kind of sketch or mockup of the user interface; however, we can still make adaptations during the implementation phase. In most cases, the originally designed user interface will not be the one that the users finally see to explore their data. We typically learn during the design process [13] how to improve it but we might get even more hints to improve it when real users are working with it.

What we are going to do is creating some kind of prototype [77, 101] of the user interface, in the best case, also including some functionalities. The prototype is something like a template, to allow producing the tool based on a certain visual agreement. This step is even more necessary in cases in which the designers and the software developers are two different groups of people who more or less work independently. The coders have to know what to code to achieve the desired result. Each prototype is something like an interactive mockup that can have any degree or level of fidelity [77], although a mockup is sometimes not regarded as a real prototype. No matter how complex a prototype will be, the goal is always to explore issues like used material, costs, developers involved, time to create the tool, or in which way the tool will be developed, with which components and which functionalities.

By creating a prototype, we get a better understanding of the final product and which modifications must be made, in any stage during the development phase to keep the tool in the desired form. Also aspects like consistency and structuring are required during the development phase. Moreover, it might be of particular interest to think about which output device or display (see Section 2.5.3) the user interface will be shown on and which technical functionalities are possible, for example, from the perspective of interactions, we might consider mouse, keyboard, voice, gesture, or gaze interactions, just to mention a few (see Section 2.5.2).

A prototype can be hand-drawn, or it can be created by means of a software. If we draw a prototype (or mockup, sketch) by hand, we have a higher degree of flexibility than if we used an external software for which we have to understand the useful features first. Drawing by hand is something that we already learn in the first years of our lives, hence we might feel more comfortable with that. The fidelity [77] describes how detailed a prototype is, for example, is it just a static picture or is it already dynamic, and we can interact with it to some degree. The fidelity gives an impression of how far we are away from the final product [96]. With a prototype, it is easier to imagine the final product than when reading pages of text describing all the components, features, and functionalities. By showing a prototype it is also easier for possible customers to imagine how the final product will look like and if they are confident with the design developed so far; hence, it accelerates the decision making of the customers. A prototype is something like a visual language that both the designers and the customers understand, to come to a common agreement before starting the development phase. Actually, there are several ways to create a form of a prototype, depending on the fidelity, that is, how far we can get to the final product. Those could be described as a sketch or hand-drawing, a wireframe, a mockup, a real prototype with lots of functions, and after that, we reach the final software with all of its functions and interactions.

There is a list of design tools and software to support the designers when creating user interfaces [16]. Those tools range from classical graphic drawing programs for 2D and 3D graphics to more prototype-like software systems full of features. Some of the tools are Justinmind, Mockplus, Adobe Photoshop, Sketch, Adobe XD, Figma, UXPin, InVision, Omnigraffle, Axure, Lucidchart, Proto.io, Marvel, Microsoft Visio, Miro Moqups, AFFINITY Designer, Adobe Illustator, Inkscape, Xara Designer Pro X, MockFlow, Gravit Designer, Fireworks, or Cinema 4D, just to mention a few from a really long list.

Exercises

- Exercise 2.4.4.1: Describe and discuss the benefits and drawbacks of designing a user interface by hand, including visualization techniques.
- Exercise 2.4.4.2: Draw a user interface for visually depicting social networks consisting of people who are related to some extent.

2.5 Interaction

Without interaction a visualization would just be a static picture that can, in its static form, be powerful as well but awaking it to life by allowing interactions [258] provides many more opportunities to dig deeper into the visualized data, to navigate in it, to modify views, to filter the data, and to inspect the data from several, even linked, perspectives [200, 222]. Interactions do not only depend on the used visualization techniques, also on the displays and the experience levels of the users, also on the fact if the users might suffer from visual, perceptual, or physical disabilities. For example, interacting on a small-scale display when using a smartphone is much different than interacting on a medium-scale computer monitor while a large-scale powerwall display [210] even allows walking around during interactions. There is no best display for interactions, each of them has its benefits and drawbacks and requires suitable technologies to make the implemented interaction techniques run smoothly, for the task at hand. Not all interaction modalities like gaze, touch, mouse, keyboard, gestures, and the like, can be applied to any kind of display, for example, on a small-scale smartphone display it is more likely to interact by touch than by using a computer mouse. Moreover, on a large-scale powerwall display, it is beneficial to allow gesture, gaze, or body motion interactions than relying on touching the powerwall with one's fingers. Touch means standing very close to the display which, on the other hand, would mean walking around a lot in front of the powerwall, with a high chance to miss important details due to a lack of overview.

Even more advanced technologies like virtual, augmented, or mixed reality can bring new challenges for interaction techniques. In particular, the field of immersive analytics [173] demands for a combination of interaction modalities, also requiring to be applicable on many linked displays, maybe with various users in front of those displays [80], with the goal to visually and algorithmically allow explorations and analyses of data from a multitude of application domains. Not only the ingredients directly related to interaction like the displays, modalities, the users, or the linking of the user interface components are crucial ingredients, also the data processing and transformation, running in the background build a huge and crucial part of a visualization tool. If the data structures and algorithms are not properly chosen and implemented, interactions cannot run smoothly and quickly, hence the interactive responsiveness would suffer from the badly designed algorithmic approaches when it comes to data handling like storing, accessing, and manipulating it, either offline or online as a real-time data visualization. We argue that creating a visualization tool or a dashboard for data exploration and data analysis is some kind of interdisciplinary field that requires expert knowledge in many related disciplines like visualization, interaction, user interface design, perception, but also in data structures and algorithms, programming, software engineering, and many more. Making design mistakes in any of such related disciplines can cause performance issues that might make a visualization tool unusable.

In this section we describe major interaction categories that we can find in nearly any data visualization tool (Section 2.5.1). These interactions can be combined in various ways, typically depending on the user tasks. Moreover, Section 2.5.2 illustrates which kind of modalities exist and in which scenario they might be the best options to integrate with a visualization tool. The most important ones might be given by gaze, touch, mouse, keyboard, or gesture. Also the display on which a visualization tool should be shown plays a crucial role (Section 2.5.3), not only for the visualizations alone but also for the interaction techniques and interaction modalities. Finally, data can be explored best if it is shown from several perspectives, bringing multiple coordinated views into play. Those are described in more detail in Section 2.5.4.

2.5.1 Interaction categories

Each individual interaction falls into a specific interaction category that describes the way how we interact, not on which display and with which interaction modality. For example, changing a visual variable in a visualization, like the color from a blue-to-red color scale to a topographic one, could be considered another visual encoding, hence it is showing something new about the data. This means that all changes in color scales, but even more, all changes of the visual encoding fall into this specific interaction category. Following this idea, we might come up with at least seven different interaction categories [258] that can be described as selecting, exploring, reconfiguring, encoding, abstracting, filtering, and connecting. Moreover, an eighth interaction category might be useful to include all changes to the exploration process itself, not directly to the visualization, which takes into account interactions like undo or redo, those that are typically more high-level interactions being applicable to sequences of interactions. The history of interactions also plays a role here, for example, to allow jumping back to a certain point during the exploration process, allowing to step back to any kind of former visualization tool configuration. This eighth category of interactions is typically applicable from the user interface directly and in most situations, shortcuts can be used to faster apply them, in case the users became more and more familiar with a visualization technique or user interface, that is, they changed their roles from nonexperts to experts in some way.

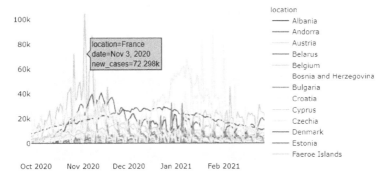

Figure 2.23   On a visualization depicting value changes over time, we can select a certain point, for example, to get detail information or to further use the selected data point in the exploration process.

The seven standard interaction categories include selecting visual elements (see Figure 2.23) as one of the most basic interaction techniques. Without selecting an element, we are typically not able to apply further interactions; hence, interactions build something like an interaction chain or interaction sequence. In cases, we even allow the undo of interactions we do not get a sequence of interactions anymore but something that looks more like an interaction hierarchy. Actually, not the interactions create a hierarchy, but more the states of the visualization tool that we are going to modify during the interaction process. Even more, allowing to reach the same state again after having applied many of those interactions, we get a graph or network of tool states that describes which states are reachable by which interactions that model the edges of this graph/network [41]. Exploring means to look around, that is, to change the view, for example, when scrolling or panning in a visualization that does not fit on the display. This interaction category helps when an overview cannot be provided in one view. Reconfiguring describes the effect of changing a visualization to make it usable for a certain task that could not be solved without the change. For example, adjusting visual elements to a common scale to make them comparable would be a useful feature, maybe using a baseline adjustment technique. Encoding actually allows to modify the visual variables to get a different perspective on the data while abstracting means to show more or less detail, like in zooming techniques. In cases in which only parts of the data are shown, maybe only those parts that follow a certain user-defined condition, we talk about filtering. Finally, connecting describes the way we link views in a visualization tool, with the goal to inspect the data from several perspectives at the same time, that is, simultaneously, for example, in a multiple coordinated view [200] described in Section 2.5.4.

Exercises

- Exercise 2.5.1.1: How would you design an interaction technique for selecting one point, several points, connected regions, or points in a previously selected region?
- Exercise 2.5.1.2: How would you design an interaction technique to select a pixel, a group of pixels, a line, or a group of (possibly intersecting) lines?

2.5.2 Interaction modalities

When interacting with a visualization tool, we need some kind of input channel as well as an output channel, both are required to allow a dialogue between a system and its users. As an example we might consider mouse clicks as the inputs and the visible impact of these clicks on a computer monitor, that is, this input–output build a modality when interacting on a computer monitor in a mouse-based user interface. Human–computer interaction defines a modality as a class of an individual channel of sensory input/output between a machine and human users [12] while there exists a difference between allowing only one modality (unimodal) or several of them (multimodal). There is a list of modalities ranging from keyboard, joystick, mouse, pointing device, touchscreen, speech recognition system, motion- or gesture-based system, or gaze-based ones, just to mention a few very popular modalities.

Unimodal modalities might be easier to apply and easier to implement in a visualization system, but can also become a limitation for certain tasks. For example, only using gaze-based interaction can cause problems due to the so-called Midas Touch problem [239] which is quite popular in the field of eye tracking [44, 86, 123]. Hence, further modalities are integrated like speech recognition, meaning if a person is looking around in a user interface nothing is activated by gaze only, but speaking out a certain kind of command, for example "press button" can start a specific interaction. This is somehow related to modern mobile phones on which speech recognition is implemented in the form of deep learning approaches, for example awakening a mobile phone to life by just saying "Hey Siri." Such a wake word [103] concept opens another way of interacting with such a system, although it slept before in a stand-by mode and only allowed the more traditional interaction modalities with the phone.

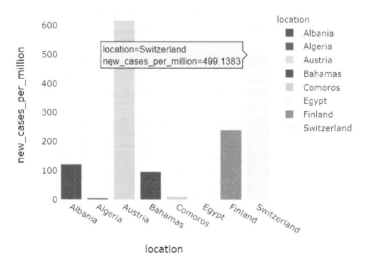

Figure 2.24   Interacting by using a computer mouse is one of the standard interaction modalities for visualization tools displayed on a classical computer monitor.

In a visualization tool we typically find the classical interaction modalities like a computer mouse (see Figure 2.24) and a keyboard, but also touch is possible depending on the fact that a touchscreen is used. However, touch can be problematic due to the humans' fingers that might cover certain tiny visual objects of pixel size and hence, the underlying information cannot be explored anymore [189]. A mouse cursor is much better in this scenario since it does not cover that much information than a human finger would do. Negatively, we can identify the problem of having a mouse not directly connected to the visualization system, that is, we have to understand the properties of a mouse on the desk first before we can apply it to the computer monitor. Touching with the finger is much more natural but it also brings new challenges into play, apart from the covering effect it creates some indirect body-to-body touch effect between human users, for example in cases in which many people use the same service like a ticket machine placed in a train station. This might cause negative issues, in particular during the COVID-19 pandemic, trying to avoid as many human-to-human contacts as possible [240]. Sure, we cannot ask people to bring their own computer mouse but we could integrate other interaction modalities like gaze-based interaction or speech recognition, however speech might be a problem in a noisy background like in the scenario of a ticket machine in a crowded train station and gaze causes problems related to the Midas touch problem and technological issues related to fixation accuracy.

Exercises

- Exercise 2.5.2.1: What are typical scenarios in a visualization tool that might be good candidates for using speech recognition as an interaction modality?
- Exercise 2.5.2.2: Imagine you have a visualization tool in which gaze-based interaction is integrated. What could be a challenging problem here? Hint: Midas Touch problem.

2.5.3 Displays

Each visualization tool must be presented somewhere, meaning a certain kind of display [165] is required to let the users see where they can apply an interaction for example and which impact such an interaction will have on the diagrams but also on the visual components of the user interface. There are various ways to display the visualizations that have been created, typically depending on the tasks to be solved and which visualizations are finally integrated into a visualization tool. For example, if many users are required we should create a web-based visualization tool that runs on a mobile phone, possibly being able to recruit many people since many of us own a mobile phone, even allowing crowd-sourcing user experiments [197]. However, the display itself is much smaller than the one of a standard computer, hence

Figure 2.25   Showing a geographic map on a large-scale display while the observer is equipped with an eye tracking device for either exploring where he is paying visual attention or for using the eye tracker as gaze-assisted interaction (figure provided by Lars Lischke).

the visualization tool itself must be designed in a different way than the one designed for the standard computer monitor. If many users have to explore a dataset visually at the same time, it might be a good idea to use a large-scale display [166], that is, a powerwall [210], allowing many people to collaboratively work on similar data analysis and visualization problems. A large display can also be useful for one observer, in cases in which an overview has to be given with many small integrated details (see Figure 2.25 for a geographic map on a large-scale display). The biggest issue here might be to merge the different findings of all the collaborators to find a common result, maybe in form of visual patterns that graphically model data patterns. The display plays a crucial role during the design but also the implementation phase. Large-, medium, and small-scale displays can make a difference not only for the visual and interface design but even more for the interaction design. Not every interaction technique that is applicable on a computer monitor can be applied in the same way on a mobile phone or on a powerwall.

Whether or not an interaction modality makes sense and is useful on a certain type of display depends on several aspects, also on the environment like noise in the background making speech more difficult to be applied, but there are some scenarios in which it is clear that a certain setup is not meaningful, for example using a computer mouse on a powerwall display (see Table 2.1 for a general overview about meaningfulness).

Table 2.1   Displays for which standard interaction modalities make sense or not: (++) very meaningful, (+) meaningful, (o) not clear, (-) not meaningful, and (–) not meaningful at all.

Display types and interaction modalities		
Small-scale	Medium-scale	Large-scale
Mobile phone	Computer monitor	Powerwall
Mouse	−	++	−
Keyboard	+	++	−
Joystick	−	+	-
Touch	++	+	+
Gesture	-	o	++
Speech	+	+	++
Gaze	+	+	+

Exercises

- Exercise 2.5.3.1: Discuss the differences of the usefulness when integrating interaction modalities like touch, gaze, mouse, keyboard, joystick, or gesture into different types of displays like small-scale displays (mobile phones), medium-scale displays (computer monitors), and large-scale displays (powerwalls).
- Exercise 2.5.3.2: Which kinds of displays are most useful for visualization tools, that is, dashboards? Discuss benefits and drawbacks.

2.5.4 Multiple coordinated views

A visualization tool rarely contains just one view on the data, it merely consists of many perspectives with different diagram types based on a multitude of parameters. In cases in which multiple of those views are integrated and in which the views are connected while the users are interacting we denote them as multiple coordinated views [200]. Depending on how large our display is we can integrate more or less views on the data being connected in the background in efficient data structures making a data handling possible to provide a fluent interactively responsive user interface. One specific interaction concept denoted by brushing and linking [243] is typically included, allowing to select a certain number of visual elements in one view that are then visually highlighted in all of the other views in which they are represented as well.

Brushing can be regarded as the operation of selecting one or a number of visual elements, maybe selected in a region, while linking describes the effect of seeing them in all of the other views in which they are existent, hence the multiple views are coordinated in some way, also depending on the users and the fact how they use the coordination. Multiple coordinated views (see Figure 2.26) can be found in user interfaces in medium- or large-scale displays [158], but less in small-scale displays like mobile phones due to the limited display sizes. By using multiple perspectives we hope to show visual patterns in different ways making them pop out in some views and in some others they might be invisible. Hence, the chance of seeing the visual patterns gets higher when providing multiple views instead of just one.

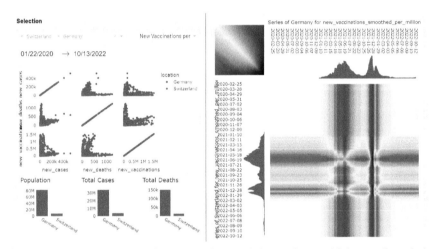

Figure 2.26 Several perspectives on a COVID-19 dataset in a multiple coordinated view (figure provided by Sarah Clavadetscher).

A big challenge for multiple coordinated views comes from the fact that the data handling has to keep all of the views up-to-date, that is, a certain control mechanism has to run in the background that updates all of the views when just one gets changed. Such a model-view-controller architecture can be quite useful in such situations. The controller keeps track of the changes and sends updates to keep the visualization tool consistent in all of the perspectives and views. This can also include user interface components not just the views in the visualization tool. For example, updating a visualization could also cause to modify or update the visual appearance of buttons or sliders, in cases in which the range of values got changed based on a user interaction it would make sense to also avoid that the users can select the wrong value ranges in cases in which the range sliders would not have been updated. Views should not be changed abruptly since this would destroy the users' mental maps [150], hence in case changes have to be made to one or several views, those should be done smoothly, for example including some kind of smooth animation [242] to allow users keeping track of the changes, a typical scenario in which arrangements of visual elements have to be made, maybe caused by a new ordering or alignment strategy.

Exercises

- Exercise 2.5.4.1: Which role plays the data handling running in the background when interacting in multiple coordinated views?
- Exercise 2.5.4.2: How many views can be integrated in a visualization tool at the same time? Discuss.

3

Python, Dash, Plotly, and More

There are various ways to implement a visualization tool, even in the form of an interactive dashboard [255]. The focus of this book is on the programming language Python [160], combined with Dash and Plotly which will be described in detail in the following sections. Python is a popular high-level programming language with a specific focus on code readability by making use of mandatory indentation rules. It supports a certain number of programming paradigms, typically the functional and object-oriented ones. One of the great benefits of designing and implementing visualization tools as dashboards in Python is the fact that the created tool can be made publicly available in an easy way by deploying it on a server, hence making it accessible for a number of people all over the world [201]. This again requires a user-friendly design solution that takes into account the various differences in spoken and written languages, cultures, signage, and the like, which is also reflected in the eight golden rules for designing user interfaces (see Section 2.4.3) [217]. Moreover, other design rules, focusing on the visual design (see Section 2.4.1) [232], are also crucial ingredients when building such web-based solutions for data visualization tools.

Including the important aspects from the field of visualization, visual analytics, interaction, algorithmics, and the many related disciplines of this interdisciplinary topic [144], we are now prepared to learn about the concepts required to actually start building a tool [172], once the design phase has been completed. This does not mean that the design phase is really over. In many scenarios, we still learn about the usefulness of a certain feature when it is really applied in the running tool or even when we think about it again in a discussion, and hence, there should always be an option to redesign what we have created before (at least partially), until we and our end users are confident with the results [214]. This actually brings into play user evaluation [152], that is, the users can either be on board during the design phase and even implementation phase or they can test the final product, that is, after it has been completed, based on the design criteria and requirements that we got so far. This again means that starting with an original sketch, mockup, or prototype (Section 2.4.4), we are able to modify this prototype based on user interventions until all involved parties are confident with the result. To reach this goal of a running tool, we actually provide the major ingredients in this chapter before we discuss code examples in the programming language Python in its own chapter (see Chapter 4).

First of all, we introduce the necessary technologies, programming languages, and libraries (Section 3.1) like Python, Dash, and Plotly, as well as further ingredients and concepts, before we move to important installations and options to actually get started to efficiently and effectively develop and implement what we have designed (Section 3.2). Here, we look into different modes like the interactive one, including the Jupyter Notebook mode, and the integrated development environment (IDE) mode. The interplay between all of the formerly described implementation concepts is illustrated in Section 3.3 with the subconcepts of data reading and parsing, data transformation, Dash core components, Dash HTML components, cascading style sheets (CSS), Plotly, and callbacks that more or less build the interface between the visualization techniques and the user interface, that is, the dashboard. The web-based solution is described in Section 3.4, with several options to get it running online.

3.1 General Background Information

There are several ways to create a visualization tool, full of algorithmic functions and interactive graphics, with the human users-in-the-loop. In this book, we mostly focus on the programming language Python, Dash, and Plotly to describe one possible way to build such tools. Python is chosen since it is taught in many university courses and hence, students are already familiar with the most important programming constructs [52]. Plotly as a way to create interactive diagrams, is based on Python code and can be learned easily, in particular, if the suitable visualization techniques are already introduced and described earlier as in this book (see Section 2.3). The same holds for the interaction techniques [258] that are integrated to some extent into the corresponding Plotly diagrams. Interaction techniques have been described in this book as well (see Section 2.5.1). Finally, Dash is a way to create dashboards, consisting of various interactive diagrams, algorithmic concepts, and user interface components, with the goal to build tools for data analysis and visualization, that is, visual analytics tools as well. Dash is some kind of framework focusing on the programming languages Python, R, and Julia.

In this section, we first introduce general aspects of the programming language Python (Section 3.1.1). The more programming-specific code constructs that are required to create our dashboards, given in Chapter 5, will be explained in a tutorial in more detail in Chapter 4. We will also focus on the framework Dash in Section 3.1.2 before we describe and illustrate some Plotly diagrams in Section 3.1.3. Finally, we will discuss further not already described ingredients that might be interesting to create dashboards (Section 3.1.4).

3.1.1 Python

The programming language Python already exists for quite a while, and it was developed in the late 80s by Guido van Rossum while 1991 it got released as version 0.9.0 [236]. Python 2.0 and 3.0 followed in the years 2000 and 2008, respectively, including further improvements and extensions. During the writing of this book, Python 3.10.4 and 3.9.12 were available. Python is considered a high-level programming language that can be applied in various application domains, with data science [223] as one of the major ones in these days. Popular features of the language are the use of explicit indentation to make the code more readable and maintainable. For example, Python also avoids many opening and closing parentheses due to its indented code structure. The type system of Python is described as being dynamic, meaning data types do not have to be explicitly specified as in other programming languages like Java or Pascal. Moreover, several programming paradigms are integrated into Python with functional and object-oriented styles, as being the most obvious ones. Also, the procedural, aspect-oriented, or logic programming paradigms can be found here and there. Libraries can be imported to extend the degree of functionality a program can understand, ranging from classical algorithmic data processing libraries to graphics libraries and many more. Given the fact that Python is frequently used from data scientists, it is typically considered as one of the most well-known languages with a large programmer community, eager to help when programming issues occur that cannot be solved by one's own knowledge and experience. However, Python code is typically quite clear and reduced to a minimum (see Listing 3.1 for an example consisting of a few lines of Python code).

```
1  colors = ["red", "blue", "green", "yellow"]
2  cars = ["BMW", "VW", "Mercedes"]
3
4  for x in colors:
5      for y in cars:
6          print(x, y)
```

Listing 3.1   A code example for a running Python program printing 12 pairs of colors and car brands in code line 6.

Exercises

- Exercise 3.1.1.1: Find other programming languages in which a dashboard or a visualization tool can be implemented. What are typical libraries required to create a visualization tool?
- Exercise 3.1.1.2: What are typical negative issues when using Python for creating a visualization tool?

3.1.2 Dash

Dash does not cost anything, is available as open source, and is created by the company Plotly as a framework to build web applications, typically with a focus on data analysis, visualization, and visual analytics tools. The major programming language which is supported in Dash is Python but also other ones like R or Julia are imaginable. Dash is actually created on React, which describes a well-known web framework in the programming language JavaScript. Moreover, it is also based on Flask, which is a well-known web server focused on Python. Before working with Dash, we have to make some installations, for example, when using conda (see Listings 3.2 and 3.3). In cases, Anaconda is not already installed, we refer to Section 3.2.

```
1  pip install dash
```

Listing 3.2   One way to install Dash on your computer.

```
1  conda install dash
```

Listing 3.3   Another way to install Dash is by using conda. Make sure that conda is already installed.

A very simple code example will generate our first application (line 4 in Listing 3.4) after having imported Dash and the Dash HTML components that are required in the layout of our webpage, given by app.layout in line 6. At the moment, this just contains a headline in H6 HTML size saying "Hello

World in Dash" but in the future, this is the place in which we can integrate many more HTML features, just like in the case when structuring a webpage like our own homepage. Finally, in line 9 of Listing 3.4, we will start the server.

```
1  import dash
2  from dash import html
3
4  app = dash.Dash(__name__)
5
6  app.layout = html.H6(children="Hello World in Dash")
7
8  if __name__ == "__main__":
9      app.run_server(debug=True)
```

Listing 3.4 An application showing how to create a simple layout and to start the server with further required ingredients such as needed imports at the beginning.

We could even compile or execute this program, for example, by using a Jupyter Notebook [184], which hopefully results in a message returning a URL for using in a web browser to see the results of our program. This message tells us that we started a Flask server on our own computer, that is, locally not remotely, which is typically run under the URL http://127.0.0.1:8050. You can start this program only on your own computer since this URL belongs to the so-called localhost. We have created our first webpage, but we have to admit that it is still too early to speak of any success in the sense of having implemented a dashboard. However, with this simple example, we are already prepared for much more complex dashboards.

Exercises

- Exercise 3.1.2.1: Modify the code example in Listing 3.4 to show a much larger text saying, "Hello, now the headline is bigger."
- Exercise 3.1.2.2: Why is HTML alone not the best choice for creating a user-friendly and aesthetically appealing dashboard?

3.1.3 Plotly and Plotly Express

Also, Plotly is available as open source and describes a library usable in the programming language Python. Based on a lot of experience in visualization and programming courses at several universities we can say that Plotly is easy to understand and makes it simple to get started in dashboard programming [42, 43, 52] since the newcomers in the field do not have to learn to create visualizations pixel-by-pixel but Plotly already comes with fully fledged diagrams equipped with the most important interaction techniques [258]. This saves a lot of time in a visualization course [45] that would otherwise be wasted when trying to build diagrams or charts from scratch. Plotly.express, on the other hand, describes some kind of wrapper for Plotly to make it even simpler to use and to equip it with even more features. Plotly.express also allows to create a visualization in one or a few lines of Python code, for the same result, we might have needed many more lines of code in other programming languages like Java or C++. We might say that with Plotly.express the writing of the code is simpler due to its easier syntax in use, meaning instead of coding a few lines one after the other, typically just one line of code is required with the desired parameters given in parentheses (see Listing 3.5 for an example of code with which we can create a simple bar chart in Plotly.express, the corresponding diagram is shown in Figure 3.1). After the installation of Plotly Express (or Plotly.express) we only need to import it in our Python code (see line 1 in Listing 3.5) to get started for creating interactive visualizations in Python.

```
1  import plotly.express as px
2
3  df = px.data.tips()
4
5  fig = px.bar(df, x="smoker", y="total_bill", color="tip")
6  fig.show()
```

Listing 3.5   A simple example of code for creating a bar chart in Plotly from the tips dataset with extra categories like "smoker" versus "nonsmoker" and color coding based on tips.

Plotly Express comes with a lot of benefits but on the negative side it also has to deal with problematic issues. On the beneficial side we can mention that each plot can be built with just one or a few lines of code, just parameters, attributes, and flags have to be adjusted to obtain the desired functionality and the visual variables of interest like a specific color coding, certain shapes, or sizes, and the like (see Section 2.2.1). Moreover, the generated plots are already equipped with interaction techniques ranging from selection, zoom and filter, or details-on-demand (see Section 2.5.1). Even animated diagrams [84, 233] can be created for a certain variable in use, for example, a time attribute or any other attribute that is given with different values or value categories. The Plotly Express world would be wonderful if it had not some major flaws that might make someone think about using other options for creating interactive graphics in Python or even in a totally different programming language. One big negative issue comes from the fact

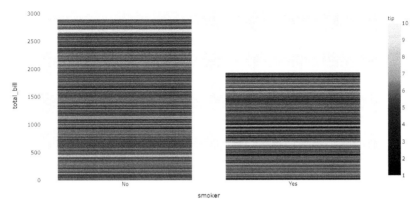

Figure 3.1 The result when executing the code in Listing 3.5. A color coded bar chart distinguishing between two categories smokers and nonsmokers as well as different tips for total bills.

that Plotly Express does not support all possible features that one desires. Although color coding works, for example, it can be a disaster if someone wants to assign exactly the same colors to pre-defined categories each time a plot is created again and again. Also for the zooming feature there is no way to solve the focus-and-context or overview-and-detail problems [195] as other advanced visualizations typically do. Plotly Express is mostly used by data scientists who need a quick visual support to their data science problems at hand, hence it is more focused on exploratory data analysis, missing many features that visualization or visual analytics experts would require for their data analyses.

Exercises

- Exercise 3.1.3.1: Modify the code in Listing 3.5 to show male versus female instead of smokers versus nonsmokers. The attribute for this is called "sex" instead of "smoker." Visually explore the created diagram.
- Exercise 3.1.3.2: Modify the code in Listing 3.5 to show the tips on the y-axis and the total bill in the color coding of the diagram. Compare the new plot with the one in Figure 3.1.

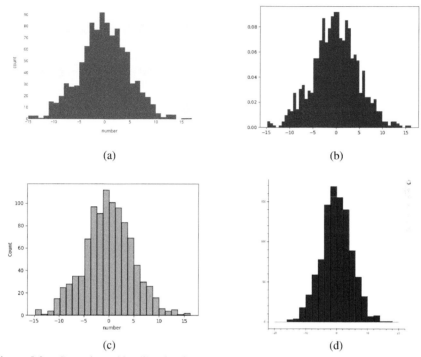

Figure 3.2   Several graphics libraries for creating diagrams in Python: (a) Plotly Express. (b) Matplotlib. (c) Seaborn. (d) Bokeh.

3.1.4 Further ingredients and concepts

Apart from Plotly Express we can find more graphics libraries in Python [120], all of them having advantages and disadvantages (see Figure 3.2 for a comparison of the same diagram type plotted by means of several graphics libraries, Figure 3.3 shows a visual result for a geo-related library). Some of the popular ones are matplotlib, Seaborn, ggplot, geoplotlib, or Bokeh. Actually, based on feedback from more than 1000 students in visualization courses [52], we can say that none of the aforementioned libraries is really difficult to use, given the fact that the users already have some prior expertise in programming (they do not have to be experts), in particular in Python. The only question that remains is which library is the best one for which purpose, a question that is quite difficult to answer. However, we can at least provide some kind of discussion on a comparable basis. Some of the aforementioned libraries already exist for quite some years

Figure 3.3   Using Geoplotlib [79] for geo-related visualizations.

while Plotly Express came on the market in 2019. Matplotlib is one of the most used visualization libraries in Python, not only because it is quite old, compared to the others but also because it supports interactions in a multitude of simple diagrams like histograms, scatterplots, pie charts, and many more (see Section 2.3). Seaborn actually makes use of the Python structures for handling data such as pandas and numpy. Moreover, it also supports simpler charts, for example for statistical approaches and results. ggplot is actually based on an R implementation of ggplot2 while ggplot is also beneficial for simple plots while at the same time allowing to integrate visual variables like color, size, shape, and so on, however, the interactions are quite limited. The specific application domain of geography is supported by geoplotlib that offers many ways to depict geographical data in maps. Bokeh is also popular, but its charts and plots are rendered by making use of HTML and JavaScript, making it a good choice when creating web-based visual solutions.

Exercises

- Exercise 3.1.4.1: Create a scatterplot with each of the visualization libraries. Which one do you think is the most aesthetically appealing one?
- Exercise 3.1.4.2: Which of the diagrams from above allow interactions and which kinds of interaction categories [258] do they support?

3.2 Installations and Options

Before we can start, we should bring our working and programming environment to a suitable state to implement the designed dashboard [145]. For this reason, it is important to take into account all possible ingredients to setup the programming tools in the right order. Python can be run in several ways, for example in an interactive mode, in a Jupyter Notebook mode, that is, interpreter-like mode, or in an integrated development environment (IDE) such as PyCharm or Spyder. Depending on which operating system we are using, like Windows, Linux, or MacOS, it might make a difference to get Python running on our computer. Anyhow, we recommend to install Anaconda (https://docs.anaconda.com/anaconda/install//) first while we might verify our installation afterward (https://docs.anaconda.com/anaconda/install/verify-install/). Table 3.1 illustrates for each of the popular operating systems how to find and start Anaconda. Once Anaconda is started we can find useful tools to implement and debug Python code.

Table 3.1   Finding Anaconda to get started in the desired operating system.

Anaconda in a specific operating system	
Operating system	How to find Anaconda?
Windows	Start $\Rightarrow$ Anaconda Navigator
Linux	Terminal $\Rightarrow$ anaconda-navigator
MacOS	Launchpad $\Rightarrow$ Anaconda Navigator

In this section, we will focus on three modes in which we can start implementing Python programs. Not all of them are suitable for developing a fully fledged dashboard but depending on the experience level of the programmer and the purpose of programming, one or the other might be beneficial. Section 3.2.1 illustrates what we call the interactive mode by directly working in a powershell or terminal, only offering a limited, but working, environment. In Section 3.2.2, we discuss an interpreter-like mode, focusing on Jupyter Notebook, an environment that is already quite flexible to implement Python programs but that only allows smaller pieces of code. We mention it in its own section in the book since we consider it as one of the most popular environments for data scientists. Jupyter Notebook is also considered an IDE, but we think it has less options than other IDEs like PyCharm or Spyder for example. In Section 3.2.3, we talk about many more integrated development environments (IDEs) [135] that are powerful tools for implementing Python code, even larger programs consisting of various files and functions which might not be that handy in Jupyter Notebook. Also,

GitHub (Section 3.2.4) can be of great help, in cases, some programmers work together on the same problem, in a so-called collaborative manner.

3.2.1 Interactive mode

It is possible to create runnable Python programs without the installation of advanced integrated development environments, just by using a terminal or a powershell (see Figure 3.4). Typing in source code line by line and finally let run this code will yield a result, in cases, the code is syntactically correct. Modifying this piece of code is a daunting task, in particular, if the code gets longer and longer with more and more functionality, even spread over several classes in object-oriented programming [176]. Moreover, it is impossible to easily store the implemented code, for example, in a text file to further develop it later on or to send it to someone else, for example, to share it with others in a collaborative source code development like it is done in larger software projects [11]. The terminal is something like a command-line interface but to accelerate our everyday programming work, we wish to have something that comes close to a graphical user interface [226] for solving typical programming tasks, focusing on mental map preservation and a reduction of cognitive efforts, aspects that are hard to take into account in command-line interfaces. Although a command-line powershell interface allows to write and run code in an interactive mode, that is, the code will be evaluated immediately on-the-fly after pressing return, for example, just like an interpreter does, all of the code will be lost each time we close or exit the powershell. This is an unsatisfactory behavior. Storing the code in a file and calling this file in a powershell is also possible, but that requires to store the file each time and to evaluate it each time. A better option would be to directly let the code evaluate while at the same time keeping the code content in a data file, a strategy that is shown in a Jupyter Notebook mode in Section 3.2.2.

Exercises

- Exercise 3.2.1.1: Open a powershell or terminal and implement Python code to experiment with this option. Discuss the benefits and drawbacks of this option.
- Exercise 3.2.1.2: Try to modify your code from Exercise 3.2.1.1 several times. What is the obvious problem here?

Figure 3.4 Programming in Python in a powershell is one way to create, compile, and run programs. Unfortunately, it comes with a list of negative issues.

3.2.2 Jupyter Notebook mode

Jupyter Notebook [184], also being an integrated development environment (IDE), can be used as a web-based tool for implementing and evaluating Python programs in an interactive style (see Figure 3.5 for the same example Python code as in Figure 3.4). Writing code in a Jupyter Notebook is similar to creating documents, with the difference that the documents can be interpreted and the result is given in cases the code is syntactically correct. The user interface of a Jupyter Notebook consists of text field-like entries containing Python code followed by results in form of textual, numerical, and graphical outputs. One benefit compared to the traditional way of using the interactive mode in a powershell comes from the fact that the code is storable, typically in a file with a .ipynb file extension. Moreover, the code can be modified, extended, while it can be re-interpreted, text field by text field, just to keep all the variable values up-to-date. It is also possible to artificially "decorate" Python code in a Jupyter Notebook by integrating HTML-like texts, for example, for providing headlines to several code fragments. Since such a notebook is running in a web browser, it can even be translated in other document formats including HTML or pdf. However, a Jupyter Notebook is still missing a lot of functionality and features that we would typically expect from classical modern integrated development environments like PyCharm or Spyder.

Figure 3.5   The same code as in Figure 3.4 is illustrated here in a Jupyter Notebook.

Exercises

- Exercise 3.2.2.1: Start a Jupyter Notebook and extend the Python code from above by changing the range of the for-loop to be between 5 and 25. Run the new code in the Jupyter Notebook.
- Exercise 3.2.2.2: Store the code in the Jupyter Notebook in a file and find the file on your computer. Which file extension does it have?

3.2.3 Integrated development environment (IDE)

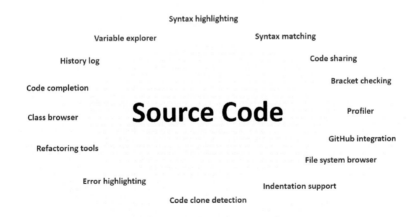

Figure 3.6   Several important aspects around source code and source code quality.

An integrated development environment (IDE) can be regarded as software that helps programmers to implement code, in particular, in larger programs by providing various tools, that is, software like an interpreter or compiler, a debugger, an editor with syntax highlighting and code formatting, a variable tracker, a version control and the like, each of them focusing on a certain functionality during software development [82]. Hence, they provide more functionality in a so-called multiple coordinated view [200] user interface than the interactive or Jupyter Notebook mode can offer. There are various IDEs, but actually software developers are mostly focusing on a specific one and hardly change this one during their lives, unless there is a really good reason to do that [110]. In Python, there is a list of such IDEs consisting of an editor and functionality to create and debug code. The most important and useful ones might be PyCharm, Spyder, Visual Studio Code, Atom, Jupyter Notebook, LiClipse, Vim, GNU Emacs, Sublime Text, and Thonny, to mention a few. Most of them can be used in the popular operating systems, hence they work in Windows, Linux, and MacOS. Some of them have more, some others less functionality, but all of them can be regarded as integrated development environments to some degree, also Jupyter Notebook, although we have described it already in Section 3.2.2 separately. Working with an editor like Emacs or Notepad can also be an option, but most of the Python-based debugging functions would be missing, functions that IDEs typically offer. Jupyter Notebook is somehow located between an IDE and an editor due to the many missing but important IDE functions. The more experience a programmer gets, the more interesting such IDEs will get, making programming more efficient. Important functions focusing on code quality improvements might be listed as follows (see Figure 3.6): syntax highlighting, syntax matching, bracket match checking, variable explorer, error highlighting, indentation support, code completion, code clone detection, refactoring tools, profiler, file system and class browser, history log, code sharing, GitHub integration, and many more.

Exercises

- Exercise 3.2.3.1: Install the integrated development environments mentioned above, experiment with them, and create a list with benefits and drawbacks for each IDE. Which one is the preferred one, and why is it suitable for developing dashboards?

- Exercise 3.2.3.2: Implement a small Python program in each of the IDEs and include a bug or a wrong indentation in the code on purpose. Describe how the IDEs react on the bug and the indentation problem.

3.2.4 GitHub

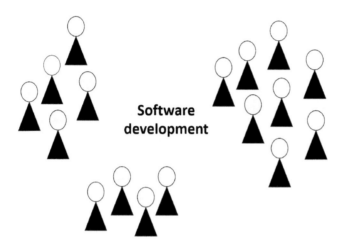

Figure 3.7   Larger software systems are implemented by developers in a collaborative process.

Software development is typically not an individual's job, in an isolated environment, but today's software systems are quite large, consisting of many files and classes, with a multitude of functions, too large that many developers and coders (see Figure 3.7) are required to solve the problems at hand in a collaborative manner [53]. GitHub is a good option to work together in larger projects [167] while also a version control is integrated to let the developers checkout the latest implementations to their workspace, to commit updates to the repository, and to set back the code to an earlier state, in cases this is needed. Also, further features apart from version control are useful during software development such as bug tracking, error databases, or change logs. The software projects in GitHub can be provided in an open source manner, letting the community taking part to some extent. GitHub already reached the sheer size of supporting nearly 100 million developers all around the globe since its development started already in 2007. GitHub also includes primitive visualizations to visually explore the developer activity in some kind of graph representation [82], but the visual support is definitely one of the weaker points in this powerful tool. Since the dashboards we are designing and implementing in this book are rather small software projects, we will not make use of GitHub, we are just introducing GitHub as an option for many developers, in cases dashboards with a multitude of functions and interactive visualizations have to be developed by several developers.

Exercises

- Exercise 3.2.4.1: Create a new dashboard project by using GitHub.
- Exercise 3.2.4.2: Invite some collaborators to your project who will help you with coding the dashboard.

3.3 Interplay between Dash, Plotly, and Python

Creating dashboards requires knowledge and experience in many subtopics, at least involving Dash, Plotly, and some programming in Python. One of the first steps is to get the data into the visualization tool, typically stored in one or several data files or in a database. The data alone is, in most of the scenarios, not usable in the given format or in the given order and structure, that is, it has to be transformed into suitable data formats, understandable by the tool, and a meaningful structure has to be computed to allow data patterns to be detected by means of powerful interactive visualization techniques [178, 258]. For the visualizations, there exist several graphics libraries (see Section 3.1.4), but the user interface [217] is as important as the visualizations themselves. The visualizations we are going to create in this book are mostly based on Plotly and the user interface focuses on Dash with its Dash HTML and Dash Core Components, visually improvable and adjustable by using the right CSS commands. The actual dialogue between the users and the visualization tool is built by so-called callbacks, standing for the interface between the user input in the user interface and the visual, tabular, and textual outputs in the user interface is given by visualization techniques, tables with textual and numerical information, and textual information itself like labels or details-on-demand and the like (see Figure 3.8 for an illustration of the ingredients for creating a dashboard).

This section is organized in some kind of ordered structure with dashboard implementation playing a key role, starting with the data in use that

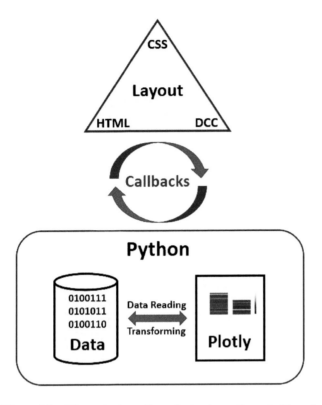

Figure 3.8 The major ingredients for implementing a dashboard.

has to be read first since the data builds a certain core ingredient in each data visualization tool (Section 3.3.1). Transforming the data is important to bring it in the right data format but also in the right data structure to derive data patterns (Section 3.3.2). In Section 3.3.3, we describe the Dash core components, while in Section 3.3.4, we will look into the corresponding HTML components that are required to layout and decorate the dashboard. The cascading style sheets (CSS) to allow aesthetically and user-friendly dashboards are discussed in detail in Section 3.3.5. Popular visualization techniques are introduced in Section 3.3.6 with explanations about how Plotly can be integrated into a dashboard code. Finally, we will talk about the very crucial callback mechanism (Section 3.3.7) to create some kind of dialogue between the users and the user interface with all of its components and visualizations by allowing inputs/outputs in the user interface, modifying the

Dash core components that can come in the form of menus, sliders, text fields, and date pickers, but also in the typically visually more detailed diagrams, charts, and plots that are also considered as Dash core components but those are based on Plotly code in this book.

3.3.1 Reading and parsing in a dashboard

Data can come in a variety of forms (see Section 2.1.1), ranging from simple data types like quantitative, ordinal, or categorical/nominal data to more complex data types like relational/hierarchical, uni-, bi-, tri-, or multivariate/tabular, textual, or trajectorial data, also with a dynamic, that is, time-varying nature [4]. Depending on the data types it might be stored on different data files in various data formats. However, reading and parsing the data by using Python code is necessary to get the data in a usable form into the dashboard, that is, to allow graphical depictions of it. Reading data can be done in a standard method by just reading a text or binary file in the traditional way (see Section 4.8) or in cases the data exists in a tabular, Excel table-like, form with rows and columns, it can be read by a so-called Pandas DataFrame [169]. This is also possible for data that is updated regularly as real-time data [228]. Even more, the data might be stored locally, on one's own computer, or remotely on a server, making a remote access via a URL to a possible solution. No matter how the data exists and where it is stored, we should be able to store the data in certain data structures and variables to make it processable and accessible quickly and effortlessly, that is, efficiently and effectively.

Table 3.2   Some rows and columns with attribute values serve as an example dataset for the following code.

An example tabular data with several attributes				
Name	Gender	Age	Smoker	Hobbies
Lucas	Male	45	No	Football, Tennis, Jogging
Emma	Female	38	Yes	Cooking, Swimming
Bob	Male	52	Yes	Baseball, Walking
Martha	Female	32	No	Hiking, TV
Roy	Male	40	Yes	Theater, TV

```
1  import pandas as pd
2
3  df = pd.read_csv("hobbies.csv")
```
Listing 3.6   Reading a csv file containing people with some personal attributes.

As we can see in Listing 3.6, reading tabular data (like the example tabular data in Table 3.2) is not a big issue in Python, in case, this table is given in a csv format, that is, in a comma-separated-values format (stored as a file with name "hobbies.csv"). We can make use of a Pandas DataFrame to read the data file in exactly that format in just one line of code. It may be noted that the correct file path must be specified in order to get positive reading results. However, in this form, the data is still sleeping in a DataFrame and has to be transformed and visualized, but fortunately, doing the plain vanilla transformations and visualizations is also not very difficult, as we will see later (again).

Exercises

- Exercise 3.3.1.1: Create a new table with rows and columns similar to the given data table from above and read it by using a Pandas DataFrame.
- Exercise 3.3.1.2: Read an arbitrary text file, for example, a page from a book. Also, read a file that contains an image from one of your last holidays. Is there a difference between reading text and image files?

3.3.2 Data transformation in a dashboard

Only reading and parsing the data into a specific format are actually crucial but also boring operations, a data transformation finally helps to compute the most important data patterns algorithmically. For example, preprocessing the data to aggregate it or to interpolate between two numerical values to fill data gaps are data transformations. Transforming data could mean everything we apply to data that modifies it by restructuring it in some way [247]. Also more complex operations might be imaginable like clustering [254] the data or projecting [235] it to a lower dimension in case it is a multivariate or high-dimensional dataset. Also, a matrix reordering [20] belongs to such data transformations, meaning to permutate the rows and columns of a matrix, like an adjacency matrix for networks [106], to compute some kind of structure and order among the network vertices based on their relations among each other (see Tables 3.3 and 3.4 for a reordering strategy to derive some meaningful group patterns among the matrix entries). There are various data transformation strategies, typically being applied for solving one or several tasks at hand to compute some structures in a dataset that would otherwise not be visible, hence a visualization of such unstructured data would not be meaningful to detect patterns and anomalies.

Table 3.3   An unordered matrix of zeros and ones.

An unordered matrix of zeros and ones								
	A	B	C	D	E	F	G	H
A	1	1	0	0	0	1	1	0
B	1	1	0	0	0	1	1	0
C	0	0	1	1	1	0	0	1
D	0	0	1	1	1	0	0	1
E	0	0	1	1	1	0	0	1
F	1	1	0	0	0	1	1	0
G	1	1	0	0	0	1	1	0
H	0	0	1	1	1	0	0	1

Table 3.4   An ordered matrix of zeros and ones, based on the matrix in Table 3.3.

An ordered matrix of zeros and ones								
	F	B	G	A	H	D	C	E
F	1	1	1	1	0	0	0	0
B	1	1	1	1	0	0	0	0
G	1	1	1	1	0	0	0	0
A	1	1	1	1	0	0	0	0
H	0	0	0	0	1	1	1	1
D	0	0	0	0	1	1	1	1
C	0	0	0	0	1	1	1	1
E	0	0	0	0	1	1	1	1

As mentioned before, data transformation can mean anything related to modifying the input data. The biggest challenge in this step is to implement it in an efficient way (if this is possible) and even more, put the corresponding Python code to the right place to avoid runtime issues. In some situations, the data transformations can be precomputed, that is, computed before the users of a visualization tool or dashboard explicitly request them. To reach this goal, the precomputed structures are stored somewhere on a server or locally (if space allows) to avoid computing the same values all the time again and again to reduce the computation time when the tool is running. In some other situations we cannot precompute the data since we do not know what the users are asking for, and computing all possible outcomes is impossible due to the immense amount of variations, depending on the parameter space and the decisions of the users. Consequently, the rule of thumb would be to compute anything that can be computed before and for all other computations, we have to come up with the most efficient algorithm that we can find to avoid runtime issues during the running program [36].

Exercises

- Exercise 3.3.2.1: If we had an Excel table full of numerical values what would be meaningful data transformations that we can apply, from the perspective of the rows and the columns?
- Exercise 3.3.2.2: Aggregating a list of numerical values, for example, the temperature at a place every minute, into an hourly form reduces the amount of data. Which ways can you find to compute aggregated values in a time interval?

3.3.3 Dash core components

The dash core components can be imported by the code line in Listing 3.7 and have the purpose of allowing users to modify data, hence serving as input options. Furthermore, the dash core components can even show results of a user interaction [258], that is, serving as output options as well. Classical ways for making inputs are by using menus, sliders, date pickers, text fields, and many more provided by the dash core components (see Figure 3.9 for a slider and a drop-down menu). Creating a range slider between the range 0 and 10 with the selected interval [2, 6] instead of a standard slider is shown in the code in Listing 3.8. It may be noted that all of the components can be visually decorated in some way, for example, a range slider can become more aesthetically appealing [5] and user-friendly if a scale with labels is added to it [232]. Ways to create outputs are diagrams, tables, or just textual information. The diagrams and tables can be created by means of Plotly Express (see Sections 3.1.3 and 3.3.6). But also menus, sliders, date pickers, and so on can produce outputs, for example in cases in which they change their visual appearance based on user interactions. On the other hand, diagrams and tables might also be options for making user inputs, for example, clicking on a visual element in a diagram or selecting a table entry, will generate information on which a user interface or a visual component can react. Dash core components could also be classified in, user interface components and visualization components, instead of an input/output classification. User interface components are the ones with respect to the functionality of the interface while the visualization components are those that focus on the visual output, focusing on visual data explorations by means of diagrams, charts, and plots.

```
1  from dash import dcc
```

Listing 3.7 Importing the Dash core components.

```
1  from dash import dcc
2
3  dcc.RangeSlider(
4      min=0,
5      max=10,
6      value = [2,6]
7  )
```

Listing 3.8 Creating a range slider as a Dash core component.

(a)

red

(b)

Figure 3.9 A slider (a) and a drop-down menu (b) created as Dash core components.

Exercises

- Exercise 3.3.3.1: Implement a drop-down menu as a dash core component that has five labels for cities in the world while the second and fourth city are already preselected by default.
- Exercise 3.3.3.2: Implement a slider with a range from zero to 100 while the value 20 is preselected.

3.3.4 Dash HTML components

HTML stands for the HyperText Markup Language which is a way to model, arrange, design, and display content that is shown in a web browser [90, 259]. HTML is quite simple with only a limited number of possible document features such as headlines of different (but fixed) font sizes, headings, paragraphs, line breaks, horizontal lines, lists, links, or tables, to mention a few. All of those features are indicated by so-called tags, while each feature has its own tag. Moreover, some HTML features can be nested into each other, just like a hierarchical structure [215]. Such a hierarchy is important for a dashboard design since each dashboard consists of the main web page, in which subpages or subregions are located and even more fine-granular substructures depending on the dashboard designer. HTML is guiding this structuring process; the components themselves are typically augmented by additional Dash core components. The cascading style sheets (CSS) (see Section 3.3.5), on the other hand, and further languages like JavaScript can be used to enhance the visual appearance of such browser content by allowing to adapt border sizes, paddings, and margins for example as well as colors and many more visual features. HTML is actually responsible for the interface appearance, that is, since a dashboard can be regarded as some kind of web page (or several of them in a linked manner), the HTML components and their layouts, sizes, and additional features model the structure of a dashboard. Consequently, we need a way to model a dashboard as some kind of HTML structure which is supported by the so-called Dash HTML components which have to be imported first to work with them as with the Dash core components (see Listing 3.9 for the import that is required in this case).

```
1  from dash import html
```

Listing 3.9   Importing the Dash HTML components.

```
1  from dash import html
2
3  html.Div([
4      html.H1("My first Dash HTML component")
5  ])
```

Listing 3.10   An example for an HTML headline with Dash HTML components.

Listing 3.10 shows an HTML headline as a Python implementation as a Dash HTML component. In Listing 3.11 we can see the same piece of code given in pure HTML with opening and closing tags.

```
1  <div>
2      <h1>My first Dash HTML component</h1>
3  </div>
```

Listing 3.11   HTML code for the Dash HTML component in Listing 3.10.

Exercises

- Exercise 3.3.4.1: Use the Dash HTML components to implement three different headlines of sizes H1, H3, and H5 placed below each other and stating what their size is.
- Exercise 3.3.4.2: Include a headline of size H1 and below that a drop-down menu by combining the corresponding Dash HTML and Dash core components.

3.3.5 Cascading style sheets (CSS)

Apart from pure HTML, there are further ways to visually enhance or decorate a dashboard which can be achieved by using the cascading style sheets (CSS), for example. This is a so-called style sheet language and can be applied on several levels like inline, internal, or external CSS, depending on what granularity the visual enhancement is made. CSS can affect the appearance of many elements in a dashboard ranging from formatting specifications to more complex layouts as well as simpler effects focusing on background images, visual variables [170] like colors, font sizes, shapes, or Gestalt laws [147] like visual components, element distances, similarities, and many more. CSS can even be used to allow dashboards to be shown on several output displays like small-, medium-, or large-scale displays [210] (smartphones, laptops, and powerwalls) and even more, it can also be used to adapt based on certain other modalities like speech or braille [68] for supporting blind people when reading content, a powerful concept that should definitely also be used for dashboards.

The general case for using CSS is by external .css files. However, internal or inline CSS are typically also used in smaller projects with a small number of code lines. Inline CSS is more flexible since it allows to put a CSS command to the right places in the HTML document, but negatively it creates a lot of extra text input, which could be mitigated when using external CSS. In case one property has to be changed for all components of a certain type, one has to find all places in the code and change this inline CSS, for external CSS, we only have to adapt one tag. The good thing here is that external CSS commands are overwritten by internal commands, which are overwritten by inline commands, hence the cascading effect, from external to internal to inline. As an example we could look into an inline CSS command that is responsible for setting the text color of an H1 HTML element to a certain color, in this special case the color blue (see Listing 3.12).

```
1 <h1 style="color:blue;">A text in blue</h1>
```
Listing 3.12   An example of using CSS to set a font color of an H1 headline in HTML to blue.

In a dashboard code in Python, the CSS command could be integrated like the example given in Listing 3.13 in Line 6. We see that there is some kind of syntactic difference between pure HTML and the Python code for creating dashboards.

```
1  from dash import Dash, dcc, html
2
3  app = Dash(__name__)
4
5  app.layout = html.Div([
6      html.H1("A text in blue", style = {'color': 'blue'})
7  ])
8
9  if __name__ == '__main__':
10     app.run_server(debug=False)
```
Listing 3.13   Integrating a CSS command into the code for a dashboard.

Exercises

- Exercise 3.3.5.1: Create a headline in HTML in size H3 with a green text color. Use inline, internal, and external CSS commands.
- Exercise 3.3.5.2: What are the benefits of using external CSS? What are the drawbacks?

3.3.6 Plotly in a dashboard

Diagrams, charts, plots, that is, visualizations also equipped with interaction techniques can be integrated into a dashboard by using Plotly Express (Section 3.1.3). A multitude of diagrams can be created focusing on showing patterns in data, in a dashboard implementation they can just be included by treating them as regular Dash core components (see Line 11 in Listing 3.14 for an example of a scatterplot in Plotly Express integrated into dashboard code). This fact makes them displayable just like any other component in the layout of a dashboard, while also CSS commands can be used to manipulate, to layout, to style, to visually augment, or to decorate them, even more they can be given a distance, margin, or padding with respect to other components in the dashboard, to make them aesthetically appealing and user-friendly [217]. Mostly, the diagrams serve as output components, showing the results of applying an algorithm [62] or just visually representing a dataset, while the integrated interaction techniques [258] can be useful to even regard them as input components, for example to manipulate other components based on the interactive requests or modifications users made to a Plotly diagram. This feature is a bit more complex to implement than the standard plain vanilla form of just showing the data visually while manipulating parameters in a drop-down menu or by moving a slider for example, however, lots of fancy visual and interactive enhancements are possible as we will illustrate in Chapter 5 with some runnable dashboard examples, ranging from simple ones to those equipped with many more features.

```python
from dash import Dash, html, dcc

app = Dash(__name__)

app.layout = html.Div([
    dcc.Graph(id='plot1', figure = {})
])

def update_graph():
    # Plotly Express, df = DataFrame
    fig = px.scatter(df, x='attribute1', y='attribute2')

    return fig

if __name__ == '__main__':
    app.run_server(debug=False)
```

Listing 3.14 Integrating a Plotly Express diagram into the code for a dashboard.

Exercises

- Exercise 3.3.6.1: Read a tabular dataset, for example, by using a Pandas DataFrame and include a Plotly diagram in the form of a scatterplot that shows the correlation behavior of two attributes from the tabular dataset.
- Exercise 3.3.6.2: Add another Plotly diagram in the form of a histogram below the scatterplot that shows the distribution of one attribute, that is, we should see two Plotly diagrams at the same time now.

3.3.7 Callbacks

Callbacks describe some kind of linking between the inputs and outputs, that is, each time an input or several of them are changed by the users the corresponding outputs will be updated. This can be the value of a slider (which is a Dash core component) that is updated, and hence, as a consequence, one or several Plotly diagrams (which are also Dash core components) have to be updated as well. By the callback mechanism, we create some kind of interaction possibility, that is, a dialogue between users and the dashboard or visualization tool. Without a callback, we would not have a chance to modify the visual appearance of a dashboard on users' requests, that is, it would remain a static picture which is not the effect that we are planning to have. The number of inputs and outputs is actually not limited, but if too many inputs are allowed this might cause confusion effects on the user side. In some cases, it is better to reduce the ways to modify parameters, to achieve a user-friendly [230] and nonoverloaded visualization tool. Moreover, the more modifications are allowed, causing changes to various outputs, the more complex the corresponding Python code will get, but still, Dash and its callback mechanism help to reduce the amount of programming work to get ready for even more complex dashboards with a lot of interactive features. Even multiple callbacks are possible, but we will move the explanation of them to Chapter 5, in which we show simple and complex dashboards together with their implementation details. However, before starting to create callbacks, we should import the required concepts (see Listing 3.15). A callback mechanism is illustrated in the code example in Listing 3.16.

```
from dash import Input, Output
```

Listing 3.15 Importing the Dash dependencies to allow a smooth callback mechanism

```
import pandas as pd
import plotly.express as px

from dash import Dash, Input, Output, dcc, html

app = Dash(__name__)

df = pd.read_csv("K:\\Desktop\\Data\\quakes.csv")

app.layout = html.Div([
    html.H1("Quakes", style = {'text-align': 'center'}),
    html.H4("Many Facts", style = {'text-align': 'left'}),

    dcc.Dropdown(
        id='location',
        options = [{"label": "Asia", "value": 'AS'},
                   {"label": "Australia", "value": 'AU'},
                   {"label": "Europe", "value": 'EU'}],
        multi = False,
        value='Asia',
        style = {"width": "40%"}
    ),

    dcc.Graph(id='plot1', figure = {}),
```

```
25      html.Br(),
26      dcc.Graph(id='plot2', figure = {})
27  ])
28
29  @app.callback(
30      [Output(
31          component_id='plot1',
32          component_property='figure'
33          ),
34       Output(
35          component_id='plot2',
36          component_property='figure'
37          )
38      ],
39      [Input(
40          component_id='location',
41          component_property='value'
42          )
43      ]
44  )
45
46  def update_graph(option_slctd):
47      dff = df.copy()
48      dff = dff[dff["location"] == option_slctd]
49
50      fig = px.scatter(
51          dff,
52          x='magnitude',
53          y='depth',
54          color = "depth"
55          )
56
57      fig2 = px.scatter(
58          dff,
59          x="latitude",
60          y="longitude",
61          color = "magnitude",
62          size = "depth"
63          )
64
65      return fig, fig2
66
67  if __name__ == '__main__':
68      app.run_server(debug=False)
```

Listing 3.16   Python code showing the mechanism of callbacks

Exercises

- Exercise 3.3.7.1: Implement a simple dashboard with one range slider whose values are used to update a corresponding scatterplot, that is, the range slider is used here as a numerical interval filter. What are the inputs and outputs of the callback function?
- Exercise 3.3.7.2: Implement another dashboard with two range sliders allowing to filter two numerical attributes while the effect of the filters is interactively shown in a scatterplot.

3.4 Deploying

Another important stage during the development of a dashboard is the deployment of it to make it available for everybody who has a web browser and internet access. Technically, this is easily possible but it brings various other challenges into play, also taking into account the visual and interface design. In case a dashboard is accessible from any place in the world, the users have a multitude of properties ranging from language differences, cultural habits, signage, symbols, reading directions, and many more [93], typically including the visual variables like colors, shapes, icons, all of them having different meanings depending on the users. Hence, deploying does not only mean to put the dashboard online, but it has to be done in a way that it is focusing on the users' experiences and environments. Making a visualization tool available for anybody on earth can be a difficult task if it is to fulfill all of the users' needs and requirements. Consequently, it is a good advice to consider the possible users already in the design phase to not run into problems after the tool is finally deployed. Also, the application domain can require differences in the tool's setup, for example for analyzing car traffic data it makes a difference if the traffic runs on the right or left street side. In the medical sector, there might be different diseases and viruses that require different analysis and visualization techniques, creating a dashboard for any kind of application scenario is not possible. Moreover, domain experts [257] have to be recruited to create a dashboard for specific scenarios, a fact that can come up with high costs.

In this section, we take a look at possibilities to deploy a dashboard, that is, to make it publicly available online in a web browser. Section 3.4.1 describes one popular way to do that by making use of Heroku. The challenging issue apart from the technical problems are the users themselves who are now international ones instead of national or local users with different cultures and symbol or signage understanding and interpretation (Section 3.4.2). One good aspect of online dashboards comes from the fact that we can access users with a multitude of backgrounds, helping to evaluate the dashboard and its algorithmic, visual, and interface components (Section 3.4.3). Finally, we will give a brief overview of drawbacks and benefits when creating an online dashboard that is accessible by everybody in the world (Section 3.4.4).

3.4.1 Heroku

Actually, we do not need to deploy a dashboard, that is, a Dash app. It typically runs locally, on our own machine, on so-called localhost. The URL for accessing the localhost is given after the compilation phase of the dashboard's Python code is finished. Typing in this URL in a web browser or clicking on it will successfully show the created dashboard with all of its functionality. However, to go one step further, it is of special interest to deploy the Dash app to a certain kind of server, to share it with our worldwide users, even by hiding it behind a login and a password. There are various ways to share a dashboard on a server, but one specific way to do that is by making use of a Heroku server [81]. This kind of server platform provides an easy way to deploy so-called Flask-based applications, as we have talked about already in Section 3.1.2. For more detailed instructions, we recommend to read the tutorial at https://dash.plotly.com/deployment. Actually, in summary, we only need four steps to get it running, which are in a condensed form:

1. The creation of a project folder for the dashboard
2. The initialization of this project folder
3. The initialization of the project folder with an example application
4. The initialization of Heroku

In cases, we modify and extend the dashboard code, we have to proceed with a fifth step that has to be repeated each time a modification or extension is made, which is the redeployment.

Exercises

- Exercise 3.4.1.1: Create a dashboard that reads a small tabular dataset (an Excel table) with numerical values for the attributes. The dashboard should show a scatterplot for two columns of the tabular dataset, and there should be an option to filter values. Deploy this simple dashboard to Heroku.

- Exercise 3.4.1.2: Let your dashboard run in different web browsers like Google Chrome, Mozilla Firefox, Opera, or Microsoft Edge and try to spot the differences.

3.4.2 International users

Deploying a dashboard means to make it accessible online, for everybody who has access to the internet and who has a web browser in which the dashboard is running properly. But such international users [241] bring into play a few new challenges that we are not confronted with when only working locally on our own computer. Not only challenges have to be tackled, and we can also see the international users as a great opportunity, for example, to evaluate a dashboard from a multitude of user perspectives, people with different backgrounds, knowledge, and experience.

On the challenging side, we see that our international users speak different languages, hence the best option is to keep the dashboard design in English [193] and/or allow to switch to another language-on-demand. The problem here is that we cannot easily support all possible languages and dialects in the world, technically, it is possible, but strategically, we would not suggest such a solution. Another problem comes from the reading direction, which is top-to-bottom and left-to-right in Western-civilized countries but which is not the case in Asian or Arabic countries. Actually, this is a challenge for the dashboard design that typically follows some kind of layout focusing on an exploration strategy. For example, the input parameters are placed on the left-hand side and we might fill in a form from top-to-bottom and from left-to-right. But how would Japanese people fill in the corresponding parameter values? They might be confused in the beginning. The only solution in such a scenario would be to request the desired layout from each user and setup the dashboard in a good layout or to link it to the language. It is also not only about the reading direction and the layout focusing on the interface design, and it is also about the visual design that is composed of many visual variables including color, shapes, positions, sizes, and so on. Color is a good example [245, 246] that has to be treated with care for international users. Colors can have different meanings, depending on cultural aspects, for example. Also, the signage, symbols, or icons go in the same direction and have to be adapted, depending on the fact which kind of users we are confronted with.

Positively, we must say that international users bring into play new beneficial aspects as well. The more users a dashboard has the more popular the dashboard is, and this honor falls back to the designers and implementors of the dashboard. We can record valuable feedback by asking the users in some kind of crowdsourcing user experiment [2] which features they liked and which ones not or what they consider improvable. This feedback can be collected in a textual form by letting them type in text in a feedback form in the dashboard or by showing some kind of Likert scale [221] ranging from very good (5) to very bad (1) in the dashboard to, get numerical instead of qualitative feedback. Numerical values are easier to evaluate than textual feedback, but they are also some kind of aggregated measure. Moreover, the mouse cursor can be tracked and stored over space and time as well as mouse clicks. This gives a more detailed impression of the user behavior; however, the mouse movements alone do not give us any feedback on the cognitive processes that the users are confronted with. The biggest issue here, no matter which kind of data is recorded from the international users, comes from the fact that the data itself is not reliable since it is acquired in some kind of uncontrolled user study in which we cannot control the users and in which we do not know much about the users, apart from their IP addresses. We might ask about personal details, but we can never be sure if those details are true. The recorded data itself is also a problem. It is quite hard to analyze the data for patterns, correlations, and anomalies, actually we are interested in the user behavior when they are given a certain task, that is, we want to detect design flaws in our dashboard based on the user behavior.

Exercises

- Exercise 3.4.2.1: Imagine your dashboard has to be created for an international market with users from Europe, Asia, and South America. Discuss important visual design and interface design features that have to be taken into account to make it usable for all those users.
- Exercise 3.4.2.2: If we integrate user data into the design of our dashboard, which kind of user data should be considered, and how trustworthy and reliable is such user data (since we do not know who the real users are)?

3.4.3 Online user evaluation

A user evaluation in an online setting can be beneficial if we are interested in many study participants, that is, in some kind of crowdsourcing experiment [2]. The big challenge, in this case, is the fact that the experiment happens in an uncontrolled way, meaning the recorded data might not be reliable enough to get statistically significant results. However, the recorded data might be usable as some kind of pilot study to indicate some kind of trend in the user behavior. This trend can be used as an inspiration for hypotheses and research questions that can be evaluated in follow-up experiments, maybe in a controlled user study setting, for example, in a laboratory. Consequently, recording user-related data in an online study is a good idea, but the data has to be treated with care, to not lead to drawing wrong conclusions. Another problem with the online study is that there is no concrete user task to be solved, actually the users just play around with the provided dashboard but they are not guided in a specific direction. One might say we could limit the functionality of the dashboard, but, on the other hand, we also wish to show the dashboard in its entirety with all integrated functions, features, and visual components.

The controlled studies typically limit the number of study participants since the control requires more preparation time and an experimenter who is present in the lab all the time to control whether the study participant is doing the right things. Also eye tracking [44, 87, 123] comes into play here, helping to record the eye movements of the study participants to analyze their visual attention behavior. Eye tracking could also be applied in an online web-based scenario, however, this brings us back to the uncontrolled study setting. Even more, although a lot of data about user behavior, visually, verbally, or based on performance measures is collected, we need further approaches from the fields of statistics, data science, and/or visual analytics to find patterns, correlations, or anomalies in the textual, numerical, or spatiotemporal data which is another tedious task and opens new perspectives for completely new research fields.

Exercises

- Exercise 3.4.3.1: Create a simple dashboard, deploy it, and include a text field for recording qualitative feedback of online users. How do you advertise your dashboard to get enough study participants?

- Exercise 3.4.3.2: Add a feature to the dashboard to track the movements of the mouse cursor as well as mouse clicks. Can you find some patterns in the recorded user behavior data?

3.4.4 Benefits and drawbacks of online dashboards

When summing up the facts about deploying a dashboard, that is, making it accessible to everybody on earth, we can identify several important positive and negative points. Some major benefits could be listed as follows:

- **Popularity:** Having access to a dashboard on the web increases its possible success since many more people can use it. However, we need to advertise it to give people the chance to use and test it, and maybe finally pay for the services provided by it.
- **Number of users:** An online version of a dashboard can increase the number of people using it. Hence, the large number of users can serve as some kind of stress test of the dashboard for all, the visual, the interactive, as well as the algorithmic components.
- **User behavior:** Many users means having the chance of collecting and recording data that describes the user behavior. This can come in the form of qualitative textual feedback or in the form of mouse movements and mouse clicks. Evaluating and analyzing this data can give insights in design flaws that are worth improving.
- **Application domains:** Today, there is a multitude of application domains that have to tackle data science and data visualization problems. Consequently, creating an online dashboard can be a great success if it can handle data from several application domains.

Although there are many positive aspects of deploying a dashboard, we can also find several drawbacks that we come across during the design and implementation phases:

- **Technical issues:** Deploying means integrating more visual and interface features to make a dashboard usable for everybody. Moreover, we need to "install" it on a server which requires some knowledge about this additional functionality.
- **User requirements:** Making a dashboard accessible to everybody brings new challenges into play since people have different needs and requirements depending on the fact about where they live or where they have grown up, focusing on cultural issues.

- **Ethics and privacy:** We might draw wrong conclusions from our own data just by using a dashboard designed and implemented by someone else. This might be due to a missing experience to work with a dashboard. Moreover, new questions arise asking about if it is allowed to use the data uploaded by others.
- **Environments:** Deploying a dashboard has to take into account different displays like small-, medium-, or large-scale ones. Also, the operating systems of the users can have an impact on the functionality as well as the different web browsers, also in different versions.

Exercises

- Exercise 3.4.4.1: Describe the benefits that you would have when deploying a dashboard.
- Exercise 3.4.4.2: Are the drawbacks when deploying a dashboard also depending on the application domain, that is, are there, for example, differences between geographic, medical, or educational applications?

4

Coding in Python

Writing programs in the programming language Python [236] is not that difficult as you might expect. Even if you are not an experienced programmer, there is still support to learn the most important Python constructs to finally implement the dashboard that you designed for visually exploring your or other people's data [255]. In this chapter we are trying to give a step-by-step tutorial on how to create Python programs, starting with simple instructions and more and more walking into the directions of much more complex programs including both functional and object-oriented programming paradigms. Since writing about Python programming can fill several books, we will only focus on the most relevant Python constructs to implement dashboards with some but not all possible functionalities. For the interested reader we suggest to read a more Python-specific book that provides many more insights into Python code constructs that are not used on an everyday basis, for example, to build dashboards for visually and algorithmically exploring data, or to analyze data based on machine learning and further data science concepts [28].

In the first few sections, we more or less use Python as some kind of calculator to mathematically evaluate arithmetic expressions, even Boolean expressions consisting of Boolean and relational operators as well as further arithmetic expressions. Those expressions build some kind of basic structure when writing computer programs since they describe how to put information together, how to aggregate and evaluate that to guide the control flow of a program. Unfortunately, programming is not as easy as writing expressions but more complex constructs are required like loops or conditionals, as well as data structures with one-dimensional lists being the basic ones from a longer list of possibilities including dictionaries, for example. For each subsection, we will provide some exercises that are worth solving by either using Jupyter Notebook for the simple ones or later, for the more complex ones, using an IDE like PyCharm or Spyder for example. This chapter can also be studied as an introduction into Python programming without drifting away into dashboard design and implementation, however, we have written it as a tool to understand, develop, and extend dashboard code, focusing on solving certain user-defined data exploration tasks.

We start the chapter with expressions (Section 4.1) that are important ingredients to evaluate complex combined mathematical, relational, or Boolean problems, even supporting bitwise operations. In Section 4.2, we describe the most common basic and composite data types and explain the concept of variables, constants, and conversions. In Section 4.3, we have a look into strings and characters as well as into typical functions and methods to allow meaningful operations on them. To allow branching in the control flow, we describe the use of conditionals as well as exceptions that must be handled sometimes (Section 4.4). A certain number of similar executions with varying values can be modeled by loops that can occur as definite or indefinite ones (Section 4.5). To encapsulate functionality like subroutines that are used at several locations in the code, we introduce the concept of functions in Section 4.6. A mighty concept in programming is recursion that can be used in its standard form as well as tail recursion. Also, high-order functions and lambda expressions serving as anonymous functions are worth discussing (Section 4.7). To allow a communication with the users and to support them at tasks like data reading and writing, we explain the most important operations to work with data files (Section 4.8). Apart from functional or procedural programming paradigms, we can also create classes and objects, which is typically falling into the object-oriented programming paradigm which is discussed in Section 4.9. Again, we do not focus on completeness in this chapter, and we only want to describe the most important ingredients to get started in Python programming.

4.1 Expressions

Evaluating mathematical constructs composed of arithmetic expressions by adding, subtracting, multiplying, or dividing is one of the major ingredients in nearly any computer program. Such expressions can get quite long with a multitude of operators connecting the individual parts. It is important to understand in which order such expressions are computed, for example, prioritizing some expressions by using parentheses. Understanding the laws of execution and evaluation is an important ingredient to avoid errors that might be hard to locate later on in a computer program. Each operator has some kind of precedence in Python, and in any other programming language, that decides which parts of a composite expression will be computed in which order. An expression can include a multitude of operators and operands, reducing to a certain value after its evaluation. Such values can be numerical or Boolean values, depending on the operators. All operators are given a well-defined precedence. In a composite expression, the operators of highest precedence are evaluated first. After those results have been computed, the operators of the next highest precedence are evaluated. This procedure goes on until the complete expression is evaluated to either a numerical or a Boolean value. In case operators have an equal precedence they are performed in a so-called left-to-right order, as in many other programming languages as well.

In this section, we have a deeper look into arithmetic, relational, Boolean/logical, but even in bitwise as well as mixed expressions. Arithmetic expressions (see Section 4.1.1) are typically built on arithmetic operators like addition, subtraction, multiplication, division, or exponentiation operators. Relational expressions are based on comparison operators like smaller, larger, equal, not equal, and the like while they evaluate a Boolean value (see Section 4.1.2). Boolean or logical expressions use logical operators like and, or, not, and many more combined complex ones (which can be built by using the basic ones) to evaluate to a Boolean value (see Section 4.1.3). We also describe bitwise expressions that, as the name suggests, work on bits as their basic units (see Section 4.1.4). In many cases, the different expression types can be combined to create even more complex expressions, also known as mixed expressions (see Section 4.1.5).

4.1.1 Arithmetic expressions

Expressions can come in various forms, typically built on certain types of operators and operands. The operators can be understood as some kind of connecting symbols describing how the individual expression parts should be combined. The operands, on the other hand, are the basic values on which the operators make computations. The operators hence describe how to combine and the operands what to combine. Arithmetic expressions [97] are based on so-called arithmetic operators which exist in various forms in mathematical expressions like addition, subtraction, multiplication, division, or exponentiation (see Table 4.1). In the Python programming language, those are expressed by special symbols like +, -, *, /, and **. Moreover, we can distinguish between binary operators, that is, those that take two arguments and combine them into one, and unary operators, that is, those that just work on one value and might change the sign of a value, for example, from a positive into a negative one. The good thing with expressions in Python is that they do not only work on raw values like integers and floating point numbers, but also on variables or even function calls that create a certain value as a result.

Table 4.1   A list of arithmetic operators, some examples, their meanings, and mathematical notations.

Operator	Example	Explanation	Math formula
+	$x + y$	Add x and y (addition)	$x + y$
-	$x - y$	Subtract y from x (subtraction)	$x - y$
*	$x * y$	Multiply x and y (multiplication)	$x \cdot y$
/	x/y	Divide x by y (division, type float)	$\frac{x}{y}$
//	$x//y$	Divide x by y (division, type int)	$\lfloor \frac{x}{y} \rfloor$
**	$x * *y$	x to the power of y (exponentiation)	x^y
%	$x\%y$	Divide x by y (modulo division)	$x \mod y$
-	$-x$	Negative of x (unary)	$-x$
+	$+x$	Positive of x (unary)	$+x$

As already shown in Table 4.1, we can start building arithmetic expressions by simply using the rules of arithmetic and then step-by-step connect more and more of such subexpressions to more complex ones. An example of a more complex arithmetic expression is given in Listing 4.1. Here, we also see the idea of evaluation precedence or priorities. The addition parentheses have the highest priority and express that the expressions contained inside the parentheses should be evaluated first. Then the multiplication and division operators have a higher priority than the additional and subtraction operators. If operators have the same priority level, the expression is evaluated from left-to-right. By the way, the arithmetic expression in Listing 4.1 evaluates to -42.

```
4*3+2-5*(7+3)-2*3  # evaluates to -42
```

Listing 4.1   An arithmetic expression

Exercises

- Exercise 4.1.1.1: Evaluate the following arithmetic expression:

```
(4+3*7-(3+5)*6)/3-17%3
```

- Exercise 4.1.1.2: Evaluate the following arithmetic expression:

```
3-12+4**(3-1)*0.1-15//(4+3)
```

4.1.2 Relational expressions

Apart from arithmetic expressions, we wish to make comparisons between values, typically by using operators like >, <, >=, <=, ==, or !=. Those describe relations indicating if one value is greater, smaller, greater or equal, smaller or equal, equal, or not equal to another value. The relational expressions [69] evaluate to Boolean values, that is, True or False, depending on the outcome of the comparison. If a value x is greater than a value y, the comparison $x > y$ evaluates to True, otherwise to False. Table 4.2 shows the most popular relational operators.

Table 4.2 A list of relational operators, some examples, their meanings, and mathematical notations.

Operator	Example	Explanation	Math formula
>	$x > y$	x greater than y	$x > y$
<	$x < y$	x smaller than y	$x < y$
>=	$x >= y$	x greater or equal than y	$x \geq y$
<=	$x <= y$	x smaller or equal than y	$x \leq y$
==	$x == y$	x equal to y	$x = y$
!=	$x != y$	x not equal to y	$x \neq y$

Since relational expressions evaluate to Booleans they can be combined by Boolean or logical operators (see Section 4.1.3). A more complex example than the ones given in Table 4.2 can be seen in Listing 4.2 which evaluates to False since both, the left and right side of the comparison operator < evaluate to 17. Consequently, they have the same value, no value is smaller or larger than the other. It may be noted that comparisons between integer values are safe while comparisons between floating point numbers can be problematic and error-prone, in particular, if we compare for equality of two floating point numbers.

```
(7*3-4) < (4**2)+1 # evaluates to False
```
Listing 4.2 A relational expression

Although comparison operators are binary operators in the sense that they are applied to two expressions, that is, the left and right side of the operator, they can even be used in a sequence in the sense of a chained comparison. This means we can write

```
w > x >= y > z
```

instead of

```
w > x and x >= y and y > z
```

which is something like syntactic sugar, making the implementation of the code faster. But it has an additional benefit. In the shorter relational expression with the chained comparison, the intermediate expressions are only evaluated once which is not the case in the longer relational expression including the Boolean operator and.

Exercises

- Exercise 4.1.2.1: Evaluate the following arithmetic-relational expression:

    `(4-12)/8+1 > (9**0)`

- Exercise 4.1.2.2: Evaluate the following arithmetic-relational expression:

    `(27//14) - 1 != 27-(3*(4+5))`

4.1.3 Boolean or logical expressions

Boolean or logical expressions [66] are based on operators like "and", "or", and "not." The components of Boolean expressions are Boolean expressions themselves, but the individual components can occur as arithmetic or relational expressions. When a Boolean expression is completely evaluated its result will either be True or False. Those can be regarded as "Yes" or "No," speaking in computer science words also "1" and "0." Tables 4.3–4.5 illustrate simple Boolean expressions with the operators "and", "or", and "not" and the operands themselves being of Boolean values True or False. It may be noted that the first ones are binary operators and the third one is a unary operator.

Table 4.3   The Boolean operator and.

and	True	False
True	True	False
False	False	False

Table 4.4   The Boolean operator or.

or	True	False
True	True	True
False	True	False

Table 4.5 The Boolean operator not.

x	Not x
True	False
False	True

An example of a more complex Boolean expression is given in Listing 4.3. The Boolean expression evaluates to False. It may be noted that the expression is composed of arithmetic and relational smaller expressions that build the entire expression. However, the result after the evaluation of a Boolean expression is always a Boolean value, either True or False, saying if a claim is true or not true, no matter what the smaller expressions evaluate to. The number of operators connecting expressions to Boolean expressions is unlimited, making such expressions to so-called compound expressions consisting of many components. Listing 4.3 shows such an example.

```
1 (4+3*(6+1)<13) and (4-3*2**3 == 27) or (not(24>3*2**3))
2 # evaluates to True
```

Listing 4.3 An example Boolean expression composed of some other smaller expressions that are themselves arithmetic and relational expressions

In cases in which we have a compound Boolean expression composed of many Boolean operators, we might ask whether all of the components are always evaluated. This is not the case for some special Boolean expressions. For example, a chained Boolean expression connecting all subexpressions with an "or" operator will only be evaluated completely if all subexpressions evaluate to False. Since the expression is evaluated from left-to-right, the first appearance of a True evaluation of a subexpression can stop the evaluation of all the other subexpressions since the entire expression will be evaluated to True anyways, no matter what the other subexpressions evaluate to. This strategy saves valuable computing time. This evaluation strategy is denoted by the term short-circuit evaluation [208] and was invented by John McCarthy. A similar strategy holds for a compound Boolean expression in which the subexpressions are connected by "and" operators. As soon as one subexpression evaluates to False the entire expression will evaluate to False, no matter what the evaluation of the other subexpression delivers.

Exercises

- Exercise 4.1.3.1: Evaluate the following arithmetic-relational-Boolean expression:

```
ı (4-3*11<0) and (4**4==256) and (3.13>3.12)
```

- Exercise 4.1.3.2: Evaluate the following arithmetic-relational-Boolean expression:

```
ı (12-3*4==0) or (15-3*5>-1*1.2) and (not(28//4>7.0))
```

4.1.4 Bitwise expressions

Instead of using decimal values in expressions, we can also work with bitwise expressions. Those interpret the values to be operated as sequences of binary digits, that is, values only allowing 0 and 1. Bitwise operators can modify such binary values one bit after the other in various ways as can be seen in Table 4.6.

Table 4.6   Bitwise operators, examples, their meanings, and binary versus decimal.

Operator	Example	Explanation	Binary	Decimal
&	$x \mathbin{\&} y$	bitwise and	$010 \mathbin{\&} 110 = 010$	$2 \mathbin{\&} 6 = 2$
|	$x \mid y$	bitwise or	$010 \mid 110 = 110$	$2 \mid 6 = 6$
$\sim$	$\sim x$	bitwise negation	$\sim 010 = 101$	$\sim 2 = 5$
$\wedge$	$x \wedge y$	bitwise xor	$010 \wedge 110 = 100$	$2 \wedge 6 = 4$
$\gg$	$x \gg n$	n bitwise right shift	$010 \gg 1 = 001$	$2 \gg 1 = 1$
$\ll$	$x \ll n$	n bitwise left shift	$010 \ll 1 = 100$	$2 \ll 1 = 4$

A more complex example for a bitwise expression would be something like the expression in Listing 4.4.

```
ı 16 << 3 | 255 >> 2 # evaluates to 191
```

Listing 4.4   A bitwise expression

Exercise

- Exercise 4.1.4.1: Evaluate the following bitwise expression:

```
ı 5 & 13 & 3 | 14
```

- Exercise 4.1.4.2: Evaluate the following bitwise expression:

```
ı 23 >> 2 & 23 | (~17)
```

4.1.5 Mixed expressions

Actually, expressions can exist in various forms composed of subexpressions based on operands of several datatypes like integers, floating point numbers,

Booleans, but even Strings, or more complex objects. Also, the operators themselves can fall into the categories of arithmetic, relational, Boolean/logical, or bitwise operators. Such expressions are denoted in this book as mixed expressions. In cases in which an expression has a mixed character, we must understand the precedence of the individual operators which is given as an overview in Table 4.7 from highest to lowest precedence. The precedence of the operators describes in which order an expression is evaluated. Parentheses can be used to change the order of evaluation, that is, subexpressions in parentheses have the highest precedence. During evaluation of an expression, the subexpressions are evaluated from highest to lowest precedence, in case we meet equal precedence, a left to right evaluation order is used.

Table 4.7 Operators and their precedences from highest to lowest.

Operator	Symbol(s)	Precedence
Arithmetic exponentiation	**	1
Arithmetic/bitwise plus/minus/negation	+ - ~ (unary)	2
Arithemtic mult, div	* / //	3
Arithmetic plus, minus	+ -	4
Bitwise shift	« »	5
Bitwise and	&	6
Bitwise xor	∧	7
Bitwise or			8
Relational comparisons	== != < <= > >=	9
Boolean not	not	10
Boolean and	and	11
Boolean or	or	12

A mixed expression could be composed of any kind of operators and operands, see an example in Listing 4.5 which evaluates to True.

```
1  3*5+4*(6-1) > 3 or 4*3**2 < 4<<3 and 25//4>6
2  # evaluates to True
```

Listing 4.5 A mixed expression

Exercises

- Exercise 4.1.5.1: Evaluate the following mixed expression:

```
1  4*(3-5**2)/4 > 7 and (3<<3)*7-6 == 9
```

- Exercise 4.1.5.2: Evaluate the following mixed expression:

```
1  (3+4) * (3-4) / (3**2+4**2) >= 6 and (22/4 >5)
```

4.2 Data Types and Variables

Data types and variables are a core ingredient in nearly any programming language. Each value should have a certain type which can be a basic data type or one that is more like a composite data type, allowing to put-together values of a multitude of different data types. Typically, in Python, we find classes and objects, on which also data types and variables are built. This means a data type is actually something like a template, that is, a class in an object-oriented programming language, and a variable is something like a container created from such a template or class, that is, an instance or object of this class, allowing to create as many variables of a certain well-defined data type as we need during coding a Python program. Moreover, each value can be stored in such a variable created from a class, while the variable name is fixed but the content, that is, the value of the variable is modifiable as the name already suggests. Variables do not have to be given an explicit data type when they are declared since Python is some kind of weakly typed programming language [207], which is different in strongly typed programming languages [132] like Java. Moreover, variables cannot only change their values but they can even change the data type.

In this section, we will learn about basic data types, which we consider as the numeric data types like integers (mathematically $\mathbb{Z}$), floating point numbers (mathematically $\mathbb{R}$), or complex numbers with real and imaginary part (mathematically $\mathbb{C}$). Also, Strings, characters, and Booleans will be introduced as basic data types (see Section 4.2.1). Composite data types, on the other hand, are those that behave like containers for several values, typically including values of different basic (but also composite) data types like lists, tuples, or dictionaries, to mention a few (see Section 4.2.2). In some cases it is a meaningful operation to convert between different data types, in case, it is actually possible (like converting the String 33 to the integer of value 33). The most prominent conversions are described in Section 4.2.3. To store the value of any data type, we need the concept of variables that is explained in Section 4.2.4 while we conclude the section by describing values that do not change during a program execution, called constants (Section 4.2.5).

4.2.1 Basic data types

Some basic data types [104] exist in Python which could be categorized into numeric data types like integer, floating point, or complex number. Other data types might be described as String for textual data consisting of characters and also Boolean for True and False values. Integers are those that contain whole numbers, positive ones as well as negative ones, also the zero value. Those integers can be given to a certain base which could indicate that an integer value is binary, octal, decimal, or hexadecimal, for example (see Listing 4.6). If no prefix is given, the value is interpreted as decimal which is the default setting. Other base options are b for binary, o for octal, and x for hexadecimal. It makes no difference if the prefix characters are given as capitals or not. The length of the number, that is, in terms of the number of following digits is unlimited in Python; however, the computer's memory is the limit.

```
1  0b101 == 5 # binary, base 2
2  0o101 == 65 # octal, base 8
3  0x101 == 257 # hexadecimal, base 16
```
Listing 4.6 Integer values to several bases

Apart from integer values we have to deal with real numbers which are given in Python with the so-called floating point numbers that can be recognized by a decimal point that divides the number into a prefix and a postfix. Additionally, we can use the exponent notation [19] to indicate the value of a floating point number which can be given as the letter e or E with an additional positive or negative integer expressing the exponent to the base 10 (see Listing 4.7).

```
1  13.876 == 13.876
2  .81 == 0.81
3  12. == 12.0
4  .32e5 == 32000.0
5  3.2e-3 == 0.0032
```
Listing 4.7 Examples of floating point numbers in different notations

The complex numbers consist of a real part and an imaginary part that are given in the form $r + ij$ in Python while r denotes the real part and i the imaginary part (see Listing 4.8 for examples).

```
1  1.89 + 2.1j
2  2.119 - 3.14j
3  -0.97 + 1.27j
```

Apart from the numeric values we can find textual values, typically called strings in Python. Each string has a finite length and consists of so-called characters, that is, a sequence of characters with a well-defined order. Python denotes string objects by using the data type str given in single or double quotes to make string numbers distinguishable from real numeric values, that is, the string 33 is different from the integer number 33 (see Listing 4.8).

It may be noted that an empty list is allowed in Python which is denoted by two single quotes ''. It might be seen as the equivalent to the value 0 or 0.0 for integers or floating point numbers. Moreover, with so-called escape sequences, we can include special characters in a string like \' or \", that is, the single or double quotes themselves, but even more of them like new line \n, tab \t, or carriage return \r, to mention a few. With an r prefix letter, we can avoid translating the escape sequences in a string, that is, they are just included in a string as they are.

```
1  "Hello world, how are you?"
2  "33 is a number, but here it is a string."
3  'A string can also be written in single quotes.'
```
Listing 4.8 Examples for strings

Finally, the Boolean is a data type giving support for true and for not true values, that is, denoted by True and False in the programming language Python. We have seen examples for this already in Section 4.1.3 when we introduced Boolean expressions.

Exercises

- Exercise 4.2.1.1: What is the result of adding an integer number to a floating point number?
- Exercise 4.2.1.2: Try the following expressions and describe the results:

```
1  4/0
2  4/0.0
```

4.2.2 Composite data types

Not only the simple data types are of interest, also the composite ones. Those allow a combination of values of (even) different data types into one. The most important in-built ones to be mentioned here are lists, tuples, sets, or dictionaries. We might even create our own composite data types, for example, by defining classes from which we can derive objects and instances.

A list can be regarded as some kind of container in which we throw data elements, with the deciding fact that the elements are given in a sequence hence, have an order which allows to access them via a well-defined index. The data elements in a list do not have to be of the same data type and a list can be extended, the values can be modified, as well as data elements can be removed, at any place in the list. To define a regular (one-dimensional) list, we use brackets that enclose the contained elements (see Listing 4.9). As you can see we start with one opening bracket, give the elements of the list separated by commas, and indicate the end of the list by a closing bracket. Lists in Python are zero-based, that is, the first element (the most left one) has the index 0 (and not 1 as we might start counting). Consequently, accessing individual elements from a list happens by the corresponding index on which the element can be found. This is done by putting the index into brackets, like myList[3] if the elements are stored in a list called myList. Typically, this is done by assigning the list to a variable (will be described in Section 4.2.4). To modify a value in a list at a corresponding position we can assign it a value at an index like myList[3] = 17.35. There are various other ways to access elements from a list, for example more than one at the same time. This can be done by myList[1:5], which gives back the values at indices 1–4, as another sublist. We can also give back the rest of a list starting from a corresponding index like myList[3:] which returns the elements from the given index until the end of the list. It may be noted that even two-dimensional, three-dimensional, or even n-dimensional lists are possible due to the fact that in Python we can add any kind of objects in lists, consequently also lists themselves, making them to lists of lists, or lists of lists of lists, and so on (see examples in Listing 4.10).

```
1 [3,3.14,False,-23,3+4j,"Hello"]
```
Listing 4.9 A list in Python with a few data elements

```
1 myList = [1,2,3,4,5,6,7]
2 myList[3] = 17.35
3 myList[1:5] # = [2,3,17.35,5]
4 myList[3:] # = [5,6,7]
5 my2DList = [[1,2,3,4],[5,2.11,9],[0,"Hi"]]
```
Listing 4.10 Accessing and modifying elements in a list

We can also define tuples which have a deciding difference compared to lists. It is not allowed to modify tuples in Python after their creation which can be explained by the fact that those are immutable while lists, on the other hand, are mutable (we have seen that in Listing 4.10 already). A deciding benefit of tuples compared to lists is that their content cannot be changed which is useful in situations in which we should not be allowed to modify values in a data structure. Moreover, tuples are typically faster to be processed compared to lists. This means, in cases lots of operations have to be executed on data structures, we have to consider the usefulness of tuples, in case the content of our data structures will not be modified during those operations.

Listing 4.11 illustrates how tuples are created and how we can work with them. Here we also see that tuples are built by using parentheses () instead of brackets [] as in lists.

```
1  myTuple = (3.14, "Hi", True)
2  myTuple[2]  # = True
```
Listing 4.11   Creating tuples and accessing values from them

There is one more option to structure data elements apart from lists and tuples. Sets are another way in Python to create a collection of data elements. To indicate a set, we enclose the elements in braces { }, separated by commas. One more difference to lists and tuples comes from the fact that the elements in a set are unordered (see Listing 4.12 for examples using sets). This leads to the consequence that we cannot access the set elements by using an index since indices have no meaning at all if there is no explicit order given. As in set theory in the field of mathematics we can work with several sets, for example applying the well-known set operations like union, intersection, symmetric difference, and many more (we will introduce functions and methods in Sections 4.6 and 4.9.3).

```
1  mySetA = {1,2,3,4,5}
2  mySetB = {3,4,5,6,7}
3
4  mySetC = mySetA.intersection(mySetB)  # evaluates to {3,4,5}
```
Listing 4.12   Creating sets and applying operations

The problem with sets is that we cannot access the elements contained in it by just asking about a well-defined index, that is, a position in the set. This is due to the fact that sets are unordered. However, there is one more data structure which is called a dictionary that actually also has no index but the access happens with so-called key-value pairs. This means, to access an element in a dictionary we just have to know the corresponding key, and we get the value to this key in return. Dictionary elements are also enclosed by braces, just like sets, the key-value pairs are separated by commas, and each key is separated from a value by a sign. A dictionary is also unordered but compared to sets we can access the elements by using the keys. Listing 4.13 shows some examples for dictionaries and for accessing their values from keys. Dictionaries can be modified, that is, key-value pairs can be removed, new ones can be added, and they can be changed. Table 4.8 summarizes the most important properties of lists, tuples, sets, and dictionaries.

```
1 myDict = {"Name1": "Peter", "Name2": "Pan", "year": 1976}
2 myDict["year"] # = 1976
```
Listing 4.13   Dictionaries and accessing their values

Table 4.8   Composite data types with special properties.

Data type	Enclosing	Separator	Example	Mutual
List	[]	,	[1,3,2,6]	Yes
Tuple	()	,	(1,3,2,6)	No
Set	{}	,	{1,3,2,6}	Yes
Dictionary	{}	, and :	{"A":1,"B":3,"C":2,"D":6}	Yes

Finally, classes can be implemented for creating more data structures like lists, tuples, sets, and dictionaries but for classes, objects, and instances we refer to Section 4.9.

Exercises

- Exercise 4.2.2.1: Given a list of natural numbers myList = [3,1,8,9,2]. Can you find a way to transform this list into a set with the same elements?
- Exercise 4.2.2.2: Given two lists of natural numbers myListA = [3,1,2,4,3,8] and myListB = [4,5,1,3,7]. Write Python code to create a new list that contains all elements that are contained in both lists.

4.2.3 Conversion between data types

In some situations, it is a good advice to convert one value into another one, particularly in cases where the values have different data types. Each conversion function follows a different conversion strategy, hence there is no unique conversion function for any kind of involved data type pairs. Important functions to receive an int, a float, or a string are int(), float(), or str(). However, we have to make sure that the conversion can be applied in a meaningful way. For example, imagine we are going to convert the string 'hello' into a floating point number. Is this a meaningful operation? Listing 4.14 shows some meaningful conversion examples.

```
1  int (3.14) # = 3
2  float (100) # = 100.0
3  float ('3.1415') # = 3.1415
4  str (42.99) # = '42.99'
5  set ([3.14,7,-3]) # = {3.14,7,-3}
6  tuple ({3.14,7,-3}) # = (3.14,7,-3)
7  list ('Bye Bye') # = ['B','y','e',' ','B','y','e']
8  dict (["A",1],["B",2],["C",3]) # = {"A":1,"B":2,"C":3}
```
Listing 4.14   Some meaningful conversions from one data type to another one

Exercises

- Exercise 4.2.3.1: Convert the floating point number 2.6176 into a corresponding integer.
- Exercise 4.2.3.2: Given a string '3.8821'. Convert the string into a floating point number and then into an int. Is it allowed to convert the string directly into an int?

4.2.4 Variables

A variable in Python is something like a container in which we can store values of a certain data type. When we define a variable, we make sure that some place is reserved in the memory for possible values contained in such a variable. Since each value has some well-defined data type, the variable that stores this value also carries this data type. A variable can be declared with a certain name and initialized with a certain value (see Listing 4.15). This is done by mentioning the name of the variable on the left-hand side of an equality sign and put its current value to the right-hand side of the equality sign. This order must be preserved. It may be noted that variables in Python can be redeclared at any time as well as their values can be modified, hence the name variable. Due to the weakly typed language character we can even change the data type of the same variable, for example, from an int to a string (see Listing 4.16).

```
1  length = 3.89
```
Listing 4.15   Declaring a variable and initializing it with a value

```
1  length = 3.72
2  length = "Given in meters"
```
Listing 4.16   Variable redeclaration

Variables can even exist in two special forms characterized by the way in which we can access them and modify them. This brings into play local and global variables which are discussed in more detail in Sections 4.6 and 4.9.

Exercises

- Exercise 4.2.4.1: Declare three variables called *height*, *width*, and *length*, initialize them with some floating point values, and compute the value of the variable *volume* as the product of the three variable values.
- Exercise 4.2.4.2: Declare two variables a and b, initialize them with floating point numbers. Compute a Pythagorean triple, that is, a value for a variable c that the equality $a^2 + b^2 = c^2$ holds.

4.2.5 Constants

Sometimes we would like to include values that never change during a program execution. This could be done by a traditional variable, but there is a chance that the value gets changed at some point which is not desired. Hence, we would like to give such a variable a special meaning, saying that its content should stay untouched in any scenario. This is the point in which we have to use a constant. Actually, in Python there is no special syntax for that. We just use variables, but we give them a special form by a well-defined naming convention, that is, using only capital or uppercase letters indicates that this variable is a constant, although it might be changed. Since constants are just variables (but never change the values), they can be based on any data type the standard variables are also based on. The value of a constant should not be modifiable, we can just use it in one direction, meaning reading the value it contains (see Listing 4.17 for creating constants).

```
1 PI = 3.141592
2 E = 2.7182
3 HIGHEST_SPEED = 240
```

Listing 4.17   Defining constants in Python

Exercises

- Exercise 4.2.5.1: Define a constant that contains the number of seconds per day.

- Exercise 4.2.5.2: Define a constant that stores the free fall acceleration on earth as a range interval.

4.3 Strings and Characters

Strings are the key data type when we have to deal with textual data, for example, to give feedback to users or to analyze textual content for word occurrence frequencies or semantic meanings. This does not only hold for standard text, but it could also be relevant for source code or DNA strings, both of them are based on textual entities composed of letters/characters from a given alphabet on its finest granularity level. Hence, text analytics [6] is a major application domain in the field of data science. This fact makes strings to relevant topics to study and to research. Strings and characters are special types of values but on the other hand they can be treated as numeric values as well, given the fact that we can map each character to a well-defined number, for example, based on a character table like the ASCII table. However, working with strings and characters is not as easy as working with numeric values, since the standard arithmetic operations (Section 4.1.1) cannot be applied simultaneously. Instead, there are many functions and methods that support operations on strings and characters.

In this section, we are first looking into methods to apply meaningful operations on strings and characters, however, there seems to be an endless list of such methods, too many to mention all of them here (see Section 4.3.1). Furthermore, we will have a look into character tables like ASCII and explain the order among those characters (Section 4.3.2). User input and the validation of user input, in particular with regular expressions is illustrated in Section 4.3.3. We also describe how a program should be commented which is possible in several ways (Section 4.3.4).

4.3.1 String methods

There are various functions and methods (to understand what methods are, see Section 4.9.3) that can be applied to transform, modify, analyze, split, or reverse strings, just to mention a few. Some methods work on one string only, some other methods work on several of them, some just process the string by reading it, some others transform one or more strings into one or several others. Such a string transformation could be a special kind of encoding, for example, used for passwords that should not be stored in its textual plain vanilla form in a system. No matter which kind of string problem we look at, there are various ways to get support from built-in Python methods. How to create one's own functions and methods will be explained in Sections 4.6 and 4.9.3, respectively. Moreover, we will explain the difference between functions and methods, actually at the moment, the outcome does not make a difference for us. Apart from string methods, we can also apply built-in methods or our own created methods on the major building blocks of such strings, namely characters and their internal organization in tables, for example, in an ASCII table (Section 4.3.2).

If only one string is involved, we might be interested in the length of that string, the number of lower- and uppercase letters it contains, the positions of special characters or substrings in that string, or we might actively change the string, for example, exchanging special characters or converting it into uppercase letters only or just one uppercase letter at the beginning. There are many options to apply functions and methods to strings, Listing 4.18 illustrates some examples.

```
1 originalString = 'hello how are you?'
2
3 numChars = len(originalString)
4 newString = originalString.capitalize()
5 newString = originalString.encode()
6 test = originalString.isascii()
```

Listing 4.18   String functions and methods if only one string is involved

If two or more strings are involved (see Listing 4.19), we can apply different kinds of functions and methods.

```
1 originalString = 'hello how are you?'
2 text = 'ow ar'
3
4 originalString.find(text)
5 originalString.index(text)
6 originalString.replace('are you','am I')
```

Listing 4.19   String functions and methods applied to more than one string

Exercises

- Exercise 4.3.1.1: Given a string 'Good morning everybody'. Find a way to reverse the string.

- Exercise 4.3.1.2: Given two strings 'hello' and 'how are you'. Find a way to concatenate both strings into one string.

4.3.2 ASCII code and table

The American Standard Code for Information Interchange (ASCII) [108] introduced a special encoding standard for characters as well as symbols that we typically meet during programming tasks. The idea behind ASCII is that each character, letter, or symbol is assigned a well-defined natural number, hence ASCII characters can be represented in some kind of table ordered by these unique numeric identifiers (see Figure 4.1). ASCII allows 128 characters due to the fact that each character is internally represented by a 7-bit binary string (from 0000000 to 1111111), resulting in $2^7 = 128$ different possibilities for the binary string. There are ways to switch between a character and the corresponding numeric value, for example, by using the functions ord() and chr(), illustrated in Listing 4.20. Apart from ASCII there are some other encoding schemes, one popular one is denoted by the term Unicode, supporting many more characters than the 128 in ASCII.

Dec	Hex	Oct	Char	Dec	Hex	Oct	Char	Dec	Hex	Oct	Char	Dec	Hex	Oct	Char
0	0	0		32	20	40	[space]	64	40	100	@	96	60	140	`
1	1	1		33	21	41	!	65	41	101	A	97	61	141	a
2	2	2		34	22	42	"	66	42	102	B	98	62	142	b
3	3	3		35	23	43	#	67	43	103	C	99	63	143	c
4	4	4		36	24	44	$	68	44	104	D	100	64	144	d
5	5	5		37	25	45	%	69	45	105	E	101	65	145	e
6	6	6		38	26	46	&	70	46	106	F	102	66	146	f
7	7	7		39	27	47	'	71	47	107	G	103	67	147	g
8	8	10		40	28	50	(	72	48	110	H	104	68	150	h
9	9	11		41	29	51	)	73	49	111	I	105	69	151	i
10	A	12		42	2A	52	*	74	4A	112	J	106	6A	152	j
11	B	13		43	2B	53	+	75	4B	113	K	107	6B	153	k
12	C	14		44	2C	54	,	76	4C	114	L	108	6C	154	l
13	D	15		45	2D	55	-	77	4D	115	M	109	6D	155	m
14	E	16		46	2E	56	.	78	4E	116	N	110	6E	156	n
15	F	17		47	2F	57	/	79	4F	117	O	111	6F	157	o
16	10	20		48	30	60	0	80	50	120	P	112	70	160	p
17	11	21		49	31	61	1	81	51	121	Q	113	71	161	q
18	12	22		50	32	62	2	82	52	122	R	114	72	162	r
19	13	23		51	33	63	3	83	53	123	S	115	73	163	s
20	14	24		52	34	64	4	84	54	124	T	116	74	164	t
21	15	25		53	35	65	5	85	55	125	U	117	75	165	u
22	16	26		54	36	66	6	86	56	126	V	118	76	166	v
23	17	27		55	37	67	7	87	57	127	W	119	77	167	w
24	18	30		56	38	70	8	88	58	130	X	120	78	170	x
25	19	31		57	39	71	9	89	59	131	Y	121	79	171	y
26	1A	32		58	3A	72	:	90	5A	132	Z	122	7A	172	z
27	1B	33		59	3B	73	;	91	5B	133	[	123	7B	173	{
28	1C	34		60	3C	74	<	92	5C	134	\	124	7C	174	|
29	1D	35		61	3D	75	=	93	5D	135	]	125	7D	175	}
30	1E	36		62	3E	76	>	94	5E	136	^	126	7E	176	~
31	1F	37		63	3F	77	?	95	5F	137	_	127	7F	177	

Figure 4.1   Characters and symbols with their corresponding numeric identifiers represented in the ASCII table.

```
1  character = 'p'
2
3  identifier = ord(character)
4  character = chr(identifier)
5  identifier = identifier + 5
6  character = chr(identifier) # evaluates to 'u'
```

Listing 4.20   Converting between characters and corresponding numeric identifiers based on the ASCII table

Exercises

- Exercise 4.3.2.1: What is the numeric value of the character 'M' in the ASCII table? Write code for that.
- Exercise 4.3.2.2: Given a list of characters myList = ['H','e','l','l','o']. Convert this character list into a numeric ASCII value list. Do the same with the letters occurring in your own name.

4.3.3 User input and regular expressions

In many scenarios we wish to get user input, for example to get feedback for a certain task, service, or to evaluate a visualization tool or dashboard. In its simplest form this can be done by allowing users to type in textual information to give feedback to the developer of such a tool or a service. This strategy brings some extra challenges, not only for the users but even more from a programming perspective. The textual user inputs can be strings, integers, floating point numbers and they might have certain lengths or text formats. Actually, this is not a problem at all but we have to react on any kind of user inputs to avoid our program from crashing, either directly or after a few steps during its executions, for example when a value, based on a wrong data type, has to be processed. This process can happen many steps later, hence it might become difficult to debug the program and to localize the origin of the error. The standard way to allow user inputs could be done by using the code in Listing 4.21. The function called input has the goal to output the given text in parentheses and to assign the variable on the left-hand side with the user input which is completed by pressing the return key. However, in a visualization tool, we typically provide more advanced text fields or text areas to type in some textual information, like in a mask to fill in personal information as it is known from the most popular web pages that need to collect this kind of personal information. We can be confronted by at least three major input validation concepts that we will explain in the following.

```
1 feedback = input('Please provide some feedback: ')
```
Listing 4.21　Allowing user input in textual form

- Length of the input: Actually, users can enter a quite long textual information, that is, consisting of many characters. If we wish to limit the number of possible characters, we can validate that by asking for the length of a string. The function len() has already been introduced earlier (see Section 4.3.1).
- Content/Data type of the input: An input in this form is typically given as a value in the string data type. This means if we expect integers or floating point numbers, we have to check first if the given string is convertable into such a numeric value. This concept has also been explained earlier (see Section 4.2.3).
- Specific pattern in the input: Finally, we might want to check if a string follows a certain pattern or rule. This seems to be more complex than the standard length and data type validations but actually, it is not really difficult. The powerful idea that comes into play here are so-called regular expressions [70, 225]. A regular expression can be understood as a string itself, consisting of characters that have a meaning, that is, those characters can be used to derive certain well-defined patterns in a string. In Python there is a built-in package denoted by re. Such regular expressions can be checked for several properties like meta characters (Table 4.9), special sequence characters (Table 4.10), or a set of characters (Table 4.11), without guaranteeing completeness of the tables.

Table 4.9　Meta characters and their meaning.

Pattern	Meaning	Example
.	Any character	'ho..ar..y.u?'
[]	Some characters	'[c-t]'
*	0 or more	'*n'
+	1 or more	'+l'
?	0 or 1	'?p'
{n}	n times	'{n}'
|	Either or	'yes|no'
()	A group	'(mnp)'
∧	Start with	'∧s'
$	Ends with	'l$'

To apply a regular expression to a given string, we have to know some useful functions and methods (see, e.g., Listing 4.22).

Table 4.10 Special sequence characters and their meaning.

Pattern	Meaning	Example
\s	match where white space is	'\sgd h tt'
\S	match where no white space is	'\Sgf g tr'
\b	match if chars at beginning/end	'\bha'
\B	match where chars are, not at beginning	'\Bhi'
\A	match if chars at the beginning	'\Ahel'
\d	match if digits contained	'\dtr6d1f'
\D	match where no digits are	'\Dt5rt65tr'

Table 4.11 Set of characters and their meaning.

Pattern	Meaning	Example
[b-t]	any lower case letter b to t	'f'
[01234]	any of the digits 0 to 4	'3'
[bgd]	any of the given letters b, g, d	'd'
[0-9]	any digit between 0 and 9	'7'
[∧bht]	any letter apart from b, h, t	'x'
[0-7][0-5]	any 2-digit number between 00 to 75	'68'
[a-zA-Z]	any letter between a and Z	'T'

```python
import re

inputString = 'I love programming'
matches = re.findall('o',inputString)
matches = re.search('o',inputString)

inputString2 = 'RE352'
validate = re.match([A-Z]{1,2}[0-9]{3}, inputString2)
```

Listing 4.22 Examples of functions and methods for applying regular expressions to strings

Exercises

- Exercise 4.3.3.1: Write a regular expression for strings that contain exactly one uppercase letter and end with three digits.
- Exercise 4.3.3.2: For a password validation check, we need a string of at least eight characters, and that starts with an uppercase letter and at least one digit. Write a regular expression for that.

4.3.4 Comments

The documentation in a program [227] is very important to let the developer better understand the functionality in certain parts in the code. This is, in particular, useful if we have to inspect the code many weeks later and to quickly get an impression about what is being implemented in a certain piece of code. Due to this fact, it is a good advice to keep the documentation in the form of code comments short but still informative to explain the effects of a code and why it has been implemented in exactly this way. A text line that starts with a # sign will be ignored by the compiler or interpreter, but when reading the code, it is always there (see Listing 4.23 for an example of a comment). Comments can be placed everywhere in a code, it may be noted that if they are placed at the end of a code line, the rest after the # will be ignored.

```
1 # Writing comments is not difficult
2 print('This is a commented program.')
3
4 value = 25 # A comment after a code line
```

Listing 4.23   A comment in a Python code

Comments are not limited to one line only. They can span several lines and many of them can be made at different code places (see Listing 4.24), also with so-called triple quotes indicating a comment over several lines.

```
1 # Hello
2 # These comments are placed
3 # in several lines
4 print('This seems to work')
5
6 """
7 Hello
8 These comments are placed
9 in several lines
10 """
```

Listing 4.24   Several comments spread over several lines by using triple quotes

Exercises

- Exercise 4.3.4.1: Write a one-line comment in Python code.
- Exercise 4.3.4.2: Write a multi-line comment in Python code.

4.4 Conditionals and Exceptions

In some situations we wish to branch in the program, meaning there are two ways to follow, given the fact that a condition can be evaluated in two directions: Either true or false (Sections 4.1.2 and 4.1.3). This leads to a binary kind of control flow that can handle one of both ways, depending on the outcome of a formerly evaluated conditional expression. In some cases, we even have more than two options which might be modeled by several conditionals, but, in this case, we might better take the option of allowing several cases, handling one case after the other until one matching is found, or in the worst scenario, no case is found, asking to execute a default option. In some situations, it is even a good idea to handle an exception, meaning there is a strange, unwanted, or unexpected evaluation that would otherwise let the program crash if not handled by an exception.

In this section, we will start by explaining the mighty concept of conditionals allowing a branching in the control flow (Section 4.4.1). We will also take a look at a so-called pattern matching option that allows several cases to be handled, but just one or a default one can be executed (Section 4.4.2). Finally, we describe exceptions and how they can be checked, even be treated to avoid the crashing of the program (Section 4.4.3).

4.4.1 If and else

In a so-called if-statement [113], we can check whether a condition holds or not. The if-statement evaluates some kind of logical/Boolean or relational expression (see Sections 4.1.2 and 4.1.3) to get a True or False value with which it is decided what to do, that is, if the condition allows a following code to be executed (see Listing 4.25). In this example the indented code after the if-statement is only executed in case the variable value contains a number greater than 0.0 which evaluates to True in this special example. It may be noted that there can be many more code lines after an if-statement, all of the indented ones belong to the body of the if-statement and will be executed one after the other. In Python we use this indentation principle, in other programming languages parentheses might be used.

```
1  value = 0.05
2
3  if value > 0.0:
4      print('The value is greater than 0.0.')
```

Listing 4.25 An if-condition can be used to allow code to be executed or not

By just using an if-statement, we do not have a real branching in the control flow, for this we need an else branch, meaning there is always an option, no matter how the conditional expression is evaluated, True or False (see Listing 4.26).

```
1  value = -0.05
2
3  if value > 0.0:
4      print('The value is greater than 0.0.')
5  else:
6      print('The value is smaller than or equal to 0.0.')
```

Listing 4.26 The else part of a conditional can be used as an alternative in cases the if-statement branch is not executed

In Python there is even another alternative: the elif option. This one gives a chance to proceed as another alternative in cases the if-statement is evaluated to False (see Listing 4.27).

```
1  value = 0.00
2
3  if value > 0.0:
4      print('The value is greater than 0.0.)
5  elif value == 0.0:
6      print('The value is equal to 0.0.')
7  else:
8      print('The value is smaller than 0.0.')
```

Listing 4.27 The elif option can be used as an alternative in cases the if-statement is not followed

The keyword 'pass' can even be used in cases in which there are no statements after an if-branch. The pass keyword replaces the otherwise empty code block, however, this happens only in rare cases.

Exercises

- Exercise 4.4.1.1: Write a program to test whether a natural number is odd or even.
- Exercise 4.4.1.2: Given a variable containing a string. Test whether this string contains uppercase letters and more than 10 characters.

4.4.2 Pattern matching

In Python there is no explicit switch statement as in other programming languages but instead, there is some kind of pattern matching strategy that tries to match pattern by pattern until one is found, or a default case is reached, in case no pattern matches from the given ones. The default case is indicated by an underscore pattern. This pattern matching strategy creates a branching effect that allows more than two or three possibilities (if, elif, else) by using a multitude of patterns (see Listing 4.28).

```
value = 'Mercedes'

match value:
    case 'Audi':
        print('Your car is an Audi.')
    case 'Peugeot':
        print('Your car is a Peugeot.')
    case 'Mercedes':
        print('Your car is a Mercedes.')
    case _:
        print('The brand of your car is unknown.')
```

Listing 4.28 A multitude of options are possible by using a match case pattern

Exercises

- Exercise 4.4.2.1: Write code for a pattern matching that checks different grades and outputs whether the grade is very good, good, medium, bad, or very bad.
- Exercise 4.4.2.2: Write code for a pattern matching that checks different sports activities and outputs the number of players required.

4.4.3 Exceptions

A syntax error [253] can occur if a piece of code is not properly defined to make it understandable for the compiler or interpreter. This kind of error happens before the actual program execution, that is, before runtime, already in the program translation phase. A semantic error [182] is an error that is not detected by the compiler but rather by the programmers themselves. Semantic errors create unwanted effects, those that do not produce the functionality the programmers desired. A third kind of error is an exception. A program might be syntactically and semantically correct, but there might be some places in which the code is not running properly, but just for a few 'exceptional' instances of a problem, hence those are so-called exceptions. Unlike syntactic or semantic errors, exceptions can be handled (in case one knows them). If they are not handled they can result in errors and the program might crash (see Listing 4.29 for an exception and Listing 4.30 for handling it). Apart from division-by-zero errors, there are various kinds of exceptions, typically indicated in error messages given by the compiler in cases the programs crash due to some unforeseen reasons. Python supports some built-in exceptions with clear exception information to provide some feedback about the type of error, however the programmers can also create their own exceptions.

```
1  value = 0
2  divisionValue = 6/value
```

Listing 4.29   An error caused by a division by zero

```
1  value = 0
2
3  try:
4      divisionValue = 6/value
5      break
6  except ZeroDivisionError:
7      print('Division by zero is not allowed')
```

Listing 4.30   Handling a division by zero error

To handle an exception we enclose the critical program code into so-called try-except statements. First, the try block is executed. If there is no exception, the try statement is processed, and the except part is skipped. If there is an exception, the rest of the code block after the try is skipped and the except part is executed, in case the name of the exception matches the real exception. Finally, the code of the try-except part is executed. This means, although there was some type of error in the program, the program will not crash, instead it will handle the exception, here with a printed string.

Exercises

- Exercise 4.4.3.1: After a user input we would like to proceed with the user-defined number, but unfortunately, this number is a string. Write code to handle such a conversion error.
- Exercise 4.4.3.2: In the example Listing 4.30 extend the code of the except part to provide a value for the divisionValue variable even if it generates a division-by-zero error.

4.5 Loops

To avoid implementing the same kind of functionality all the time, only differing in the size of an argument, for example, we can make use of so-called loops [159]. Those are simple constructs that repeat instructions until a certain well-defined termination condition is met. There are two types of loops: definite ones and indefinite ones. This means, for the first type of loops we know how many iterations are made until the process terminates, for the second type of loops we have no idea how many iterations have to be made until the process terminates. The termination is decided during the runtime of the loop and has to be computed in some kind of dynamic termination condition. For this reason (and maybe for some others as well) Python supports for-loops and while-loops, both of them, contain a termination condition, however it is given in two different ways. Loops can even run endlessly, in case the termination condition is never met. Moreover, loops can be implemented inside loops and the loop types can even be mixed, that is, for-loops can be contained in while-loops and vice versa.

In this section, we start by introducing the principle of definite iteration and focus on the so-called for-loops (Section 4.5.1). Apart from definite iterations we look into indefinite iterations, in this case we describe the concept of while-loops and explain termination conditions (Section 4.5.2). Finally, we illustrate how loops can be nested, meaning there is actually no limit to the number of loops contained in each other, but it may be noted that an unclever nesting can cause high runtimes (Section 4.5.3).

4.5.1 Definite iteration

The for-loop is used to process a list or set of elements. This list or set can be based not only on a real list but also on a string (which is actually a list of characters) or on a range, for example as an interval of natural numbers (which again is some kind of list). The order of the list (or sequence) is important to start somewhere and end somewhere during the processing strategy. In programming terms we say that we iterate over the sequence, hence we know exactly how many steps are needed to process all elements, which give this iteration strategy its name, the definite iteration. The first line of a for-loop just describes which elements are involved in an iteration and in which order, the rest of the for-loop, that is, its body describes what to do exactly with each of the elements, one-by-one. Listing 4.31 illustrates an example for such a for-loop iterating over a list of names and sums up the numbers of letters contained in each name string.

```
1 names = ['Marco','Michael','Heiko','John']
2 numOfLetters = 0
3
4 for name in names:
5   numOfLetters += len(name)
6
7 print(numOfLetters)
```

Listing 4.31 A for-loop illustrating a definite iteration over a list of names

There are even break and continue statements to stop the iteration if a certain element is found or has a certain property. Moreover, we do not have to stop it, but we might skip it instead and continue the iteration after it, hence the corresponding element is omitted in the process (see Listings 4.32 and 4.33).

```
1 names = ['Marco','Michael','Heiko','John']
2 numOfLetters = 0
3
4 for name in names:
5   if name == 'Michael':
6     break
7   numOfLetters += len(name)
8
9 print(numOfLetters)
```

Listing 4.32 A for-loop with a break statement

```
1 names = ['Marco','Michael','Heiko','John']
2 numOfLetters = 0
3
4 for name in names:
5   if name == 'Heiko':
6     continue
7   numOfLetters += len(name)
8
9 print(numOfLetters)
```

Listing 4.33 A for-loop with a continue statement

Apart from using a list or sequence of elements we can operate on a certain interval with natural numbers. The easiest way to get that done is by applying the range() function. This creates a sequence of numbers and then the for-loop iterates over this sequence (see Listing 4.34). Actually, the iteration can increment by one, starting from 0, between left and right interval borders, or even increment by a given value, typically specified as a third parameter. There is even an else statement which can be given after the for-loop has finished. Moreover, a pass statement can be used in cases the body of a for-loop is empty for some reason.

```
1  n = 5;
2
3  for i in range(10):
4      n+=i**2
5
6  for i in range (7,17):
7      n-=i
8
9  for i in range (10,20,4):
10     n+=i
```
Listing 4.34   A for-loop defined on the range()-function

Exercises

- Exercise 4.5.1.1: Implement a for-loop that sums up the natural numbers from 1 to 100, that is, $\sum_{i=1}^{100} i$.
- Exercise 4.5.1.2: Implement a for-loop that computes the factorial of a natural number $n \in \mathbb{N}$ given as $n! := \prod_{i=1}^{n} i$ for a value of $n = 20$.

4.5.2 Indefinite iteration

In contrast to the for-loop which is typically used for a definite iteration, the while-loop is the most frequent used concept for indefinite iteration. Actually, in cases in which it is unclear how long or how often an iteration has to run, a while-loop is suited better since it allows to start the loop without clearly specifying how long or how often it has to run. Each for-loop can be transformed into a corresponding while-loop by just using the number of iterations in the for-loop as a break up criterion in the while-loop. The other direction, transforming a while-loop into a for-loop, is more difficult, sometimes even impossible. The reason is that we cannot just use the conditional test expression in a while-loop as a sequence to iterate over. The condition itself might be dependent on side effects that we cannot easily understand when starting the loop. However, even if it is possible, we should follow the principle of using for-loops for definite iterations and while-loops for indefinite iterations. Listing 4.35 illustrates an example for a while-loop. The body of the while-loop is executed as long as the test expression in the first line is evaluated to true; otherwise, the loop stops and the control flow proceeds regularly after the last statement in the loop's body. The test expression is only checked once at the beginning, after each iteration, independent of the fact whether or not the test expression might change during executing the statements in the body of the while-loop.

```
1  value = 100
2
3  while (value % 3 != 0):
4       value = value/2
5
6  print(value)
```
Listing 4.35   A while-loop iterates in an indefinite way

Similar to the for-loop, also the while-loop allows break-statements and an else option at the end.

Exercises

- Exercise 4.5.2.1: Implement a while-loop that runs as long as the term $n := n + \frac{1.0}{n}$ is smaller than a given number.
- Exercise 4.5.2.2: Implement a while-loop that does the same as the for-loop in Listing 4.31.

4.5.3 Nested loops

The programming world would be boring if it was not allowed to create more complex loops, for example in a nested fashion. This means loops can be contained inside other loops, even as a mixture of while- and for-loops (see Listing 4.36).

```
1  for i in range(10):
2       while i*i<50:
3            i = i+1
4            print(i*i)
```
Listing 4.36   An example for nesting loops

Exercises

- Exercise 4.5.3.1: Implement a for-loop that processes a list of strings, element by element, and that processes each string character by character to count the number of uppercase letters.

- Exercise 4.5.3.2: Implement a three-dimensional list containing natural numbers. Use three nested for-loops to sum up all values in the 3D list.

4.6 Functions

Functions are the major building blocks of programming since they allow to encapsulate subroutines into code blocks. A subroutine is understood as a small algorithm that works with input and output parameters, computing something useful. The whole program is full of such subroutines, being responsible for the functionalities a software can have. Using functions makes coding much easier, with less text, and even more maintainable. For example, if the functionality of a subroutine has to be changed without using functions we have to find all locations in the code and adapt the subroutine. This is a tedious, time-consuming, and error-prone task, also with high chances to include inconsistencies in the code. For this reason, functions can be used to put such subroutines at one place. Each time we have to adapt something in the subroutine we only have to do this once, in the corresponding function, which accelerates the adaptation process and reduces the chance to include inconsistencies that would lead to the program to crash.

In this section, we describe the concept of creating one's own functions (Section 4.6.1) with and without return parameters and with an arbitrary number of such parameters, also with different data types. Section 4.6.2 illustrates how functions can be called, taking into account their parameter lists and data types as well. Apart from one, even several functions can be integrated, in some kind of nested structure, a strategy that is illustrated in Section 4.6.3. Moreover, the variables inside a function are typically used in a local way, but for some reason, we could even define them as global variables (Section 4.6.4).

4.6.1 Defining a function

Before using such self-built functions, we have to find a way to define them. This means we have to specify a name, the input and output parameters, and the computation routine itself in the body of the function. A computation routine can be as simple as finding a maximum value among a list of numeric values for projecting high-dimensional data to a lower-dimensional space [235]. No matter which functionality we create, the definition of a function always follows the same principle, depending on the problem itself, it can be more or less complex. The most important thing when defining a function is to know the Python keyword for that which is given by def, telling us that we are going to define a function. Listing 4.37 shows an example for a simple function that is named sum and gets 3 input parameters x, y, and z. Those are summed up and the result is returned as the only output parameter. It may be noted that a function can have as many input and output parameters as we like (separated by commas), also no inputs and no outputs are possible. Returning a result is done by the return statement (in the last line of a function definition). This means the function is completely processed and we will return in the control flow to the place where the function was called and process the next statements, but now we know the result of a computation (a simple or complex one) and can use it in the program.

```
1  def sum(x,y,z):
2      return x+y+z
```

Listing 4.37 A simple function definition in Python

Exercises

- Exercise 4.6.1.1: Define a function that computes the factorial of n, that is, the product of all natural numbers from 1 to n.
- Exercise 4.6.1.2: Define a function that takes two lists with numeric values as arguments and adds them element by element, returning a new list containing the sums of the elements.

4.6.2 Calling a function

Defining a function is one side of the problem, calling it is the other. However, calling a function is not difficult, in case, we know its name and its input and output parameters. Apart from the number of parameters we should also know which data types they are based on to make the call a reliable one, that is, avoid runtime errors during the program execution. The syntactic errors will typically be found by the compiler before the execution but still even if a program is syntactically correct there is no guarantee that it is also semantically correct. For example, an originally intended float data type might be mistaken for an integer data type. The program itself might be syntactically correct, for example adding two integers happens in a similar way as adding two floating point numbers, but the precision after the execution is a different one. Such a problem should be detected when calling the function, even if the definition might be syntactically correct. Calling a function happens by its name and the parameter list while the parameters are replaced by real values in the call, to allow the function to be executed and to compute a result. Listing 4.38 gives an example showing how to call a function, in this case the function sum on three arguments from Listing 4.37. The three values are given as variables and build the input parameters of the sum function. Since the function is already properly defined, it is known what to do with these values while the returned value from the function is finally assigned to another variable called result which can be seen in the main code.

```
1 value1 = 2.3
2 value2 = 4.5
3 value3 = 1.3
4
5 result = sum(value1, value2, value3)
```

Listing 4.38 Calling a function happens by using its name and its parameter list

In some cases, where we call a function with a wrong parameter list, for example, the input parameters we get an error message. Moreover, if the number of output parameters does not match with the assignment to a variable or several variables, this will also cause an error. Also a wrong order of the parameters can cause an error, in case the data types do not match, however, if the data types match for some reason, we might have the problem of wrong value assignments. This will not be detected by the compiler but we will obtain a wrong result that is caused by a semantics error, that is, a semantically wrong assignment.

There are even options in Python to call a function when the number of the input arguments might be unknown at the moment of the function call. For example, if a list of values is given as input parameters we can use the * pattern to let the function expect as many values as are given in the current situation of the function call (see Listing 4.39).

```
1 def bestStudent(*students):
2     return("The currently best student is " + students[0])
3
4 bestStudent("Michael", "Marco", "Ingo", "David")
```

Listing 4.39 Using a star to indicate an unknown number of arguments at the moment of a function call

It is even possible to explicitly assign the used variables in a function in the function call, making the ordering of the arguments irrelevant, but negatively we have to know the keys that are needed to properly make the key-argument assignments (Listing 4.40).

```
1 def bestStudent(student4, student3, student2, student1):
2     return("The currently best student is " + student1)
3
4 bestStudent(student1 = "Michael", student2 = "Marco",
      student3 = "Ingo", student4 = "David")
```

Listing 4.40   Using key-value pairs at a function call

Exercises

- Exercise 4.6.2.1: Call the function in Listing 4.37 to compute the sum of the values for each parameter by varying the value between 0 and 100. Hint: Use a nested for-loop.
- Exercise 4.6.2.2: Extend the function from Listing 4.37 to allow an unknown number of numeric arguments. Call the function by varying the number of the arguments.

4.6.3 Nesting of functions

Defining and calling a function can also be based on a multitude of other functions, in some kind of nested structure. For example, to compute a clustering from a list of two-dimensional points it might be important to compute the distance of pairs of those points, to create and to validate the computed clustering. This distance function can be implemented inside the clustering function, but it would be better to call the distance function inside the clustering function. Maybe the distance function, which is a very basic computation, has to be applied in several other functions, apart from only the one for the clustering computation. This makes the distance function more general in some way, hence it is a good strategy to create some kind of function set whose elements can be called inside each other whenever required. An example for simple nested functions is given in Listing 4.41.

```
1 def sum(x,y,z):
2     return x+y+z
3
4 def average(x,y,z):
5     return sum(x,y,z)/3
6
7 average(4.3,2.7,8.9)
```

Listing 4.41   Nesting functions can be a powerful coding strategy to avoid reimplementing the same basic functions again and again many times

Exercises

- Exercise 4.6.3.1: Define a function for computing the average length of strings in a given string list. Use the function len() to compute the length of each string.
- Exercise 4.6.3.2: Define a function to compute the ratio between maximum and minimum of a given list of floating point numbers. Use the functions min and max.

4.6.4 Local and global variables

Typically, in a function in Python we use local variables. The reason is that they cannot be accessed and modified from the outside of the function, a programming concept that is known under the term encapsulation. This mighty principle is important to avoid ugly side effects that would allow to change values inside a function from anywhere, leading to problems when maintaining the code or detecting errors. But in some rare situations it might make sense to define a variable inside a function as a global variable, that is, one that is accessible from everywhere, can even be modified, and flows into the computation inside the function. But this strategy should be taken with care since it can create unwanted side effects. Listing 4.42 illustrates how to define a variable inside a function as global. This definition uses the value of the global variable nFact from the main program inside the function which will not create the right result for the factorial of n. This error can happen if we accidentally used the same variable name somewhere in the program and now the value is used in the function without being aware of it.

```
1  nFact = 5
2
3  def nFactorial(n):
4      global nFact
5
6      for i in range (1,n+1):
7          nFact = nFact*i
8      return nFact
```

Listing 4.42   A global variable inside a function definition

Exercises

- Exercise 4.6.4.1: Define a function that computes the product of 3 natural numbers. Use a global variable to store the result of the computation.

- Exercise 4.6.4.2: Call the function in Listing 4.42 without initializing the value of the global variable nFact in the main program. What is the effect?

4.7 More Complex Functions

The functions we discussed so far are quite simple, that is, plain vanilla function definitions and calls. There are other options in Python to create functions, for example functions calling themselves until a termination condition is reached. This strategy is known as recursion [234] since a function is recursively defined on itself, starting with a problem that is solved by recursively reducing the size of the problem until it is small enough to be trivial, that is, to lead to a termination. The input and output parameters of functions can themselves be functions bringing us to the higher-order functions. Functions do not have to be named, they can even be defined and called anonymously, in so-called lambda expressions. This allows to use a function 'on-the-fly' by defining and calling it exactly at the place in the code where it is needed.

In this section, we are going to explain more complex functions by starting with recursion and tail recursion (Section 4.7.1), that is, a kind of recursion that reduces the memory consumption by more or less directly evaluating the expression that is built during the recursive process. The next recursive call is started when the expression is computed which avoids creating long recursion chains or trees. Functions with functions as input and output parameters are described in Section 4.7.2 as higher-order functions. Finally, we discuss the usefulness of anonymous functions, so-called lambda expressions in Section 4.7.3.

4.7.1 Recursion versus tail recursion

Recursion is a mighty and elegant concept that is based on the idea of functions calling themselves. A function is typically used to solve some kind of algorithmic problem, a simple or complex one. In some scenarios the situation is that simple that we just create a 'traditional' function and provide the result in one or a few well-defined steps. An example would be a function for computing the maximum of two given natural numbers, for which we do not need recursion. In cases in which the problem is quite hard but can be solved by reducing the hard problem to a little bit weaker one we are in a situation in which recursion might make sense. The idea behind this concept is that the problem can be made weaker and weaker (like using loops) until a basic case is reached for which we know the answer. Typically, this process generates a chain or tree of executions that have to be handled either during the recursion or after the recursion has terminated. In this section we look into both perspectives, the first one sometimes bringing problems with memory consumption since all of the executions might cause values that have to be stored somewhere until we reach the stage of putting everything together to obtain the result. Listing 4.43 illustrates an example of a traditional recursive function for computing the factorial of a natural number n. Be careful with the valid numbers that can be used as the input values for this function. If a negative number is given as input the result will always be 1 which is mathematically not correct, that is, undefined. A similar aspect holds for floating point numbers. Another big issue with recursion, apart from memory consumption, can be the fact that the termination condition is never reached, ending in a never-ending recursive call.

```
def nfactorial(n):
    if (n > 0):
        return n*nfactorial(n-1)
    else:
        return 1
```
Listing 4.43   A recursive function for computing the factorial of a natural number n

The recursive function for the factorial of n generates a chained expression since $n! := n \cdot (n-1) \cdot (n-2) \cdot \ldots \cdot 3 \cdot 2 \cdot 1$. For longer recursive calls this could lead to a high memory consumption. However, apart from a chain shape the recursive call could create some kind of tree-like shape, in the example in Listing 4.44 a so-called binary tree since there are always two branches in the recursive call. This means the recursion tree for this function has some kind of exponential growing. The function we are talking about here is the so-called Fibonacci function [112] that is mathematically given in Equation 4.1.

$$f_{fib}(n) := \begin{cases} f_{fib}(n-1) + f_{fib}(n-2) & \text{if } n \geq 2 \\ 1 & \text{if } n = 1 \\ 0 & \text{if } n = 0 \end{cases} \qquad (4.1)$$

```
1 def fib(n):
2     if n == 0:
3         return 0
4     elif n == 1:
5         return 1
6     else
7         return fib(n-1) + fib(n-2)
```
Listing 4.44   The Fibonacci numbers can be computed in a recursive way generating some kind of tree structure for the recursive calls

An even more fascinating example (Equation 4.2) for a recursive function is the so-called Ackermann function [175]. This function is mathematically defined as

$$Ack(m,n) := \begin{cases} n+1 & \text{if } m = 0 \\ Ack(m-1,1) & \text{if } m > 0, n = 0 \\ Ack(m-1, Ack(m, n-1)) & \text{if } m > 0, n > 0 \end{cases} \quad (4.2)$$

The Ackermann function which got its name after Wilhelm Ackermann is said to be one of its simplest examples of a function that is total computable and not primitive recursive as well [188]. From a programming perspective we can implement the function as in Listing 4.45.

```
1 def acker(m,n):
2     if m == 0:
3         return n+1
4     elif m > 0 and n == 0:
5         return acker(m-1, 1)
6     else:
7         return acker(m-1, acker(m, n-1))
```
Listing 4.45   A recursive implementation in Python for the Ackermann function

Not only the memory consumption but also the runtime of such recursive functions can be terribly high which makes them unusable in its 'traditional' implementation. This can be seen in the example of the Fibonacci numbers, but it is even more visible if we run the Ackermann function example. One problem with the recursion can be that the execution chain or tree gets really large, another problem can be that many calls get repeatedly computed again and again although the result is already known. These two problems can be solved in some cases if we use an iterative version of the recursion, sometimes also called tail recursion (or iterative recursion, repetitive recursion). The idea behind tail recursion is that the result of intermediate subexpressions is already computed before the next recursion step is done. This reduces the required memory a lot and as well the chance to recompute the same expressions all the time, that is, memory and time can be saved at the same time with this simple idea. Listing 4.46 gives an example of a tail recursive function for the Fibonacci numbers.

```
1  def fib(n, a, b):
2      if n <= 1:
3          return a + b
4      else:
5          return fib(n-1, b+a, a)
6
7  def tailrecursivefib(n):
8      return fib(n-1,1,0)
9
10 print(tailrecursivefib(10))
```

Listing 4.46   A tail recursive function for the Fibonacci numbers

The variables a and b in the listing are responsible for the intermediate computations, hence the next recursion step always needs these intermediate results to proceed. This reduces the memory consumption.

Exercises

- Exercise 4.7.1.1: Evaluate the Ackermann function for (1,1), (2,2), and (3,3). What are the results? Do you run into challenges when getting those results?
- Exercise 4.7.1.2: Define a tail recursive function for reversing a list of natural numbers.

4.7.2 Higher-order functions

A function is called a higher-order function if its input or output parameters are functions as well. Actually, such higher-order functions are treated very similarly to the standard functions apart from the fact that they can operate on other functions as well. Listing 4.47 gives an example of such a function creating another function inside its function body and returning this newly created function. Here the idea is to create a function that allows to multiply two numbers while one of the numbers is given by the function itself and the other one can be given as an argument in the newly created function.

```
1 def makeMultiplier(x):
2     def multiplier(y):
3         return x*y
4     return multiplier
5
6 multiplyBy50 = makeMultiplier(50)
7
8 print(multiplyBy50(20))  # result = 1000
```
Listing 4.47   An example of a simple higher-order function returning a function

Exercises

- Exercise 4.7.2.1: Define a higher-order function that creates a function for adding 3 floating point numbers while one of the numbers is fixed in the created function that is returned.
- Exercise 4.7.2.2: Define a higher-order function that returns two functions, one for adding and one for multiplying the two given numbers similar to the example in Listing 4.47.

4.7.3 Lambda expressions

In some situations, it is a good idea to use so-called anonymous functions. Those can be implemented in some kind of on-the-fly style due to their typical short nameless statements. They can be regarded as a programming style coming quickly to the point without first thinking about a name and a return statement, hence being a quicker way to create functions. To do this, so-called lambda expressions are used that can be added inside other expressions. Listing 4.48 illustrates some examples for using lambda expressions. Such lambda expressions or lambda functions can have any number of parameters. However, they are just small code pieces allowing one expression.

```
1 y = lambda x : x * 4
2 print(y(3))
3
4 z = lambda x, y : x**2 + 2*x*y - 4*x + 3
5 print(z(3.4, 5.1))
```
Listing 4.48   Lambda expressions can be used as some kind of anonymous functions

The good thing with lambda expressions comes from the fact that they can even be included in other functions, like the example we have shown in Section 4.7.2 on higher-order functions. Here we could modify the example in Listing 4.47 to integrate an anonymous lambda function instead of a named function with a return value (see Listing 4.49).

```
def makeMultiplier(x):
    return lambda y : y * x

multiplyBy50 = makeMultiplier(50)

print(multiplyBy50(20)) # result = 1000
```
Listing 4.49   A lambda expression inside another higher-order function

Exercises

- Exercise 4.7.3.1: Define an anonymous function for multiplying 3 numbers by using a lambda expression.
- Exercise 4.7.3.2: Define an anonymous function for checking a given input string on containing exactly 3 digits and 2 uppercase letters.

4.8 Reading and Writing Data

Not only for visualization tools [1, 49, 65, 154], it is also important to be able to read and write data. Also, for general applications in data science [235], the data itself is the major ingredient. It can come in a multitude of formats like comma-separated values for tabular/multivariate data, a Newick format for hierarchical data, or a matrix-like format for graph and network data, just to mention a few. Reading and parsing the data typically depends on the given data format, being even more complex if the data is spread over several data files. Moreover, the place from which we have to read the data makes a difference for a visualization tool's data reading strategies, for example the data could be accessible on a local machine or it might be located on a server accessible via a URL. Even more, the data could be given as text or image files or it could be stored in a database. Also, the data could be static or dynamically changing, and again the dynamics of the data could be given as a static data source but in the most challenging form it could be given as a real-time dataset that is updated from time to time, in different granularity levels ranging from seconds, to minutes, to hours, to days, or even years and decades. If an analysis and visualization is required on the finest granularity it can be quite hard to keep up with the incoming data, hence apart from loading and reading the whole dataset, in such a scenario only some kind of data sampling is done, reading and processing the data only if this is necessary, but this again brings into play other challenges.

In this section, we are going to first describe user input as a way to communicate textual information to a system. This 'user data' can then be used as a dialogue between the users and the system or it might be used to analyze user feedback about a system (Section 4.8.1). Directly reading from a file, either textual or binary data is important to get real data into a visualization tool, however, the data can come in a multitude of types and formats that have to be taken into account during reading and parsing it (Section 4.8.2). In some scenarios we might wish to write data to a data file, for example after a data exploration process when storing the relevant information (Section 4.8.3). Sometimes the data to be explored is stored on a local data source but in many more situations we can access the data from a server, online, that is, as a web-based data reading approach, also beneficial for real-time data that is regularly updated on a server and allows an up-to-date state of the visualization tool (Section 4.8.4).

4.8.1 User input

Allowing users to input information can be important, for example to ask for login or personal details as well as a password. This simple string-based data is handled by an in-built function given as input(). This function takes as argument a string and waits until a user has typed in a text and has pressed the enter key. Listing 4.50 gives an example for code asking someone for filling in his or her name and then assigning this name to a variable.

```
name = input("Please input your name: ")
```

Listing 4.50   Asking users to input a name that is assigned to a variable

One issue with the input function is the fact that Python always expects the data type String from the input. If we were asking for numeric inputs like integers or floating point numbers we are not completely lost, but we have to convert the string into the corresponding number first (see Listing 4.51).

```
text = input("Please input the exact temperature: ")
temperature = float(text)
```

Listing 4.51   Converting an input string into a numeric value

Exercises

- Exercise 4.8.1.1: Write Python code to ask users about their hobbies and store those hobbies in a list of strings.
- Exercise 4.8.1.2: Write a function that asks a user about an integer number n and then computes the factorial of n. Can you also write this function as an anonymous lambda expression?

4.8.2 Reading from a file

Reading data from a file is quite easy, however in cases we already know the data format we might have different options to get the data in an internal format to further process it algorithmically or show it visually. There is also a difference if the data has a pure textual nature or if it contains images that cannot be interpreted as pure text. Image data has a different semantic understanding than textual data has, hence it is important to read in the data depending on this aspect. Another problem to be solved is the fact where the file is located, that is, in which folder which can be given as a file path as an argument in the reading function. Moreover, the file might be stored on a server accessible via a URL or on a web page (see Section 4.8.4). Reading and parsing the data is one thing, processing it correctly another one. Listing 4.52 shows an example for reading data from a local file by using the built-in functions open() and read(). With open() we obtain a file object (see Section 4.9 for more information on object-oriented programming) while the "r" option specifies that the file is prepared for reading. With the encoding we can specify the symbol set on which the text is based, here UTF8 but we already know ASCII (Section 4.3.2). This object contains methods, one of them is the read() method with which we can read the content from the file.

```
1  file = open("C:\\Users\\Michael\\datafile.txt", encoding = "
       utf8", "r")
2  text = file.read()
```
Listing 4.52 Reading data from a local file

With read(), we always read the whole content of the file but in most of the situations we only want to read a small piece of the file, maybe line by line or even character by character. Listing 4.53 shows an example for this. Reading line by line works by using some kind of line iterator that moves one line further after each call of the function.

```
1  file = open("C:\\Users\\Michael\\datafile.txt", "r")
2  text = file.read(20)  # only reading 20 characters
3  text1 = file.readline()  # reading the "next" line (1st line)
4  text2 = file.readline()  # reading the "next" line (2nd line)
5
6  for line in file:  # reading line by line with a loop
7      textline = line
8      print(len(textline))
9
10 file.close()
```

Listing 4.53 Reading smaller pieces of a text file

If we have finished the task of reading content from a file we have to close it to avoid ugly side effects like content that is still not read due to internal issues that we cannot easily understand from a programming perspective. Such negative issues are typically caused by buffering problems or those caused by several processes reading the same file or writing on it. This cannot only happen after reading, but also after writing content to files (see Section 4.8.3).

If the data format is based on comma-separated values (csv) we can also use a so-called Pandas dataframe to read the content directly into an internal data structure. This frees us from reading the text file line by line and from carefully parsing it into corresponding data structure elements like rows and columns. The csv format reflects tabular data, typically shown to a user by using some kind of Excel table. Listing 4.54 illustrates how to read tabular data from a file by making use of a Pandas dataframe.

```
1  import pandas as pd
2
3  df = pd.read_csv("C:\\Users\\Michael\\csvfile.csv")
```

Listing 4.54 Reading tabular data by using a Pandas dataframe

There is even a difference for file reading depending on the fact if we have to read text or images. Listing 4.55 shows an example for such binary or image data. Reading regular binary data demands for adding the option letter "b" for binary to the reading option letter "r."

```
1  import imageio as imio
2
3  # Reading the image
4  image = imio.imread("C:\\Users\\Michael\\logo.png")
5
6  binfile = open("C:\\Users\\Michael\\logo.png","rb")
7  test = binfile.read(10)
8  binfile.close()
```

Listing 4.55 Reading images or binary data cannot be done by the same procedure as for reading texts

Exercises

- Exercise 4.8.2.1: Write Python code to read a given text file line by line. Then count the characters by using the len() function for each string and sum up all numbers to get the size of the file.
- Exercise 4.8.2.2: Read a given text file character by character and reverse each word in the text file.

4.8.3 Writing on a file

In some situations it can be useful to know how to write content on a file, for example in cases in which we used our data visualization tool to explore data to find patterns or anomalies which typically lets the users filter and aggregate the data. If we closed now the visualization tool and started it again in a few days, weeks, or months, our old explorations and insights are lost. This is the point in which it might be a powerful idea to let users store portions of the data, typically those that contain the found insights. Apart from the data itself also parameters might be stored to start the tool at a later point in time in exactly the configuration we stopped the exploration process. Whatever kind of storing we do we need to know how to create files and put some kind of data in a structured way to these files, with the goal to reload them later on again. Listing 4.56 gives an example about how to write data to a file, a new one or an existing one, while we can also append data to an existing file, we do not have to overwrite the content. Writing on a file is initiated by the letter "w" while appending by the letter "a." Also here we should close the file again after we have completed all file operations.

```
1 newFile = open("C:\\Users\\Michael\\test.txt", "a")
2 newFile.write("Add one more line to the existing file.")
3 newFile.close()
4
5 newFile2 = open("C:\\Users\\Michael\\test.txt", "w")
6 newFile2.write("Old content gone, replaced by this line.")
7 newFile2.close()
```

Listing 4.56   Appending and writing data to a file

When a file does not exist it will be created. In the other case the file might be overwritten accidentally. The best option is to use the "x" letter since then an error message will be given if the file already exists to avoid losing content. After the "x" option has been used the content of the file can be safely modified.

Exercises

- Exercise 4.8.3.1: Create a new file called myNewFile.txt and put the numbers from 1 to 1000 on the file.
- Exercise 4.8.3.2: Append the numbers from 2000 to 3000 to the file myNewFile.txt and output the content by directly reading from the file.

4.8.4 Reading web content

Reading data from a text file or database is important but in some situations it is good to directly access the data from a web page, for example if the web page is regularly updating its content. What we need is a mechanism that more or less automatically connects to the web page by using a URL and gets the current HTML text. This text can then be further processed, that is, parsed into a certain data format with which we can create our own real-time dataset. Listing 4.57 gives an example for this kind of data reading process.

```
1 from urllib.request import urlopen
2
3 page = urlopen("http://www.futbol24.com")
4
5 content = page.read()
6 htmltext = content.decode("utf-8")
7
8 print(htmltext)
```

Listing 4.57   Reading data from a web page

Exercises

- Exercise 4.8.4.1: Write code to read the HTML content from the online version of your favorite newspaper.
- Exercise 4.8.4.2: Write code to fill a list with numeric values by reading the scores from a web page that provides football tables.

4.9 Object-Oriented Programming

Also in Python we can find the object-oriented programming paradigm. This means we can model a program with classes that serve as some kind of template or blueprint from which we can derive objects and instances. Those objects have a state and a multitude of methods that can modify the state, that is, the values of corresponding variables or attributes. The objects follow the principle of encapsulation meaning everything is happening inside an object created by a class, that is, an object's state should only be modified by calling the corresponding methods and not just changing the values immediately. We can even let the classes inherit from each other, on several inheritance hierarchy levels and even merge them together which actually destroys the idea of a hierarchy [212], making it to a general graph structure [18]. Actually, the inheritance principle brings us to the idea of having parent and child classes, just like in real life in pedigree trees known from the field of genealogy [63]. Creating classes in object-oriented programming is a mighty principle but in some situations, it might not be the best one to find a solution to a problem by implementing a program. In some situations, it is still good to use functions and avoid the somewhat more blown-up code in object-oriented programming.

In this section, we first describe the idea of creating classes, that is, templates that model which general rules the instances of that class should follow (Section 4.9.1). The instances of a class must be built in some well-defined way to allow working with them later on (Section 4.9.2). Methods are the ways to modify the state of the objects created from classes, that is, we show how to define such methods and how they can be called (Section 4.9.3). The division into parent and child classes and the mighty concept of inheritance is illustrated in Section 4.9.4.

4.9.1 Classes

A class can be regarded as some kind of blueprint that gives us an internal structure on which each object is based that is created later by using this specific class. Classes can even be used inside other classes just like a nested structure. Each class follows some well-defined rules (see Listing 4.58). A house could be modeled as a class with properties like the number of rooms, the square meters, the floors, the address, and the like. Moreover, a house could even have some behavior like being dirty, being empty, getting built, and the like. A house could also have people living in it, that is, the people themselves can be a property of the house but the people have properties as well which can be modeled by another class as well, hence the house class could include the people class for example. A class does not contain data or values, it is just a specification which data should be integrated in the corresponding object later on. With each class we can create as many instances/objects we need in our program. As a coding convention, class names are written with an uppercase letter at the beginning to make the instantiated objects distinguishable later on from standard variables that use lowercase letters.

```
1  class House:
2      toRent = False      # class attribute
3
4      def __init__(self, rooms, smeters):
5          self.rooms = rooms       # instance attribute
6          self.smeters = smeters   # instance attribute
```

Listing 4.58 Creating a class

In Listing 4.58, we see the definition of a House class with a so-called init function that is used to initialize the later created objects with initial values for the given parameters, that is, the state of the corresponding object is set. It may be noted that init can have any number of parameters, however, the first one is always self which stands for the option to allow new attributes to be defined for this object. This can be seen in the two code lines right after the init method, actually setting or assigning the values of the attributes coming during the creation of the object. They are called instance attributes. In contrast to instance attributes we can find class attributes that carry the same value for all instances while the instance attributes are individual values for each instance of a class.

Exercises

- Exercise 4.9.1.1: Create a class Student that includes typical properties and behaviors of students.

- Exercise 4.9.1.2: Create a class University that includes typical properties of universities.

4.9.2 Objects and instances

Taking a class as a blueprint and instantiating it to create objects is a powerful idea since then the static class without included data and values gets to a dynamic object with data and modifiable values. Each object can have its own individual values describing its state by the instance attributes. The class attribute, on the other hand, can be used to describe a fact about each object, hence it is given by a class attribute. However, also the class variable value might be changed, it just serves as an initial value when the object is created to let each object start with the same value for a class attribute. Listing 4.59 shows how an object can be instantiated by just using the previously defined name of the class (e.g., the one from Listing 4.58) from which we create an instance. The simplest way to instantiate is by calling the class name with opening and closing parentheses. The parameters inside the parentheses must match those ones given in the init method that is used to initialize the values of the instance attributes, otherwise we will get an error message.

```
1  House(15,337)  # stored at a memory address
2
3  myHouse = House(11,240)  # assigned to a variable
4  myHouse2 = House(9,189)  # assigned to another variable
5
6  myHouse == myHouse2  # results in False
```
Listing 4.59 Instantiating from a class to get an object

If we create an object as shown in Listing 4.59, we will obtain this object at a memory address inside the computer which we cannot see. Creating two or more objects means that they are stored at different memory addresses which is also the reason why they are not equal although they model exactly the same objects. If we want to further process the created objects we should assign them to variables. We can do that since variables (or even constants) can carry values which are objects as well. The objects assigned to the variables myHouse and myHouse2 are now real instances from the House class, each one carrying its own values which come from the initial creation of each object in which we provided those values inside the parentheses. The self parameter is not relevant anymore in this construct, it is just used to pass the values to the instance attributes.

Exercises

- Exercise 4.9.2.1: Write a class Student and create some Student objects. They should have a name, an age, a list of grades, and a gender.
- Exercise 4.9.2.2: Write a class Car and create some Car objects. Those objects should be stored in a list.

4.9.3 Methods

Methods are a way to modify the instance attribute values from outside, that is, after an object has been created we should not modify its state by directly accessing and changing the values, but instead everything should happen via methods, a special type of functions that actually belong to instances of a class. For example, we could directly access the values of the rooms and smeters instance attribute from the House object myHouse as shown in Listing 4.60. For class attributes this works in the same style.

```
1  rooms = myHouse.rooms
2  squareMeters = myHouse.smeters
3
4  isRentable = myHouse.toRent
```

Listing 4.60   Accessing the values of some instance attributes without using methods

Apart from accessing those values they can even be changed in a similar way just like assigning values to variables. However, this strategy does not follow the encapsulation principle, the values should only be accessed and modified by so-called instance methods. Those methods are also defined and coded in the body of a class and can be used for each instance of that class in the same way, just like the instance variables. They also start with the self parameter as a first one in the parameter list which works in the same way as for the instance variables (see Listing 4.61). The calling syntax, however, is a bit different than those from standard Python functions. Methods are always bound to an object, hence they are called by stating the name of the object first, followed by a dot, followed by the corresponding method name (see Listing 4.62).

```
1  class House:
2      toRent = False    # class attribute
3
4      def __init__(self, rooms, smeters):
5          self.rooms = rooms      # instance attribute
6          self.smeters = smeters  # instance attribute
7
```

```
 8      def getRoomNumber ( self ) :
 9          return self.rooms
10
11      def getSquarePerRoom ( self ) :
12          return self.smeters/self.rooms
```
Listing 4.61 Adding methods to a class

```
1  myHouse = House (8 ,209)
2
3  rooms = myHouse.getRoomNumber ()
4  roomAverage = myHouse. getSquarePerRoom ()
```
Listing 4.62 Creating an object from a class and calling methods

Exercises

- Exercise 4.9.3.1: Create a class Student, add class and instance attributes, and complete the class with several methods allowing to get and set the values of the instance attributes.
- Exercise 4.9.3.2: Add another method to the class that returns the name of the student in capital letters.

4.9.4 Inheritance

In some real-world scenarios we find objects or persons with similar properties but they still differ by some other properties. But somehow the core of each object or person is the same. In such a scenario we wish to have a strategy that avoids reimplementing the core properties as well as the functionality all the time. It seems as if the additional properties must be some kind of new implemented code while the core, that is, the same properties might be somehow reused from existing code. The principle behind this idea is called inheritance since it can categorize classes into parent classes and child classes that get all of the properties and functionality from the parent classes but they can have more properties and functionality than the parent classes. This concept forms some kind of hierarchy, however in Python we can also merge classes, similar to the real-world situation between humans, but in programming this inheritance concept is even more flexible. Although the child classes inherit the attributes (properties) and methods (functionality) from the parent classes they can even use the inherited aspects in a more specific form while they can also extend their functionality. Listing 4.63 shows examples to create child classes from the parent class House from before. Those children could be TinyHouse, Hotel, TreeHouse, and so on. All of them have rooms and a total number of square meters. However, each of them could have additional properties and functionality, a hotel might have guests and room prices.

```python
class TinyHouse(House):
    pass

class Hotel(House):
    pass

class TreeHouse(House):
    pass

hotelCalifornia = Hotel(250,8346)
smallHouse = TinyHouse(1,5)
natureHouse = TreeHouse(2,8)
```

Listing 4.63 Parent and child classes for using the principle of inheritance

Exercises

- Exercise 4.9.4.1: Define another kind of house that inherits from the House class.
- Exercise 4.9.4.2: Define another kind of hotel that inherits from the Hotel class.

5

Dashboard Examples

We can compose a dashboard in various ways, based on one specific dataset or even more of them in a linked manner focusing on the specific interests of the data analysts and users and on the tasks they are planning to solve by means of interactive visualizations. The design of the graphical user interface and the design of the visualizations equipped with various interaction techniques [258] play major roles to finally obtain a runnable and user-friendly tool [127] with which we can explore and analyze our data-at-hand. In the previous chapters, we described the ingredients from several perspectives like data (Section 2.1), algorithms (Section 2.2), visualizations (Section 2.4.1), user interfaces (Section 2.4.3), interactions (Section 2.5), and the coding ingredients based on the Python programming language (Section 4). In this chapter, we try to combine all of the previously learned concepts to create a dashboard for interactive visualizations, allowing user interventions as some kind of dialogue between users and the provided user interface as well as the individual visual components in form of interactive diagrams. The chapter can be studied as a stand-alone chapter but we also provide references to previously explained concepts to let the reader step back to unknown concepts and components, however we try to describe each individual stage in the code for creating one's own dashboards. We look at such dashboards from two perspectives, the design as well as the implementation, that is, if a dashboard is designed as some kind of mockup, we need to implement the functionality and the visual components and let them play together which requires some knowledge in Python, Dash, and a graphics library like Plotly Express or even go for creating graphics objects in Plotly.

The chapter is structured as follows. In Section 5.1, we introduce a simple first example of a dashboard for showing a histogram in which a color parameter can be modified. We extend this dashboard to one that can show two diagrams, a histogram and a scatter plot while allowing to filter values with a slider (Section 5.2). Moreover, the concept of bootstrap is used to define a good layout. Section 5.3 describes a dashboard in which two plots can be controlled while also separate tabs are supported. Moreover, we introduce a simple external CSS file to show how the interface parameters can be controlled globally to have an additional mechanism apart from the inline CSS that can become a tedious task when the user interface components appear in numerous ways and have to be visually enhanced one-by-one. Also Plotly templates are introduced in this example. In Section 5.4, we show how to let an interactive diagram be an input option for another plot. This concept allows to react on user interactions in the visualizations by interactively modifying other visualizations which shows a first step of the popular brushing and linking [243] feature in the research field of information visualization [245]. The callback mechanism can be based on an arbitrary number of input and output parameters which is also shown in this dashboard example. As an add-on to the Plotly diagrams we will use go objects as an alternative to pure Plotly diagrams. An even more complex dashboard example is explained in Section 5.5 integrating several plots in the user interface while also supporting tabs to switch between two visual alternatives. For example, in a scatter plot we can select point clouds that are then shown in a density heatmap and the categories of the point distribution is also shown in a color coded bar chart. Even some more input features are implemented as dash core components.

To run the dashboard codes successfully we recommend to use the package versions python 3.9, dash 2.11.1, numpy 1.25, pandas 2.0.3, dash-bootstrap-components 1.4.1, and scikit-learn 1.3.0. The Python codes can also be found in a GitHub repository https://github.com/BookDas hboardDesign. In case the readers have questions they can send them to BookDashboardDesign@gmail.com to get answers or useful hints.

5.1 Modifying the Color in a Diagram

We are starting this section with a very simple example of a dashboard that is based on randomly generated data. This data is visually explored for its distribution [213], that is, we are interested in a visualization that shows this distribution, that allows some basic interactions [222, 258], and as a user input, the color of the diagram should be modifiable between a few standard colors [29, 199]. The diagram type that is best suited for such a scenario showing distributions of a univariate dataset is the so-called histogram. With that we can put a numeric scale on the x-axis and the number of data elements falling in each pre-defined interval on the y-axis. Looking at the distributions can provide insights into the data, not only from a perspective of a statistician who is familiar with these kinds of diagrams. We first start with some kind of hand-drawn mockup to get a better visual idea of what is expected from such a dashboard (Section 5.1.1). As a next step we illustrate the Python code for getting this dashboard running (Section 5.1.2). As a last step, we describe what we will see and which interactions are possible when letting the code run, that is, we see our designed and implemented dashboard in action (Section 5.1.3).

5.1.1 A simple dashboard with a histogram

Before implementing a dashboard, it is a good idea to think about its design, that is, the design [13] of the user interface with all of its components but also the design of the incorporated visualization techniques. Moreover, the layout and the aesthetics [38], that is, visual decoration of all of the components is of importance. To get an impression about all the components and their locations in the display as well as possible interaction techniques and how the components are linked to each other it might be good to draw the dashboard, in the best case by hand since that allows the highest degree of flexibility [250] (see Section 2.4). Figure 5.1 gives a visual impression about the ingredients in the dashboard, however, the interaction techniques must be described in textual form since it is difficult to illustrate them visually due to the lack of animation in a book.

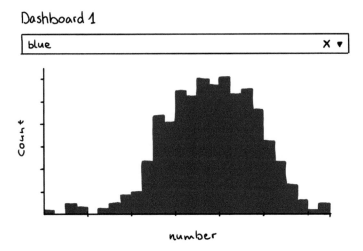

Figure 5.1   A hand-drawn mockup of a dashboard for interactively modifying the color of a histogram (drawn by Sarah Clavadetscher).

There should already be some basic interactions [258] in the dashboard which can be listed as follows:

- Select: A drop-down menu can be used to select a color for the histogram from a pre-defined list of colors.
- Encode: The modification of the color itself can be regarded as some kind of visual encoding.
- Zoom: Since we use interactive Plotly diagrams we have a zooming function already included in the histogram.
- Reconfigure: Even an aggregation of the histogram might be possible in a Plotly diagram which is also some kind of rearrangement feature.

For creating such a basic dashboard example we just need a few ingredients like Python (Section 3.1.1 and Chapter 4), Dash (Section 3.1.2), and Plotly (Section 3.1.3) while we must have our design concept in mind which we have made visible as a hand-drawn mockup (Figure 5.1).

Exercises

- Exercise 5.1.1.1: Design a dashboard that uses a box plot instead of a histogram to show the data distribution.
- Exercise 5.1.1.2: Design a dashboard that integrates a value slider to select options for colors like 0 for red, 1 for green, and 2 for blue.

5.1.2 Coding details

Listing 5.1 shows the coding details to implement the dashboard shown in Figure 5.1 with the integrated interaction techniques described above. Lines 1 to 4 show the modules that need to be imported, with Dash, the Dash core and HTML components, Input, Output, and the callback mechanism (Line 1), followed by Plotly Express (Line 2), numpy (Line 3), and pandas (Line 4).

The modules and their functionality in this dashboard implementation can be briefly described as follows:

- Dash: This module is required for the web development, that is, making the dashboard publicly available in a web browser.
- dcc: The dash core components module contains various interactive elements for integrating in a user interface like drop-down menus, sliders, date pickers, and many more.

- html: The dash HTML components module is useful for HTML commands to, for example, layout and decorate the dashboard, for example, by adjusting sizes, colors, and distances.
- Input: The input is needed to handle the elements that go into a callback.
- Output: The output is needed to handle the elements that are returned from a callback.
- callback: This module is responsible for the communication between the inputs and outputs.
- plotly.express: The visualizations in form of interactive diagrams are provided by this graphics module.
- numpy: This library allows to work with complex mathematical functions to artificially create, transform, or manipulate data. It focuses on efficient computations.
- pandas as pd: This package is typically used for data reading and parsing tasks, useful in the data science and machine learning domain.

```
1  from dash import Dash, dcc, html, Input, Output, callback
2  import plotly.express as px
3  import numpy as np
4  import pandas as pd
5
6
7  app = Dash(__name__)
8
9  # generate random normal distributed data
10 # and store it in a Pandas DataFrame
11
12 df = pd.DataFrame({'number':
13                     np.random.normal(loc=0,
14                                       scale=10,
15                                       size=1000)})
16
17 app.layout = html.Div([
18     html.H1("Dashboard 1"),
19     dcc.Dropdown(options=['red', 'green', 'blue'],
20                  value='red',
21                  id='color',
22                  multi=False),
23     dcc.Graph(id="graph")
24 ])
25
26 @callback(
27     Output("graph", "figure"),
```

```
28        Input("color", "value")
29  )
30
31  def update_graph(dropdown_value_color):
32
33        fig = px.histogram(df,
34                           x="number",
35                           color_discrete_sequence=
36                                   [dropdown_value_color])
37        fig.update_layout()
38        return fig
39
40  if __name__ == '__main__':
41        app.run_server(debug=True)
```

Listing 5.1   A dashboard example with a histogram and a modifiable color parameter

The dashboard or app gets actually started in Line 7 with the creation of a Dash object. Since each visualization needs some kind of data we generate our own artificial dataset [134] which allows us some flexibility in the dataset size, structure, and complexity and we are not restricted to a specific dataset case. In Line 12, the data generation process is illustrated by using a Pandas DataFrame that consists of random normal distributed data, that is, it is actually univariate data just mapping a number to each data object while each object can be represented on a numerical scale. As we already know, one traditional and prominent diagram for this type of data is the so-called histogram which we will also use in the dashboard. Lines 17 to 24 illustrate how the dashboard's layout can be built. Since our dashboard is similar to a web page, we can make use of HTML and in particular, the division element (div) to hierarchically structure the web page. We can see some components, the first one given in Line 18 as a title of the dashboard in H1 font size. Lines 19 to 22 add a drop-down menu for the three color options as a dash core component with some additional properties. In Line 23 we also add a graph as a dash core component which can actually be any diagram but we already decided to integrate a histogram for the univariate data.

The callback mechanism is coded in Lines 26 to 29. We see that it is composed of inputs and outputs, in this simple dashboard we only allow one input (a drop-down menu) and one output (a diagram which is a histogram in this special case). The following function that is responsible for updating the dashboard and which corresponds to the callback mechanism is located right below the callback (Lines 31 to 38) and must have the same signature as the callback itself, otherwise it runs into compilation errors, or even semantic errors in case the input and output types are the same but the values are mixed in some way. The update function can be named as the developer likes but it may be noted that in case we have many callbacks and many such update functions they should have different, that is, unique names. In the update function in this example we see an input parameter which gives the color value that is modifiable in the drop-down menu (Line 31) as well as one return parameter which is the updated figure, in this case a histogram (Line 38). The histogram itself gets the artificial dataset as a dataframe (Line 33), an attribute named number (Line 34), and a color coding (Lines 35 and 36). In Lines 40 and 41 the dashboard is started on a server, which is in its current implementation the localhost.

Exercises

- Exercise 5.1.2.1: Implement a dashboard that shows a box plot for which we can interactively manipulate the color by using a drop-down menu.
- Exercise 5.1.2.2: Implement a dashboard that uses a slider instead of a drop-down menu to select the colors with options like 0 = red, 1 = green, and 2 = blue.

5.1.3 Dashboard in action

Executing the code from Listing 5.1 will return a URL that we can click on or copy into one of our available web browsers. Since a dashboard is some kind of web page we can work with it in any newer web browser. It may be noted that an implemented dashboard should be tested on several web browsers first before making it accessible to the public. This test avoids the effect that some people in the world might see a strange layout or a reduced functionality which is not caused by the code itself but just by the fact that the browser version or browser itself is not suitable. Hence, after such a test we should state which web browsers in which versions are supported. Anyhow, if we have a look at our first implemented dashboard in a suitable web browser we should get the visual result in Figure 5.2.

We see that there are just two components in the dashboard (as we desired), a drop-down menu and a histogram showing the distribution of a univariate randomly generated dataset. Admittedly, the dashboard is not very aesthetically appealing but it contains the desired functionality. We can find a drop-down menu for selecting a color, negatively the drop-down menu is horizontally stretched although the text entries for the color names are only

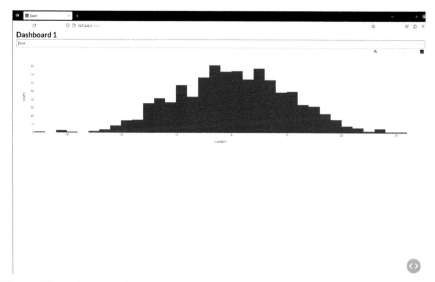

Figure 5.2   After executing the dashboard code we get this graphical user interface (dashboard) with a drop-down menu and a blue colored histogram.

spanning a few pixels in horizontal direction. This gives room for further layout improvements and adjustments later on. We can find the same negative issue in the histogram which is currently horizontally stretched. In the next implementation iterations, we will incorporate more and more functionality, but we also look into aesthetic improvements and visual decorations.

Exercises

- Exercise 5.1.3.1: Check the features provided in the dashboard given in Figure 5.2. How would you add more options for colors in the dashboard?
- Exercise 5.1.3.2: For the dashboard in Figure 5.2, we could also integrate other diagram types apart from a histogram. Which ones do you consider useful for the same dataset and how do you integrate them in the dashboard?

5.2 Two Diagrams, Bootstrap, and Value Filter

We extend the dashboard from Section 5.1 by adding one more input option as well as one more diagram. Moreover, we introduce bootstrap as a way to allow more flexibility for the layout of the dashboard. The input options are a drop-down menu and a slider with which a numeric value can be selected that has an impact on one or several diagrams showing data in a visual way. A histogram is useful for univariate data, that is, data which is just measured under one attribute. A scatter plot, on the other hand, can be used to show correlations between two chosen attributes, that is, bivariate data. Each data element is measured under two, typically numeric, attributes which allows some kind of spatial representations for each of the two-dimensional data points. The distribution of the points in the two-dimensional plane can be visually explored for patterns, for example positive or negative correlations. However, a static scatter plot will only tell us half of the truth, hence it is a good idea to allow interactions like filtering for a certain numeric value. The section is organized as follows: In Section 5.2.1, we introduce our design idea coming as a hand-drawn mockup with descriptions about the individual components and interaction techniques. Then in Section 5.2.2, we explain the code to implement such a dashboard while finally, we show the result of the running code as a screenshot (Section 5.2.3).

5.2.1 Extension with a scatter plot and slider

The next level of dashboard implementation can be reached by allowing more than one input and more than one output. In this example we are going to integrate a drop-down menu for selecting one category, that is, one color from a repertoire of given colors. Moreover, we would like to provide a slider with which we can select a value from a numeric value scale. The selected value in the drop-down menu should have an impact on the histogram while the selected numeric value in the slider should have an impact on the scatter plot. These two types of inputs should be applied independently by the users, hence we need to split the callback mechanism into two callbacks with two separate update functions. Since we have four components now, two inputs and two outputs, we can already get a more complex layout for our dashboard interface. We would like to have the inputs in the top row and the outputs in the form of diagrams in the bottom row, but each input–output horizontally aligned (see the mockup in Figure 5.3).

In addition to the previous dashboard, the users should also be able to interact with the user interface but also with the two diagrams as explained in the following:

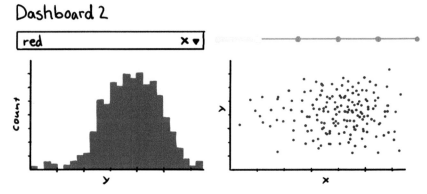

Figure 5.3　A mockup of a dashboard with a drop-down menu and a slider for manipulating the color of a histogram and for filtering a scatter plot (drawn by Sarah Clavadetscher).

- Numeric filter: A slider can be used to select a value in a given range. The selected value can be used as a filter to reduce the number of data elements in the scatter plot.
- Geometric zoom: Since we use Plotly diagrams a geometric zooming function is supported in the scatter plot as well.
- Undo: The zooming interaction can be made undone by double clicking in the plot.

We can implement this extended dashboard by using the dashboard example from before and by just adding the new functionality and features at the right place (see Section 5.2.2).

Exercises

- Exercise 5.2.1.1: Design a dashboard that integrates a range slider instead of a regular slider for the scatter plot.
- Exercise 5.2.1.2: Design a dashboard that shows the scatter plot on the left-hand side and the histogram on the right-hand side. Moreover the inputs in form of a drop-down menu and a slider should be placed below the diagrams and not above them.

5.2.2　Coding details

Listing 5.2 shows the code for the extended dashboard. The imports are quite similar to the previous dashboard but we have two more modules imported that can be listed as follows:

- math: This module is needed for mathematical functions like ceil, floor, factorial, comb, and many more.
- dash_bootstrap_components: This library consists of so-called bootstrap components with the purpose of styling dashboards and apps, that is, with a focus on user interface layouts for example.

```
1  import math
2  from dash import Dash, dcc, html, Input, Output
3  import plotly.express as px
4  import numpy as np
5  import pandas as pd
6  import dash_bootstrap_components as dbc
7
8  app = Dash(__name__,
9              external_stylesheets=[dbc.themes.BOOTSTRAP])
10
11 # generate random normal distributed data for x and y
12 # and store it in a pandas DataFrame
13
14 df = pd.DataFrame({'y': np.random.normal(loc=0,
15                                           scale=10,
16                                           size=1000),
17                    'x': np.random.normal(loc=10,
18                                           scale=2,
19                                           size=1000)})
20
21 app.layout = html.Div([
22     html.H1("Dashboard 2"),
23
24     dbc.Row([
25         dbc.Col([dcc.Dropdown(options=['red',
26                                        'green',
27                                        'blue'],
28                               value='red',
29                               id='color',
30                               multi=False)], width=6),
31         dbc.Col([dcc.Slider(min=math.floor(df['y'].min()),
32                             max=math.ceil(df['y'].max()),
33                             id="min_value")
34                 ], width=6)
35     ]),
36
37     dbc.Row([
38         dbc.Col([
39             dcc.Graph(id="graph_1")
```

```
40            ] ,  width=6) ,
41
42            dbc . Col ( [
43                 dcc . Graph ( id=" graph_2 " )
44            ] ,  width=6)
45        ])
46
47  ] ,  className="m-4 " )
48
49
50  @app . callback (
51      Output ( " graph_1 " ,  " figure " ) ,
52      Input ( " color " ,  " value " )
53  )
54  def  update_graph_1 ( dropdown_value_color ) :
55
56      fig  =  px . histogram ( df ,
57                           x=" y " ,
58                           color_discrete_sequence=
59                                   [ dropdown_value_color ] )
60      fig . update_layout ( )
61      return  fig
62
63
64  @app . callback (
65      Output ( " graph_2 " ,  " figure " ) ,
66      Input ( " min_value " ,  " value " )
67  )
68  def  update_graph_2 ( min_value ) :
69      dff  =  df [ df [ ' y ' ]>  min_value ]
70      fig  =  px . scatter ( dff ,  x=' x ' ,  y=' y ' )
71      fig . update_layout ( )
72      return  fig
73
74  if  __name__  ==  ' __main__ ' :
75      app . run_server ( debug=True ,  port=8000)
```

Listing 5.2   Including a histogram and a scatter plot in a dashboard with additional bootstrap for the layout

After all imports have been made the rest of the code describes the functionality and features of the dashboard. Lines 8 and 9 initialize the dashboard and include the bootstrap to improve the layout of the user interface. The data is artificially generated in Lines 14 to 19 as a Pandas DataFrame with 2 attributes called 'x' and 'y'. The data has the additional property that it is normally distributed in both data dimensions. The layout of the dashboard is created in Lines 21 to 47 making use of the bootstrap by allowing two rows, each having 2 columns, resulting in a 2 times 2 grid layout (see Figure 5.4). The first row includes the inputs in form of a drop-down menu and a slider while the second row includes the two Plotly diagrams in form of a histogram and a scatter plot which is actually not further specified here, just the type is given which is some kind of graph. The drop-down menu works similarly as in the previous dashboard example while the slider ranges between a minimum and a maximum value for which the math functions are needed for value rounding purposes. Both inputs get unique identifiers which are important for the callback mechanism at a later point in time. Those identifiers are 'color' and 'min_value' respectively. The graphs also get identifiers just called 'graph_1' and 'graph_2'. All components are set to a fixed width of 6.

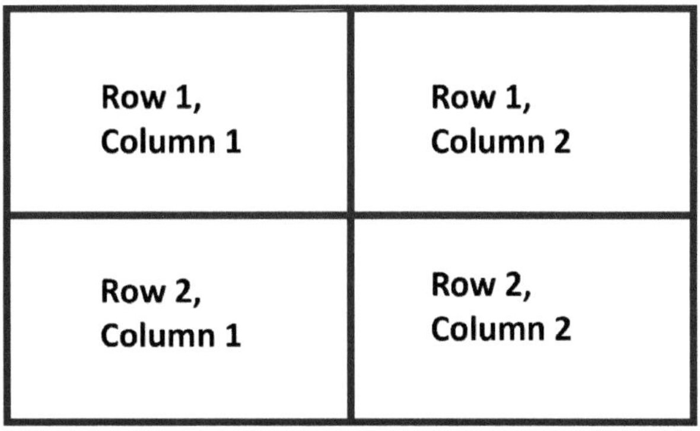

Row 1, Column 1	**Row 1, Column 2**
Row 2, Column 1	**Row 2, Column 2**

Figure 5.4   A grid layout may consist of a number of rows and columns, like 2 of them as in this case.

In this example we have two callback mechanisms which is a different strategy compared to the previous dashboard example with only one callback. The first callback can be found in Lines 50 to 53, followed by the corresponding update function in Lines 54 to 61. This first callback is responsible for updating the histogram, that is, it gets a color value from the drop-down menu as input and outputs the corresponding histogram. The detailed instructions for this update are shown in the function called 'update_graph_1' in Lines 54 to 61. The second callback can be found in Lines 64 to 67, followed by the corresponding update function in Lines 68 to 72. Here the callback gets a value from the slider and outputs a corresponding updated scatter plot with the filtered values. The details for this update function are given in Lines 68 to 72 in the 'update_graph_2' function. The value filter is also implemented in this update function given in Line 69. The rest of the program was already described in the previous dashboard example with the extension that the port 8000 is used.

Exercises

- Exercise 5.2.2.1: Modify the dashboard code in a way that the scatter plot can be filtered with a range slider allowing an interval of numeric values.
- Exercise 5.2.2.2: Change the input–output mechanism: The scatter plot should allow to modify its color by a drop-down menu and the histogram should be filtered for value intervals, on the x-axis but also on the y-axis.

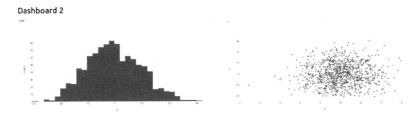

Figure 5.5   The extended dashboard will show a few more features than the one given in Section 5.1.1. Now, we can see a slider and a scatter plot as well. Moreover, we also have to care for a good layout of the components although we just have 4 of them at the moment.

5.2.3 Dashboard in action

Figure 5.5 shows the result when executing the dashboard code given in Listing 5.2. We see the title Dashboard 2 which was generated by an HTML H1 component. Then, the layout is split into 2 rows and 2 columns (see Figure 5.4), that is, some kind of grid layout with the inputs in the first row. On the left-hand side the drop-down menu is located for the color selection while on the right-hand side, we see the slider for the numeric filter. The bottom row consists of the histogram in a selected color on the left-hand side while the right-hand side is reserved for the scatter plot which is currently filtered for the selected numeric value in the slider input. Although the layout is already a bit more complex than in the previous dashboard example it is still not very flexible. There are various options to improve the layout, make it more dynamic and flexible, and even interactively modifiable.

Exercises

- Exercise 5.2.3.1: Modify the scatter plot in the dashboard to let it also visually encode data in the size and shape of the points.
- Exercise 5.2.3.2: Modify the scatter plot in the dashboard to let it use intervals for the numeric values instead of discrete numbers. Each interval should be visually encoded as a point size and/or a point shape.

5.3 Dashboard with Tabs, CSS, and Plotly Template

We further extend the previous dashboard by the concept of tabs, that is, allowing each diagram to be active and in focus separately, if the users selected/activated it. If a tab is activated, the corresponding diagram and functionality can be worked with. To achieve a better and more maintainable layout and even more aesthetic features for each dashboard component we include the concept of CSS, but this time not in the traditional inline variant, this time we use a global CSS file with which all components of a certain kind can be visually enhanced, decorated, and augmented globally. CSS provides some kind of linear hierarchy in external, internal, and inline CSS, hence the cascading concept that allows to override global features with more local ones, making the styling process easier and more flexible. Even more, we introduce the concept of Plotly templates supporting special Plotly themes to graphically style the diagrams based on a common visual appearance. The section is organized in the following way: In Section 5.3.1, we describe the design idea with a hand-drawn mockup again as well as explanations of the individual components and interaction techniques. This is followed by Section 5.3.2 explaining the individual code parts and lines to give the programmer a starting point for creating own dashboards in this style. Finally, we show a screenshot of the running dashboard in Section 5.3.3 and explain the visual features.

5.3.1 Histogram and scatter plot separately

Sometimes it is a good idea to keep the functionality, features, and diagrams in a separate tab, to create functionality groups that reduce the cognitive effort for the users when finding individual features to solve a certain task. The users can switch between those groups to allow a more structured exploration strategy. This means one region in a dashboard might be given a specific focus indicating that only the functions and visualizations in this region are active at the moment on users' demands, that is, users' current workspace is exactly there while the other features and functionalities are still reachable in a quick way, just by clicking on one of the other provided tabs. Such a concept will be illustrated in the dashboard in this section while from a visualization perspective we will focus again on simple visualization techniques like a histogram and a scatter plot. The readers can create now their own visual features and exchange the existing ones with their own ones. The histogram's color can still be modified by using a drop-down menu with colors while the scatter plot values can be filtered by a slider. The functionality is clearly separated, that is, the drop-down menu belongs to the histogram and the slider belongs to the scatter plot. Figure 5.6 illustrates how such a dashboard can be imagined before we can implement its functionality in form of user interface components, diagrams, and interactions. We also integrate CSS as a concept to globally guide the appearance and layout of the individual components. The Plotly diagrams can now be based on a certain template as well, for example to let all of them look consistently, this idea might be regarded as a similar idea to CSS while with CSS we actually guide and equip the user interface components with additional features, not primarily the visualizations and diagrams.

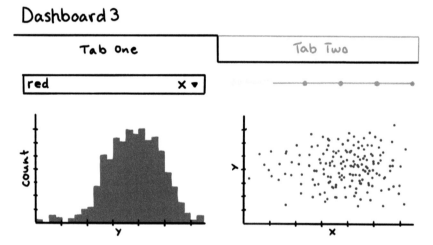

Figure 5.6   A hand-drawn mockup of a dashboard for displaying data in a histogram and a scatter plot while both diagrams and their inputs can be given a specific focus by a tab mechanism (drawn by Sarah Clavadetscher).

From the interaction perspective, we focus now on additional ways to create a dialog between our users and the dashboard's user interface and visualization components. Also, special features related to those interactions can be found:

- Separate interactivity: Instead of allowing all components to be interactive we can even specifically set a component or region in a dashboard to be active, that is, to be able to accept interactions from the user side. One idea is to use the concept of tabs.
- Setting Focus: When starting interacting with a component we can explicitly set the focus to this component by using tabs which lets organize the features and functionality into active and inactive components allowing some kind of structured exploration strategy.
- Highlighting: The component or even visualization in focus can be highlighted to show the users which component is actually active and which ones are not active at the moment.
- Graying out: The counterpart of highlighting might be the graying out of a component or several of them. Graying out means it is inactive at the moment but it is still partially visible for an overview or even for contextual information.

After the design phase we can start implementing this kind of dashboard with the given visualizations, user interface components, as well as interaction techniques and interaction-related aspects. The implementation details can be read in Section 5.3.2.

Exercises

- Exercise 5.3.1.1: Design a dashboard that contains four tabs with four diagrams and corresponding interaction options like a drop-down menu, a slider, a text field, and a date picker.
- Exercise 5.3.1.2: Which kinds of features might be important to dynamically adapt in a dashboard, that is, on users' demands? Discuss!

5.3.2 Coding details

Listing 5.3 shows the external CSS file for the dashboard. We can see that there are three subsections including the header, the content, and the tab_content. The first part sets the margins in the header, that is, in all four orientations top, bottom, right, and left. Top is set to 0 px while all others are set to 25 px. The margins are also set for the content (second part) in the same manner while the third part just sets the margin to the top to 60 px which is the tab content. Actually, in the CSS file, we can define nearly any kind of additional property a certain user interface component should have, not only the margins but also colors, font sizes, border sizes, backgrounds, and many more.

```css
.header {
  margin: 0px 25px 25px 25px;
  /* margin-top margin-right margin-bottom margin-left */
}

.content {
  margin: 0px 25px 25px 25px;
}

.tab_content {
  margin-top: 60px;
}
```

Listing 5.3   A CSS file for improving the layout and aesthetics of the user interface of the dashboard

Listing 5.4 illustrates the code for the dashboard shown in the hand-drawn mockup in Figure 5.6. The imported modules are already familiar from the previous dashboard examples, consequently we will directly jump into the Python code.

```python
import math

from dash import Dash, dcc, html, Input, Output
import plotly.express as px
import numpy as np
import pandas as pd
import dash_bootstrap_components as dbc

# new: Tabs for a better overview

# new: external CSS -> main.css
# (nothing must be changed in the code
# if css file in folder 'assets'

# new: plotly template="plotly_white"
# https://plotly.com/python/templates/
```

```
17
18 app = Dash(__name__,
19                external_stylesheets=[dbc.themes.BOOTSTRAP])
20
21 # generate random normal distributed data
22 # for x and y and store it in a pandas DataFrame
23
24 df = pd.DataFrame({'y': np.random.normal(loc=0,
25                                          scale=10,
26                                          size=1000),
27                    'x': np.random.normal(loc=10,
28                                          scale=2,
29                                          size=1000)})
30
31 app.layout = html.Div([
32     html.Div(
33         [html.H1("Dashboard 3")],
34         className="header"),
35     html.Div([
36         dcc.Tabs(id="tabs",
37                 children=[
38                     dcc.Tab(label='Tab One',
39                         id="tab_1_graphs",
40                         children=[
41                         html.Div([
42                             dbc.Row([
43                                 dbc.Col([dcc.Dropdown(
44                                     options=['red',
45                                              'green',
46                                              'blue'],
47                                     value='red',
48                                     id='color',
49                                     multi=False)],
50                                     width=6),
51                                 dbc.Col([dcc.Slider(
52                                     min=math.floor(
53                                         df['y'].min()),
54                                     max=math.ceil(
55                                         df['y'].max()),
56                                     id="min_value")],
57                                     width=6)
58                             ]),
59                             dbc.Row([
60                                 dbc.Col([
61                                     dcc.Graph(id="graph_1")],
62                                     width=6),
```

```
63                                        dbc.Col([
64                                            dcc.Graph(id="graph_2")],
65                                                    width=6)
66                                    ])
67                            ], className="tab_content"),
68                        ]),
69                        dcc.Tab(label='Tab Two',
70                                id="tab_2_graphs",children=[
71                                    html.Div([],
72                                    className="tab_content")
73                                ]),
74                    ])
75        ], className="content")
76  ])
77
78  @app.callback(
79      Output("graph_1", "figure"),
80      Input("color", "value")
81  )
82  def update_graph_1(dropdown_value_color):
83      fig = px.histogram(df,
84                         x="y",
85                         color_discrete_sequence=[
86      dropdown_value_color])
86      fig.update_layout(template="plotly_white")
87      return fig
88
89  @app.callback(
90      Output("graph_2", "figure"),
91      Input("min_value", "value")
92  )
93  def update_graph_2(min_value):
94      if min_value:
95          dff = df[df['y'] > min_value]
96      else:
97          dff = df
98      fig = px.scatter(dff, x='x', y='y')
99      fig.update_layout(template="plotly_white")
100     return fig
101
102 if __name__ == '__main__':
103     app.run_server(debug=True, port=8000)
```

Listing 5.4   A dashboard using tabs and CSS as well as a Plotly template

The code for this dashboard is a bit more complex than the codes for the two dashboards before. This is due to the fact that we included more features and concepts, with CSS, tabs, and Plotly templates among them. In Lines 18 and 19, we initialize the dashboard by including external stylesheets with the bootstrap mechanism. Lines 24 to 29 are responsible for generating artificial data based on a random normal distribution. In cases we need other artificial data or real-life data, this is the place in the code how to put any kind of data into a Pandas dataframe.

With Line 31, we begin setting the layout of the dashboard by using the HTML division element again. This div element is split into two subelements allowing to split the display area for our dashboard (typically the computer monitor) into two actually equally-sized subregions that we can fill with components separately. The first subregion in Lines 32 to 34 is just creating some kind of title for the dashboard followed by the CSS styles coming from the main.css file given in Listing 5.3 by using the className variable set to "header." The header information can be found in the CSS file in the corresponding section. The next subregion is introduced in Line 35 with the next div element. This time the subregion looks a bit more complex starting with the dash core component Tabs given the id "tabs." This component can have as many children as we like, in our case just two, representing the two tabs we are planning to integrate. Each tab itself can be added as a core component (dcc) starting with tab one in Line 38 giving it a label and an id again, to later reference and access it with our callback mechanism. Also the tab itself can be suborganized by again using the HTML div component. Now the bootstrap comes into play organizing the dashboard's user interface into rows and columns including the drop-down menu and the slider in the first row and the two diagrams in the second row (Lines 42 to 67). It may be noted that the drop-down (Lines 43 to 49) can be decorated on designers' demands as well as the slider (Lines 51 to 56). The CSS styles are based on the tab_content section from the main CSS file in Listing 5.3. The second tab (Lines 69 to 74) is just shown for illustrative purposes, at the moment there is not much functionality, but in the next dashboard we will also fill this tab with more functionality. The entire style of this dashboard component is based on the style given by the "content" section of the CSS file (Line 75).

In this dashboard we can find two callbacks, one for the dialogue between the histogram and the user via a drop-down menu and one for the user dialogue via a slider with the scatter plot. The first callback starts in Line 78 and defines one input value for the color selection and one output value for the corresponding figure which is a histogram in this special case (Lines

78 to 81). The update function for this callback can be seen in the following code lines (Lines 82 to 87). We see that a histogram is created with Plotly with the data as a Pandas dataframe and further parameters. In Line 86 we additionally find the template information given as "plotly_white." Finally, the created figure is returned. The second callback starts in Line 89 with an input value for the filter and a corresponding figure (a scatter plot) as return value. The corresponding update function describes how this filter value has to be handled and which impact it has on a created scatter plot (Lines 93 to 100).

Exercises

- Exercise 5.3.2.1: Implement functionality and features for the second tab in the dashboard application and test it.
- Exercise 5.3.2.2: Create a dashboard with three tabs instead of two.

5.3.3 Dashboard in action

Figure 5.7 shows the result when executing the code above with the external CSS in mind. This should be located in a folder called "assets." We can see that tab one is currently active since it is not grayed out. This means that the histogram and the scatter plot are visible in this scenario. Currently, the color red is chosen for the histogram while the scatter plot is not filtered due to the fact that the slider is turned to the leftmost position. Still, the dashboard is quite simple but the code already contains some useful features with some functionality.

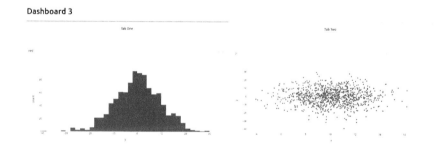

Figure 5.7   A dashboard showing two tabs while tab one has the focus at the moment. Two diagrams are integrated: A histogram (left) and a scatter plot (right).

Exercises

- Exercise 5.3.3.1: Create a dashboard with four tabs in which each tab should be used to switch to a new diagram. You can use the same data generator as in the dashboards explained before.
- Exercise 5.3.3.2: Modify the external CSS file to also adapt the background colors of the tabs. Moreover, use a different Plotly template instead of "plotly_white" to get another visual appearance of the diagrams.

5.4 Inputs from a Plot and Plotly Go

To go one step further and to also allow inputs from an interactive diagram to be the output for a different diagram, we will create another dashboard on top of most of the already existing features and functionality. The relevant feature from information visualization that comes into play here is called brushing and linking, meaning a certain subset of visual elements in one diagram can be selected (and highlighted) and, as a consequence, all of the selected visual elements will be highlighted in all (visible) diagrams as well. This feature is a very important one in information visualization since it connects several plots based on a selection feature. In this extended dashboard, we also look into another way of using Plotly, this time by means of so-called Plotly go objects, while go stands for graph objects that are more flexible but also require more code to implement. In this section we first introduce the dashboard design by a hand-drawn mockup (see Section 5.4.1). Actually, the user interface of the dashboard with the required features looks very similar to the already shown dashboards, but in the background, we have to implement more code to get the functionality running. The corresponding code can be found in Section 5.4.2. Finally, we conclude the section by showing the results of the running code with a dashboard screen shot (Section 5.4.3).

5.4.1 Selecting point clouds for an overview

Figure 5.8 shows a mockup for a dashboard's graphical user interface that consists of two visualizations of an artificially generated dataset for trivariate data. On the one hand, we would like to see the data as a scatter plot for detecting correlations between the two numerical data attributes and the one categorical data attribute, on the other hand we wish to see a distribution of the data split by its categorical information given as the color of the points in a corresponding bar chart. The new idea in this dashboard is based on supporting the spatial selection of point clouds in the scatter plot while at the same time updating the selected point cloud and the distribution of points as a bar chart. This brushing and linking feature is very popular in the field of information visualization, in most cases for more than one plot as we demonstrate in this simple dashboard example.

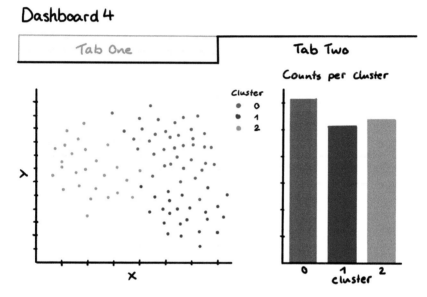

Figure 5.8   A hand-drawn mockup for a user interface of a dashboard with a scatter plot, allowing to select a point cloud for which we see the point distribution in a linked and color coded bar chart (drawn by Sarah Clavadetscher).

In this dashboard we support one new interaction technique among the already existing ones from before. This is defined as brushing and linking in the field of information visualization:

- Brushing and linking: In cases in which a visualization tool consists of several visualizations/diagrams showing views and perspectives on the same dataset, we can interactively connect/link those visualizations. This means in particular that a selection of data elements in one view has an impact on all other views in which those data elements are visually represented as well.

Exercises

- Exercise 5.4.1.1: Integrate a fourth color in the drop-down menu. Extend the dashboard by this new color.
- Exercise 5.4.1.2: Apart from the visual variable color we could also add the shape of the points in the scatter plot. Extend the dashboard to also allow colors and shapes, for the drop-down menu, for the scatter plot, and for the bar chart.

5.4.2 Coding details

In Listing 5.5, we can read the code for the dashboard designed in Figure 5.8. There are some new concepts integrated like more than one plot in a callback mechanism, brushing and linking, making one plot the input for another plot, and the Plotly go objects. To let the code run reliably we need to import a few modules which we have not imported before in the previously described dashboards. Moreover, we use the same external CSS file as in the previous example given in Listing 5.3. Two more modules are required in this example:

- plotly.graph_objects as go: This module contains a figure scheme organized in some kind of hierarchy consisting of Plotly classes. With this concept we can create so-called graph objects which are actually instances of the Python classes.
- sklearn.datasets: With this package we can use some existing datasets from different application domains. This means the data is already in a prepared and well-known data format and several other researchers might have analyzed the same dataset creating some kind of ground truth or golden standard.

```
1  import math
2
3  from dash import Dash, dcc, html, Input, Output
4  import plotly.express as px
5  import plotly.graph_objects as go
6  import numpy as np
7  import pandas as pd
8  import dash_bootstrap_components as dbc
9  from sklearn.datasets import make_blobs
10
11 # new: more than one plot in a callback
12 # new: one plot as an input for another plot
13 # new: plotly go object
```

```
14
15 app = Dash(__name__,
16             external_stylesheets=[dbc.themes.BOOTSTRAP])
17
18 # generate random normal distributed data
19 # for x and y and store it in a pandas DataFrame
20
21 df = pd.DataFrame({'y': np.random.normal(loc=0,
22                                          scale=10,
23                                          size=1000),
24                    'x': np.random.normal(loc=10,
25                                          scale=2,
26                                          size=1000)})
27
28 # define cluster colors
29
30 COLORS = {'0': "red",
31           '1': "blue",
32           '2': "grey"}
33
34 X, y = make_blobs(n_samples=100,
35                   centers=3,
36                   n_features=2,
37                   random_state=0)
38 cluster_df = pd.DataFrame(data=X,
39                           gcolumns=["X", "Y"])
40 cluster_df['cluster'] = [str(i) for i in y]
41
42 app.layout = html.Div([
43     html.Div(
44         [html.H1("Dashboard 4")],
45         className="header"),
46     html.Div([
47         dcc.Tabs(id="tabs",
48             children=[
49                 dcc.Tab(label='Tab One',
50                     id="tab_1_graphs", children=[
51                         html.Div([
52                             dbc.Row([
53                                 dbc.Col([
54                                     dcc.Dropdown(
55                                         options=['red',
56                                                  'green',
57                                                  'blue'],
58                                         value='red',
59                                         id='color',
```

```
60                                          multi=False)],
61                                       width=6),
62                          dbc.Col([
63                              dcc.Slider(min=
64                                  math.floor(
65                                      df['y'].min()),
66                                  max=math.ceil(
67                                      df['y'].max()),
68                                  id="min_value")
69                              ], width=6)
70                          ]),
71                      dbc.Row([
72                          dbc.Col([
73                              dcc.Graph(id="graph_1")
74                              ], width=6),
75                          dbc.Col([
76                              dcc.Graph(id="graph_2")
77                              ], width=6)
78                          ])
79                      ], className="tab_content"),
80                  ]),
81              dcc.Tab(label='Tab Two',
82                  id="tab_2_graphs",
83                      children=[
84                          html.Div([
85                              dbc.Row([
86                                  dbc.Col([
87                                      dcc.Graph(
88                                          id="graph_3")
89                                      ], width=8),
90                                  dbc.Col([
91                                      dcc.Graph(
92                                          id="graph_4")
93                                      ], width=4)
94                                  ])
95                              ], className="tab_content")
96                          ]),
97                  ])
98          ], className="content")
99  ])
100
101 @app.callback(
102     Output("graph_1", "figure"),
103     Input("color", "value")
104 )
105 def update_graph_1(dropdown_value_color):
```

```
106        fig = px.histogram(df,
107                              x="y",
108                              color_discrete_sequence=
109                                 [dropdown_value_color])
110        fig.update_layout(template="plotly_white")
111        return fig
112
113 @app.callback(
114      Output("graph_2", "figure"),
115      Input("min_value", "value")
116 )
117 def update_graph_2(min_value):
118      if min_value:
119          dff = df[df['y'] > min_value]
120      else:
121          dff = df
122
123      fig = px.scatter(dff, x='x', y='y')
124      fig.update_layout(template="plotly_white")
125      return fig
126
127 @app.callback(Output("graph_3", "figure"),
128                Output("graph_4", "figure"),
129                Input("graph_3", "relayoutData")
130 )
131 def update_graph_3_and_4(selected_data):
132      if selected_data is None or
133          (isinstance(selected_data, dict) and
134           'xaxis.range[0]' not in selected_data):
135          cluster_dff = cluster_df
136      else:
137          cluster_dff =
138              cluster_df[(cluster_df['X'] >=
139                  selected_data.get('xaxis.range[0]')) &
140              (cluster_df['X'] <=
141                  selected_data.get('xaxis.range[1]')) &
142              (cluster_df['Y'] >=
143                  selected_data.get('yaxis.range[0]')) &
144              (cluster_df['Y'] <=
145                  selected_data.get('yaxis.range[1]'))]
146
147      fig3 = px.scatter(cluster_dff,
148                          x="X",
149                          y="Y",
150                          color="cluster",
151                          color_discrete_map=COLORS,
```

```
152                    category_orders=
153                        {"cluster": ["0", "1", "2"]},
154                    height=750)
155
156    fig3.update_layout(template="plotly_white",
157                       coloraxis_showscale=False)
158    fig3.update_traces(marker=dict(size=8))
159
160    group_counts =
161        cluster_dff[['cluster', 'X']].
162            groupby('cluster').count()
163
164    fig4 = go.Figure(
165        data=[go.Bar(
166            x=group_counts.index,
167            y=group_counts['X'],
168            marker_color=
169                [COLORS.get(i) for i in group_counts.index]
170        )])
171
172    fig4.update_layout(height=750,
173                       template="plotly_white",
174                       title="<b>Counts per cluster</b>",
175                       xaxis_title="cluster",
176                       title_font_size= 25
177                       )
178
179    return fig3, fig4
180
181 if __name__ == '__main__':
182     app.run_server(debug=True, port=8012)
```

Listing 5.5 A dashboard with more than one plot in a callback and additionally the Plotly go object

The major implementation concepts in the code after the imports can be described as follows. In Line 15, the dashboard is initialized with the external style sheets from the dash bootstrap components. Lines 21 to 26 generate an artificial dataset based on a random normal distribution. A constant named COLORS is defined in Lines 30 to 32 with the colors mapped to numeric information, for the colors of individual point clusters later on in the visualization. The following code in Lines 34 to 40 creates clusters of data.

The layout of the dashboard is built with Line 42 and the next ones, again based on splitting the display area with the HTML div element. This layout strategy is quite similar to the one in the previous dashboard. There is a tab one with two rows and two columns (see Figure 5.4). The first row contains the dash core components for the user input like a drop-down menu and a slider while row two integrates the two diagrams in form of a scatter plot and a bar chart. Tab two just contains one row with two columns for two more diagrams. It may be noted that the widths are arranged differently in the second tab with an 8-to-4 ratio while in tab one we had an equal 6-to-6 ratio.

There are three callback mechanisms in this dashboard code. The first one starts in Line 101 having one input as a color value from a drop-down menu and one output as a figure, that is, a diagram which is a histogram in this special case as we can see in the corresponding update function (Lines 105 to 111). Moreover, the figure uses a special update of its layout based on a template called "plotly_white" which was already described in the previous dashboard example. The second callback (Lines 113 to 116) with its corresponding update function (Lines 117 to 125) is responsible for reacting on the slider input, that is, if the user interactively changes a value by using the slider, this value is directly passed to the corresponding scatter plot as desired with a filter function implemented. This filter works on a copy of the Pandas dataframe (Lines 118 to 121). The filtered data is then given to the scatter plot while again the template is set to "plotly_white" (Line 124).

The third callback starting in Line 127 with its update function starting in Line 131 is the most complex one compared to the previous two callbacks, including some new concepts and features. First of all, we see one input which stems from a graph called "graph_3" and which is passed to two outputs, that is, the "graph_3" itself and a different graph called "graph_4." This is the idea of allowing brushing and linking, meaning the selected data elements in a diagram can be the input for a different diagram which actually sends data between diagrams and not just "pure" inputs from dash core components in the form of sliders, menus, date pickers, and many more. Lines 132 to 145 define the selected data and create a cluster variable "cluster_dff" based on an original variable "cluster_df." The updated diagram (Lines 147 to 154) is then based on this filtered data, that is, the selected data elements are actually color coded by using the defined colors from the COLORS constant in Lines 30 to 32. In Lines 156 to 158, we set the layout of the diagram based on the template again, and we update the traces. To create the corresponding bar chart with which the scatter plot is linked we first need to count the number of selected points together with their category, that is, color. This is done in Lines 160 to 162 and stored in a variable "group_counts." Lines 164 to 170 create the bar chart by a new concept which is based on the so-called graph objects in Plotly. Those go objects have a different syntax than the pure Plotly express diagrams as we can see in the code lines. Finally, in Lines 172 to 177, the layout of the bar chart is updated by setting the height, the template, the title, the description on the x-axis, and additionally a font size to the value 25. In Line 179, both diagrams (the scatter plot and the bar chart) are returned which is inline with the corresponding callback mechanism in Lines 127 to 130 (one input, two outputs).

Exercises

- Exercise 5.4.2.1: The selected data points in the scatter plot should also be represented in a new scatter plot, only showing the selected points.
- Exercise 5.4.2.2: Reimplement the dashboard to let the selected data points appear in a highlighted yellow color.

5.4.3 Dashboard in action

In Figure 5.9, we see that tab two is currently selected. In this tab, we get the scenario of selecting data elements in a scatter plot which are then visualized in a bar chart by using their categories to group them. Moreover, the color of the data elements is integrated in both plots as some kind of visual linking or visual correspondence.

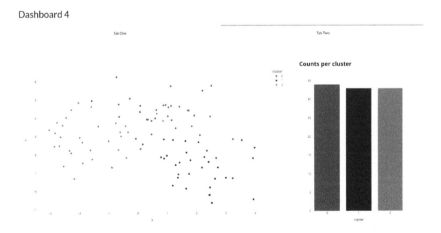

Figure 5.9 Tab two is active in this dashboard showing a scatter plot with color coded data points and a linked bar chart in which the selected point clouds are visually encoded and categorized by their colors/categories.

Exercises

- Exercise 5.4.3.1: Add a third tab in which we can see the distribution of the selected data elements from the scatter plot based on their occurrence on the x- and y-axis.
- Exercise 5.4.3.2: Create a three-dimensional scatter plot and integrate a point selection mechanism. Discuss the usefulness of three-dimensional visualizations in information visualization.

5.5 Two Tabs, Three Plots in One Tab, and Several Inputs

In this next dashboard example, we would like to extend the previous ideas by a separate tab that supports the interactive and visual exploration of trivariate data by means of a color coded scatter plot. These points are embedded in the two-dimensional plane with an additional color coding that visually encodes the third attribute while the other two of the trivariate data are encoded in the x- and y-axes. The scatter plot allows brushing and linking and the selected data points are shown in a corresponding bar chart reflecting the data distribution of the selected point clouds separated in their color categories. Moreover, we require a third diagram that can display the density information of the selected point clouds in the scatter plot based on the powerful concept of heatmaps [30]. As illustrated in this even more complex dashboard example, the designer and implementor can build more and more features and functions, linked to each other, structured into feature and function groups by so-called tabs. However, it may be noted that we should not create too many of such tabs to avoid an information overflow and an increase of the cognitive efforts and a steep learning curve for our users.

The section is organized as follows: In Section 5.5.1 we introduce a hand-drawn mockup showing the major features in this dashboard. We mainly focus on the visual components and the additional interaction techniques compared to the previously described dashboards. In Section 5.5.2, we look into the details of the corresponding Python code and describe the most important code components to get the dashboard running in its desired form. In the last part (Section 5.5.3), we show the visual outputs of the code after we let it run to give the readers an impression about how the dashboard will look like after executing the code. We recommend the readers of the book to test the code by themselves, modify it and check the new results. Extending the code step-by-step might help to understand the dashboard design and implementation on an experimental basis.

5.5.1 Scatter plot as a density heatmap

The general idea of this dashboard is to create a visual way to explore the number of points in a scatter plot. This can be done by selecting point clouds and inspect their distribution in a bar chart. Although this is a good strategy we cannot see the spatial distribution of the points in the bar chart anymore. Hence, an improved solution would be another kind of scatter plot that shows the density information of the points which is in particular useful in cases in which many points are plotted on top of each other. But still we need the bar chart to see the categorical distribution which is given by the color coding in the scatter plot. The plots should be linked somehow by a brushing and linking feature, a visualization concept that can also be implemented with Dash, Plotly, and Python. Figure 5.10 illustrates how such a dashboard might look like. The reader might think about further extensions of the dashboard, for example with further diagrams, interactions, and even other datasets from real-world applications.

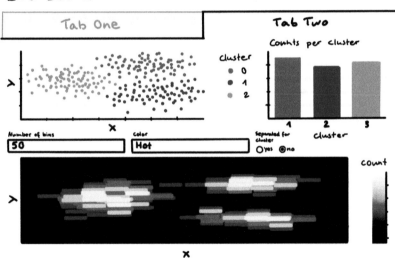

Figure 5.10 A hand-drawn mockup of a dashboard with several linked visualizations: A scatter plot, a bar chart, and a density heatmap to visually explore the spatial distribution of the points in 2D (drawn by Sarah Clavadetscher).

Exercises

- Exercise 5.5.1.1: Design a dashboard with six different visualization techniques showing the same dataset from six different perspectives.
- Exercise 5.5.1.2: Which interactions are important for such a dashboard scenario and which of your diagrams should be linked and in what way?

5.5.2 Coding details

We describe two options to implement such a dashboard, the first one based on CSS (Listing 5.7) and the second one based on bootstrap (Listing 5.8). For the CSS version we need an external CSS file which can be found in Listing 5.6. Before we start discussing both of the code options we take a closer look into the CSS code and briefly describe its components. The CSS defines the padding, margin, and box sizing with fixed values (Lines 1 to 5) for example. Nothing is mentioned about the HTML (Lines 7 and 8) in this specific example. However, the body sets the font family to Lato and sans-serif and the font weight to 400 while the margins left and right are set to 15 px respectively (Lines 10 to 15). The container is set to a margin of 0 and a maximum width of 2000 pixels in Lines 17 to 20 while the header title is fixed to a top margin of 20 pixels and a bottom margin of 10 pixels (Lines 22 to 25). Also the tabl main container gets a few additional settings which are the display type as grid and the grid template columns are set to 1fr (Lines 27 to 30). In the remaining definitions we set the graph to a maximum width of 100 %, the height to 700 pixels, and the margin top to 15 pixels (Lines 32 to 36). Further definitions for the graph control set the maximum width to 50 %, the margin to 0, and the margin top to 50 pixels (Lines 38 to 42). The main container for tab two is set to a grid display with grid template columns set to 1fr, a column gap to 20 pixels, a row gap to 10 pixels, and a margin top to 50 pixels (Lines 44 to 50). Graph 3 gets an additional grid column setting to 1/-2, while graph 5 is set to 1/-1 (Lines 52 to 58). Finally, graph 5 gets an additional feature for the label and the last child whose margin is set to 20 pixels (Lines 60 to 62). This CSS example should illustrate that there are various options possible to guide the layout and the appearance of dashboard components. The reader is recommended to read further details in the corresponding CSS literature, mentioning all of the CSS features would go beyond the fence of this book.

```
 1  *{
 2      padding: 0px;
 3      margin: 0px;
 4      box-sizing: border-box;
 5  }
 6
 7  html {
 8  }
 9
10  body {
11      font-family: Lato, sans-serif;
12      font-weight: 400;
13      margin-left: 15px;
14      margin-right: 15px;
15  }
16
17  .container {
18      margin: 0 auto;
19      max-width: 2000px;
20  }
21
22  .header--title {
23      margin-top: 20px;
24      margin-bottom: 10px;
25  }
26
27  .tab1--main-container {
28      display: grid;
29      grid-template-columns: 1fr 1fr;
30  }
31
32  .graph {
33      max-width: 100%;
34      height: 700px;
35      margin-top: 15px;
36  }
37
38  .graph-control {
39      max-width: 50%;
40      margin: 0 auto;
41      margin-top: 50px;
42  }
43
44  .tab2--main-container {
45      display: grid;
46      grid-template-columns: 1fr 1fr 1fr;
```

```
47        column - gap :  20px ;
48        row - gap :  10px ;
49        margin - top :  50px ;
50  }
51
52  . graph _ 3  {
53        grid - column :  1  /  - 2 ;
54  }
55
56  . graph _ 5  {
57        grid - column :  1  /  - 1 ;
58  }
59
60  . graph _ 5 _ separated  label : last - child  {
61        margin :  20px
62  }
```

Listing 5.6   The external CSS file for a dashboard

Listing 5.7 starts again with the import of the relevant modules (Lines 1 to 8). Most of them we have used already in the dashboard examples before. A new one in the code is:

- helpers: This module allows to import data-related functionality like the generation of random data, the generation of cluster data, or the update of selected data.

We define a color constant again in Lines 18 to 20 and use external stylesheets in Lines 22 to 25 which are included in Lines 28 and 29 when starting the app. The random data is generated in Line 31 with a seed of value 8 and in Line 32 we create additional clusters. The layout of the dashboard is then defined starting in Line 34 with the HTML division element again that creates a header and another division element (Line 37). In this container we start building tabs (Line 38) with several subtabs organized as children. In tab 1 (Lines 39 to 69) we find again the HTML div elements to organize and layout the dash core components which are a dropdown menu (Lines 42 to 51) and a graph which stands for a Plotly diagram (Lines 52 to 54). The variable className are used to attach the external CSS file features to the corresponding core components in the dashboard. A second subcomponent of tab 1 is built by the slider (Lines 57 to 63) and by another graph representing a Plotly diagram (Lines 64 to 66). As we can see in this example there are several className variables attached to the used components, always defining additional layouts and visual properties.

Tab 2 is coded in Lines 70 to 127 and is much more complex than the code for the functionality provided by tab 1. Again we split the features and functions by defining children of the tab environment and we use an HTML div element on the highest level in the tab (Line 72). Moreover, several other division elements are used to subcategorize and layout the tab's content. We start with two graphs called graph_3 and graph_4 (Lines 73 to 76) followed by another division element containing even another division element with a label (Lines 79 to 81) and a drop-down menu (Lines 82 to 89). This is repeated again with further features (Lines 90 to 105) and again for a label and a RadioItems component (Lines 108 to 119). The last part builds a graph component for graph_5 (Lines 120 to 122).

The following lines describe the callbacks starting with one that takes a color value as input and that outputs a figure identified by graph_1 (Lines 130 to 133). The corresponding update function is placed below this callback (Lines 135 to 141). It is responsible for updating the histogram in a certain user-selected color value. The next callback (Lines 143 to 146) takes a min_value as input and outputs a graph_2. The corresponding update function can be found in Lines 148 to 156. It is responsible for the filtering of the scatter plot based on the minimum value that is user-selected by a slider. Then, a more complex callback can be found in Lines 158 to 160 that takes some graph-related input and outputs two other graphs. The idea in this callback is to allow inputs from a diagram and make its outputs in other diagrams. The update function is coded in Lines 162 to 202. Another callback (Lines 204 to 210) takes four values as inputs, 3 numbers and one graph-related property while it just outputs one new figure. The corresponding update function can be found below (Lines 212 to 228). The code is completed with the already known commands in Lines 230 to 231.

```
1  from dash import Dash, dcc, html, Input, Output
2  import plotly.express as px
3  import plotly.graph_objects as go
4  import math
5  from helpers import generate_random_data,
6                       generate_random_cluster_data,
7                       update_selected_data
8  import dash_bootstrap_components as dbc
9
10 # New: same functionality like previous example
11 # but this time without inline styles and without bootstrap
12 # this time much more CSS in main_dashboard4.css
13
```

```
14  # New: Exporting data generation in own function
15
16  # define cluster colors
17
18  COLORS = {'0': "red",
19            '1': "blue",
20            '2': "grey"}
21
22  external_stylesheets = [
23      "'https://fonts.googleapis.com/css2?family=
24              Lato:wght@400;700&display=swap'"
25  ]
26
27  # own .css from folder assets integrated
28  app = Dash(__name__,
29             external_stylesheets=external_stylesheets)
30
31  df = generate_random_data(seed=8)
32  cluster_df = generate_random_cluster_data()
33
34  app.layout = html.Div([
35      html.Header([html.H1("Dashboard 5")],
36                  className="header--title"),
37      html.Div([
38          dcc.Tabs(id="tabs", children=[
39              dcc.Tab(label="Tab1", children=[
40                  html.Div([
41                      html.Div([
42                          dcc.Dropdown(
43                              options=['red',
44                                       'green',
45                                       'blue'],
46                              value='red',
47                              id='color',
48                              multi=False,
49                              className=
50                                  "graph_1--dropdown
51                                  graph-control"),
52                          dcc.Graph(
53                              id="graph_1",
54                              className="graph_1 graph")
55                      ], className="graph-component"),
56                      html.Div([
57                          dcc.Slider(
58                              min=math.floor(df['y'].min()),
59                              max=math.ceil(df['y'].max()),
```

```
60                              id="min_value",
61                              className=
62                                  "graph_2--slider
63                                   graph-control"),
64                          dcc.Graph(
65                              id="graph_2",
66                              className="graph_2 graph")
67                      ], className="graph-component")
68                  ], className="tab1--main-container")
69              ], className="tab1"),
70              dcc.Tab(label="Tab2",
71                  children=[
72                      html.Div([
73                          html.Div(dcc.Graph(id="graph_3"),
74                              className="graph_3"),
75                          html.Div(dcc.Graph(id="graph_4"),
76                              className="graph_4"),
77                          html.Div(
78                              html.Div([
79                                  dbc.Label("Number of bins:",
80                                      html_for=
81                                          "graph_5_nbins"),
82                                  dcc.Dropdown(
83                                      options=[str(i) for i in
84                                          range(5, 100, 5)],
85                                      value='40',
86                                      id='graph_5_nbins',
87                                      multi=False)
88                              ]), className=
89                                  "graph_5--bins-dropdown"),
90                          html.Div(
91                              html.Div([
92                                  dbc.Label(
93                                      "Color:",
94                                      html_for="graph_5_color"),
95                                  dcc.Dropdown(
96                                      options=["Viridis",
97                                          "Magma",
98                                          "Hot",
99                                          "GnBu",
100                                         "Greys"],
101                                     value='Hot',
102                                     id='graph_5_color',
103                                     multi=False)
104                             ]), className=
105                                 "graph_5--color-dropdown"),
```

```
106                                         html.Div(
107                                           html.Div([
108                                             dbc.Label(
109                                               "Separated for Cluster:",
110                                               html_for=
111                                                 "graph_5_separated"),
112                                             dcc.RadioItems(
113                                               options=["Yes", "No"],
114                                               value='No',
115                                               id='graph_5_separated',
116                                               className=
117                                                 "graph_5_separated")
118                                           ]), className=
119                                             "graph_5--separation-radio"),
120                                           html.Div(
121                                             dcc.Graph(id="graph_5"),
122                                             className="graph_5")
123                                         ], className=
124                                           "tab2--main-container")
125                                     ], className="tab2")
126                 ])
127         ], className="tabs-content")
128     ], className="container")
129
130 @app.callback(
131     Output("graph_1", "figure"),
132     Input("color", "value")
133 )
134
135 def update_graph_1(dropdown_value_color):
136     fig = px.histogram(df,
137                        x="y",
138                        color_discrete_sequence=
139                          [dropdown_value_color])
140     fig.update_layout(template="plotly_white")
141     return fig
142
143 @app.callback(
144     Output("graph_2", "figure"),
145     Input("min_value", "value")
146 )
147
148 def update_graph_2(min_value):
149     if min_value:
150         dff = df[df['y'] > min_value]
151     else:
```

```
152          dff = df
153
154      fig = px.scatter(dff, x='x', y='y')
155      fig.update_layout(template="plotly_white")
156      return fig
157
158 @app.callback(Output("graph_3", "figure"),
159                Output("graph_4", "figure"),
160                Input("graph_3", "relayoutData"))
161
162 def update_graph_3_and_4(selected_data):
163      PLOT_HEIGHT = 400
164
165      cluster_dff = update_selected_data(
166                      cluster_df=cluster_df,
167                      selected_data=selected_data)
168
169      fig3 = px.scatter(cluster_dff,
170                      x="X",
171                      y="Y",
172                      color="cluster",
173                      color_discrete_map=COLORS,
174                      category_orders={"cluster":
175                                      ["0", "1", "2"]})
176
177      fig3.update_layout(
178          height=PLOT_HEIGHT,
179          template="plotly_white",
180          coloraxis_showscale=False)
181      fig3.update_traces(marker=dict(size=8))
182
183      group_counts =
184        cluster_dff
185          [['cluster', 'X']].groupby('cluster').count()
186
187      fig4 = go.Figure(
188          data=[go.Bar(
189              x=group_counts.index,
190              y=group_counts['X'],
191              marker_color=
192                  [COLORS.get(i) for i in group_counts.index]
193      )])
194
195      fig4.update_layout(height=PLOT_HEIGHT,
196                      template="plotly_white",
197                      title="<b>Counts per cluster</b>",
```

```
198                              xaxis_title="cluster",
199                              title_font_size=25
200      )
201
202      return fig3, fig4
203
204  @app.callback(
205      Output("graph_5", "figure"),
206      Input("graph_5_nbins", "value"),
207      Input("graph_5_color", "value"),
208      Input("graph_5_separated", "value"),
209      Input("graph_3", "relayoutData"),
210  )
211
212  def update_graph_5(nbins, color, separated, selected_data):
213      cluster_dff = update_selected_data(
214                      cluster_df=cluster_df,
215                      selected_data=selected_data)
216
217      fig = px.density_heatmap(
218          cluster_dff,
219          x="X",
220          y="Y",
221          nbinsx=int(nbins),
222          nbinsy=int(nbins),
223          color_continuous_scale=color,
224          facet_col=None if separated == "No" else "cluster",
225          category_orders={"cluster": ["0", "1", "2"]}
226      )
227      fig.update_layout(template="plotly_white")
228      return fig
229
230  if __name__ == '__main__':
231      app.run_server(debug=True, port=8014)
```

Listing 5.7   Example of a dashboard without inline styles and without bootstrap but based on CSS

Listing 5.8 shows a code example for the same features and functionality as in Listing 5.7 but this time CSS is not used but instead, we make use of bootstrap. The imports in Lines 1 to 9 are already familiar to the reader. In Line 17, we can find the first major difference compared to the code before which is the integration of the dash bootstrap components. After the data generation, color settings, and cluster definition (Lines 22 to 46), we code the layout of the dashboard based on HTML div elements but this time we use the inline style commands for the margin for example (Line 50). The structure of the code is similar to the code example before but this time we make use of rows and columns based on the dash bootstrap components (starting in Line 59 and ending in Line 149 with the last column). The rest of the code is again defining callbacks and update functions, similar to the example code before.

```python
import math

from dash import Dash, dcc, html, Input, Output
import plotly.express as px
import plotly.graph_objects as go
import numpy as np
import pandas as pd
import dash_bootstrap_components as dbc
from sklearn.datasets import make_blobs

# New: Density heatmap (2 columns) as third plot on tab 2
# with color and resolution options

# New: Everything with inline style and bootstrap (no CSS)

app = Dash(__name__,
           external_stylesheets=[dbc.themes.BOOTSTRAP])

# generate random normal distributed data for x and y
# and store it in a Pandas DataFrame (for plot 1,2, and 5)

np.random.seed(seed=8)

df = pd.DataFrame({'y': np.random.normal(loc=0,
                                         scale=10,
                                         size=1000),
                   'x': np.random.normal(loc=10,
                                         scale=2,
                                         size=1000)})

# define cluster colors

COLORS = {'0': "red",
          '1': "blue",
          '2': "grey"}

# generic cluster data (for plot 3 and 4)

X, y = make_blobs(n_samples=7500,
                  centers=3,
                  n_features=2,
```

```
42                          random_state=0,
43                          cluster_std=0.75)
44
45  cluster_df = pd.DataFrame(data=X, columns=["X", "Y"])
46  cluster_df['cluster'] = [str(i) for i in y]
47
48  app.layout = html.Div([
49      html.Div([html.H1("Dashboard 6")],
50              style={'margin': '10px 25px 25px 25px'}),
51
52      html.Div([
53          dcc.Tabs(id="tabs",
54              children=[
55                  dcc.Tab(
56                      label='Tab One',
57                      children=[
58                          html.Div([
59                              dbc.Row([
60                                  dbc.Col([dcc.Dropdown(
61                                      options=['red',
62                                              'green',
63                                              'blue'],
64                                      value='red',
65                                      id='color',
66                                      multi=False)
67                                      ], width=6),
68                                  dbc.Col([
69                                      dcc.Slider(
70                                          min=math.floor(
71                                              df['y'].min()),
72                                          max=math.ceil(
73                                              df['y'].max()),
74                                          id="min_value")
75                                          ], width=6)
76                              ]),
77                              dbc.Row([
78                                  dbc.Col([
79                                      dcc.Graph(id="graph_1")
80                                  ], width=6),
81                                  dbc.Col([
82                                      dcc.Graph(id="graph_2")
83                                  ], width=6)
84                              ])
85                          ], style={"margin":
86                                  "100px 25px 25px 25px"}),
87                      ]
```

```
88      ),
89      dcc.Tab(
90          label='Tab Two',
91          id="tab_2_graphs",
92          children=[
93              html.Div([
94                  dbc.Row([
95                      dbc.Col([
96                          dcc.Graph(id="graph_3")
97                      ], width=8),
98                      dbc.Col([
99                          dcc.Graph(id="graph_4")
100                     ], width=4)
101                 ]),
102                 dbc.Row([
103                     dbc.Col(html.Div([
104                         dbc.Label(
105                             "Number of bins:",
106                             html_for=
107                             "graph_5_nbins"),
108                         dcc.Dropdown(options=
109                             [str(i) for i in
110                             range(5, 100, 5)],
111                             value='40',
112                             id='graph_5_nbins',
113                             multi=False
114                         )
115                     ]),width={"size": 3},),
116                     dbc.Col(html.Div([
117                         dbc.Label("Color:",
118                             html_for=
119                             "graph_5_color"),
120                         dcc.Dropdown(
121                             options=["Viridis",
122                                      "Magma",
123                                      "Hot",
124                                      "GnBu",
125                                      "Greys"],
126                             value='Viridis',
127                             id='graph_5_color',
128                             multi=False)
129                     ]),width={"size": 3,
130                         "offset": 1},),
131                     dbc.Col(html.Div([
132                         dbc.Label(
133                             "Separated
```

```
134                                     for Cluster:",
135                                     html_for=
136                                     "graph_5_separated"
137                                     ),
138                                     dcc.RadioItems(
139                                     options=["Yes",
140                                                 "No"],
141                                     value='No',
142                                     id=
143                                     'graph_5_separated')
144                                 ]),width={"size": 3,
145                                             "offset": 1},
146                                     )
147                             ]),
148                         dbc.Row([
149                             dbc.Col([
150                                 dcc.Graph(
151                                     id="graph_5")
152                             ], width=12)
153                         ])
154                     ], style={"margin":
155                                 "10px 25px 25px 25px"})
156                 ]),
157             ])
158         ], style={"margin": "10px 25px 25px 25px"})
159 ])
160
161 def update_selected_data(selected_data):
162     if selected_data is None or
163         (isinstance(selected_data, dict) and
164         'xaxis.range[0]' not in selected_data):
165             cluster_dff = cluster_df
166     else:
167         cluster_dff =
168             cluster_df[
169             (cluster_df['X'] >=
170                 selected_data.get('xaxis.range[0]')) &
171             (cluster_df['X'] <=
172                 selected_data.get('xaxis.range[1]')) &
173             (cluster_df['Y'] >=
174                 selected_data.get('yaxis.range[0]')) &
175             (cluster_df['Y'] <=
176                 selected_data.get('yaxis.range[1]'))]
177     return cluster_dff
178
179 @app.callback(
```

```
180      Output("graph_1", "figure"),
181      Input("color", "value")
182 )
183
184 def  update_graph_1(dropdown_value_color):
185      fig = px.histogram(df,
186                         x="y",
187                         color_discrete_sequence=
188                             [dropdown_value_color])
189      fig.update_layout(template="plotly_white")
190      return  fig
191
192 @app.callback(
193      Output("graph_2", "figure"),
194      Input("min_value", "value")
195 )
196 def  update_graph_2(min_value):
197
198      if  min_value:
199          dff = df[df['y'] > min_value]
200      else:
201          dff = df
202
203      fig = px.scatter(dff, x='x', y='y')
204      fig.update_layout(template="plotly_white")
205      return  fig
206
207
208 @app.callback(Output("graph_3", "figure"),
209               Output("graph_4", "figure"),
210               Input("graph_3", "relayoutData"))
211 def  update_graph_3_and_4(selected_data):
212
213      PLOT_HEIGHT = 400
214
215      cluster_dff = update_selected_data(
216                    selected_data=selected_data)
217
218      fig3 = px.scatter(cluster_dff,
219                        x="X",
220                        y="Y",
221                        color="cluster",
222                        color_discrete_map=COLORS,
223                        category_orders=
224                            {"cluster": ["0", "1", "2"]})
225
```

```python
226      fig3.update_layout(
227          height=PLOT_HEIGHT,
228          template="plotly_white",
229          coloraxis_showscale=False)
230      fig3.update_traces(marker=dict(size=8))
231
232      group_counts = cluster_dff[
233          ['cluster', 'X']].groupby('cluster').count()
234
235      fig4 = go.Figure(
236          data=[go.Bar(
237              x=group_counts.index,
238              y=group_counts['X'],
239              marker_color=[
240                  COLORS.get(i) for i in group_counts.index]
241      )])
242
243      fig4.update_layout(height=PLOT_HEIGHT,
244                         template="plotly_white",
245                         title="<b>Counts per cluster</b>",
246                         xaxis_title="cluster",
247                         title_font_size=25
248                         )
249
250      return fig3, fig4
251
252  @app.callback(
253      Output("graph_5", "figure"),
254      Input("graph_5_nbins", "value"),
255      Input("graph_5_color", "value"),
256      Input("graph_5_separated", "value"),
257      Input("graph_3", "relayoutData"),
258  )
259  def update_graph_5(nbins, color, separated, selected_data):
260      cluster_dff = update_selected_data(
261                      selected_data=selected_data)
262
263      fig = px.density_heatmap(
264          cluster_dff,
265          x="X",
266          y="Y",
267          nbinsx=int(nbins),
268          nbinsy=int(nbins),
269          color_continuous_scale=color,
270          facet_col=None if separated == "No" else "cluster",
271          category_orders={"cluster": ["0", "1", "2"]}
```

```
272    )
273    fig.update_layout(template="plotly_white")
274    return fig
275
276
277 if __name__ == '__main__':
278    app.run_server(debug=True, port=8014)
```

Listing 5.8 Example of a dashboard with more functionality like tabs and interactive visualizations as well as the inline style and bootstrap but no CSS

Exercises

- Exercise 5.5.2.1: Add one more row and one more column in the dashboard code. Do this in both code variants with CSS and bootstrap.
- Exercise 5.5.2.2: Discuss which code variant is better. Take into account criteria like code understanding, code maintenance, code extension, and find some more criteria.

5.5.3 Dashboard in action

Figure 5.11 shows a screenshot of the dashboard after executing either the code example in Listing 5.7 or in Listing 5.8. We can see three partially overlapping point clusters in the upper left part colored in gray, red, and blue. The distribution of the selected points is shown in the corresponding bar chart in the upper right part indicating that the points seem to be equally distributed in the three categories. The lower part shows the spatial distribution of each point cloud as a density scatter plot in form of a heatmap-like diagram. The color coding visually encodes the density value, that is, the denser the point cloud the brighter the color.

We hope that we could give some useful examples for creating dashboards. It may be noted that there are lots of variations in the design and implementation phases. Each designer and developer has his/her own ideas and concepts in mind, meaning this chapter just served as a starting point showing some fruitful ideas which build the basis for new dashboards to be created on.

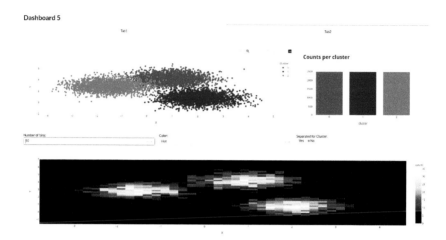

Figure 5.11   Executing the dashboard code and activating tab 2 to interactively explore the trivariate data in a scatter plot linked to a bar chart and a density heatmap.

Exercises

- Exercise 5.5.3.1: Find your own dataset on the world wide web and design and implement your own dashboard to visually explore this data.
- Exercise 5.5.3.2: For a user-defined (or selected) mathematical function $f : \mathbb{R} \longrightarrow \mathbb{R}$ we would like to see the plot of the function as well as additional information like minima, maxima, gradient function, area under the function in a certain interval, and many more. Design and implement a dashboard to support a mathematician at these tasks.

6

Challenges and Limitations

Although a dashboard is a good concept to build an interactive visualization tool [1, 50, 61, 155] for a multitude of data consisting of various data types we still find many challenges during the design and implementation, but also the execution phase. In this chapter we will take a look on several aspects that bring into play challenges during the design of a dashboard in Python. To mention a few but important ones we come across several perspectives like the design, implementation, the execution of the code, and the testing phase that can be done after the implementation or during it in an iterative way. As we learned before, the design includes the visual [232] and interface design [217] but also aspects like aesthetics [38]. The implementation phase takes into account the software [82], the development environment (IDE), the developers themselves [53, 54], the operating systems, but also the web browsers to let the users explore their data with an online version of the dashboard. In the execution phase we are confronted by aspects including the data, algorithms, interactions, visual, and perceptual scalability. In the testing phase we look into typical performance issues with respect to the runtime performance of the tool with all its algorithms but also the user performance when giving tasks to solve with the dashboard. The user performance includes the users themselves but also aspects regarding usability, user-friendliness as well as user evaluation with and without eye tracking [44, 87, 123].

This chapter is organized as follows: In Section 6.1, we will discuss the major challenges when designing a user interface as well as visualization techniques, typically following well-defined rules to focus on user-friendliness, efficiency, and effectiveness for data exploration tasks. Implementation challenges can occur in various forms, in particular when using the programming language Python, Dash, and Plotly. Those are also based on the operating systems, development environments, but also on web browsers in cases a dashboard should be run online (Section 6.2). When using the dashboard, that is, after execution of the implemented source

213

code we can run into problems concerning data, algorithmic, visual, or perceptual scalability aspects, typically those challenges are detected when the dashboard is ready to be used, that is, during its runtime (Section 6.3). We also take a look into performance issues that can come from the software but also from the users' perspectives which could be evaluated in controlled or uncontrolled user studies with and without eye tracking (Section 6.4).

6.1 Design Issues

When creating a dashboard for interactive visualizations [13] we have to focus on at least two design perspectives. The first one comes from the graphical user interface (GUI) with all its components like sliders, menus, buttons, text fields, and so on, presented in a suitable and user-friendly layout. The second one is based on the visualization techniques with its integrated interaction features. The visualizations in use depend on the datasets with their data types on the one hand and the tasks the users have in mind for which they plan to use the visualization tool to explore and analyze the data. On top of this we have to deal with a multitude of interaction techniques, in each individual visualization technique but also connecting two or more of them in some kind of brushing and linking concept. Apart from just looking at the standard design rules for the user interface and the visualization techniques we have to keep in mind that there also exist aesthetic rules that focus on readability aspects but also on beauty [15, 38]. Those two aspects stand in some kind of trade-off criterion, that is, the nicer a visualization is the less readable it becomes, the more readable a visualization is for solving exploration tasks the less beautiful it is.

In this section, we start our discussion on limitations and challenges by looking into interface design issues. This can be done by at least two perspectives, the static components and their layouts but also dynamic interface features like interactions that are possible with buttons, sliders, drop-down menus, date pickers, and the like (Section 6.1.1). Moreover, we continue by taking into account the problems that occur when thinking about a visual design including the visualization techniques with the interactions in each individual visualization technique but also in a linked manner (Section 6.1.2). Visualization tools do not only focus on providing interactive and readable visualization techniques, they also take into account aesthetics in the sense of creating a visually attractive and beautiful appearance of both, the interface and the visualization techniques, however there is some kind of trade-off between both concepts (Section 6.1.3).

6.1.1 Interface design challenges

One of the first steps when creating a dashboard for an interactive visualization tool is to think about the required components, where they are located in the display, which size each individual one will get, if they are static or dynamically modifiable, or which additional features they will be equipped with. This task is quite challenging and can come with a multitude of problems, typically asking the designers to only focus on a limited number of components and either throw away the others or allow to show them on users' demands. What we actually do is to generate a list of possible component candidates that all have some kind of priority depending on a certain task to be solved. Hence, the design of the user interface is linked to the tasks at hand that the final dashboard should support. We should try to come up with a solution based on a principle including the must haves, should haves, and could haves, creating a three-stage categorization of all the features that are required in the dashboard. However, in most situations, we only concentrate on the most important ones. Hence each dashboard only provides a limited number of functions that are useful for solving the tasks.

Designing an interface can be done individually or in a group of team members, but actually no matter who the designers are, we have to consult the end users. They are the ones who are our customers and who might buy our final product. We can create the most impressive dashboard ever with a multitude of components, functions, features, interactions, visualizations, and so on, linked together and put into a good layout. However, the users decide if the created product is really useful and meets their needs. Hence, also here we need already some kind of user evaluation [152] that uncovers the bottlenecks, drawbacks, and design flaws on which an improvement phase should be based. Typical tasks in a user study related to the interface design focus on the major ingredients like the buttons, sliders, and menus and their interplay as well as the layout of the GUI to decide whether the locations of the individual components are well chosen. However, this is already a difficult problem since the design space with all of its parameters cannot be covered in one individual user experiment. Many more have to be conducted, each one varying and checking only a few parameters as independent variables into the study while the created dataset from the study results can already be quite large needing another kind of analysis or visualization tool to find insights in the study data, in particular, if spatiotemporal eye tracking data [44] or verbal feedback is also recorded as a dependent variable in the study.

Exercises

- Exercise 6.1.1.1: Imagine your dashboard should have 20 user interface components. How do you decide which of them are the most important ones and where do you place them in the layout?
- Exercise 6.1.1.2: Which general options do you have to support 20 visualization techniques in a dashboard?

6.1.2 Visual design challenges

The design of the visualization techniques is based on a composition of visual variables like color, size, position, orientation, texture, and so on. The biggest challenge here is to decide which ones are appropriate to generate a visual solution for the tasks at hand. Even if the visual variables seem to be good candidates there is no guarantee that there are better visual variable combinations; however, we have already learned some visualization techniques (Section 2.2.1) that are beneficial for certain data types and user tasks. Just in case we are planning to design our own visualization techniques we need to check if those are better candidates than existing ones, otherwise the users might not be confident with the chosen visualizations, in particular, if they are visualization experts who know better examples. In case we have created a new visualization technique we can compare the usefulness, efficiency, and effectiveness by checking it against a ground-truth visualization technique in a comparative study, based on performance measures but also based on user performances in a user experiment with typical user tasks. However, this evaluation strategy can cost some valuable time during the design phase, but actually, it is necessary to avoid design flaws later on that we were not aware of without having asked the users.

The visual design (as already discussed in Section 2.4.1) also focuses on further more complex principles which are based on the composition of the visual variables but which also take into account user tasks. Those are chart junk, the lie factor, as well as visual clutter. Creating a visualization technique that takes into account all three of them at the same time is a challenging task, in particular, if line-based diagrams have to be drawn, we mostly run into a visual clutter problem [202] for larger datasets. In many visual situations, we should exploit the Gestalt laws [147] to follow a good visual design since they consist of a rule set with natural aspects related to how we interpret a diagram as a whole and not as composed of its parts which contradicts somehow the aforementioned idea of composing visualization techniques by a number of visual variables. Here, we have to take into account that the composition is the visual encoding while the Gestalt laws work into the other direction, i.e. as a visual decoding. As a challenge, we have to find a visual encoding that is powerful enough to serve as a visual decoding, that is, an interpretation of the visual patterns to visually explore the encoded data.

Exercises

- Exercise 6.1.2.1: Find diagrams on the web that contain visual design flaws and discuss how to get rid of them.
- Exercise 6.1.2.2: Discuss whether chart junk, the lie factor, or visual clutter is bad for a designed diagram.

6.1.3 Aesthetics criteria

Since we design and develop a visualization tool for exploring and analyzing data, we first look into the aspect of readability of the created visualizations and the usefulness of the integrated interaction techniques. This plays the major role and has the highest priority when building such an interactive tool for data exploration. However, a second, but actually equally important role is played by aesthetics that makes a visualization tool attractive to the viewers, that is, aesthetically appealing [38] with a certain value [237]. The biggest challenge in this area comes from the fact that both aspects stand in some kind of trade-off behavior, that is, increasing the readability typically happens at the cost of less aesthetics while increasing the aesthetics in the sense of making a user interface and the integrated visualization technique more beautiful comes at the cost of less readability (see Figure 6.1).

Measuring readability can be done by user performance measures but measuring aesthetics is a much more difficult problem since each user might understand aesthetics differently and has a different feeling for aesthetics. However, there are some general rules to measure aesthetics of a visualization given by facts that focus on symmetry or certain shapes that might be liked more than others like curved diagrams which might be preferred over noncurved diagrams [15]. But still, it is quite challenging to input a visualization in an aesthetics computing algorithm that comes up with a value for the degree of aesthetics in the visualization. One idea in this direction might be a regression problem solved with a neural network that is trained to compute a percentage value from a given repertoire of visualization candidates, however the model for such a neural network has to be trained

Figure 6.1   Readability and aesthetics cannot be integrated into a diagram at the same time to a full extent. There is always some kind of trade-off situation.

on labeled data while the labels come again from an original aesthetics judgment of viewers, a fact that brings us back to the old problem that users are required to judge the aesthetics of a visualization before a machine can do it.

Exercises

- Exercise 6.1.3.1: Which diagrams do you think are nicer: Two-dimensional versus three-dimensional ones, or Cartesian versus radial ones, colored versus gray-scale ones, static versus animated ones?
- Exercise 6.1.3.2: What makes a diagram look aesthetically appealing? What makes a graphical user interface look aesthetically appealing?

6.2 Implementation Challenges

After the design phase, we have to start to implement the created dashboard. This will again bring into play many challenges, but this time related to programming issues. The design is more flexible since it is based on humans' creativity while following some well-defined rules. The implementation phase, on the other hand, shows up as being more restricted due to the fact that we have to rely on the features that a programming language and its libraries offer [82]. In some situations the desired functionality might not be available as an already implemented function, hence we either have to adjust our design or we need profound knowledge to implement the desired feature by ourselves. Whatever way we decide to take, there are various other challenges that come our way, related to the bottlenecks of the integrated development environment, the underlying operating system, the internet connection and power of the servers, in case the dashboard has to be deployed as an online version, or the web browsers that come in a multitude of forms with different versions. Moreover, the developers themselves play a crucial role and are a challenge by themselves, typically based on their experience levels.

In this section, we first look into challenges related to software and libraries that come across our way (Section 6.2.1). A second stage is to understand which bottlenecks and drawbacks integrated development environments can have, avoiding to successfully build a dashboard (Section 6.2.2). The developers should choose the software, libraries, and IDEs not only on the dashboard design, but also on their experience levels, otherwise they might fail in the implementation phase (Section 6.2.3). Also, the operating systems can mean a problem during the implementation, in particular, if some developers have different operating systems causing inconsistencies during the implementation (Section 6.2.4). If we plan to provide our dashboard as an online visualization tool, we must make it available online, that is, on a server which typically requires some knowledge about web-based development (Section 6.2.5). Even if we were successful in all the aforementioned stages, the dashboard might still have problems when opening it which might be due to the fact that the web browsers on the users' sides have a number of awkward features that let the dashboards look differently for each user and even some features cannot be executed as expected (Section 6.2.6).

6.2.1 Software and libraries

The biggest issue when using existing libraries, for example graphics and visualization libraries, comes from the fact that they only provide a limited functionality. This has to be understood first to make it applicable to the problems at hand which turns out to be a challenging task for a developer. Moreover, it quickly happens that the desired functionality is not available as a function or method in the library, hence there remain two options in this case: Either reduce the dashboard by the desired functionality or implement the functionality by oneself which again requires more profound knowledge in programming than is needed when just relying on the functions given by a library. A good example for such library challenges in the field of visualization is given by the feature of brushing and linking in multiple coordinated views [200] which requires that two or more diagrams are interactively connected. In Plotly Express, it is quite easy to create interactive diagrams based on certain data types, however linking two or more of them is a tedious task. Actually, the standard diagrams are not connected to each other, they just work in isolation, each one separately.

Not only the visualization libraries may cause such problems when individually developing a dashboard for a specific application. Also other libraries related to data analytics, for example, popular algorithmic concepts like clustering, dimensionality reduction [235], or data mining [98] can cause such negative issues. For example, if we wish to modify an algorithm to make it applicable to a specific dataset while the algorithm has to take into account some more parameters than specified in the function given by the library, we run into the problem of transforming the algorithm, which turns out to be a challenging task. Moreover, external software could be a solution, in particular, for data preprocessing but it is questionable if the external software is able to work with the data format and which kind of new data is produced. Even more, we cannot easily call an external software from the dashboard, we have to guarantee that this software is accessible and puts the preprocessed data to the right place to make it loadable into the visualization tool. An example would be a statistics software that is given a table with numeric values and that returns classical values related to the median, standard deviation, or variance, just to mention a few.

Exercises

- Exercise 6.2.1.1: Integrate two Plotly diagrams into a dashboard and connect them. This could be a scatter plot on which an axis interval is selected while the distribution of the points in the selected interval is shown as a histogram.
- Exercise 6.2.1.2: Integrate a drop-down menu in a dashboard that lets you execute external software, for example, a statistics tool.

6.2.2 Integrated development environments (IDEs)

There is a list of integrated development environments (Section 3.2.3) for implementing Python code for interactive visualization tools and dashboards. Some of the prominent and oftentimes recommended ones are PyCharm and Spyder, however, there are some others. Although one IDE might be powerful and user-friendly for one developer it might be the opposite effect for the other developer. The rule of thumb is that everybody should work with an environment that meets one's needs best in order to efficiently and effectively create the dashboard. The biggest problem with IDEs is the fact that they are overloaded with functions and features that it is hard for the newcomer to immediately understand all the provided functions and features. There is definitely a learning curve for the newcomers; hence it is recommended to start with one IDE and try to implement and debug the code with the provided IDE features, but once the IDE is fully understood, it might be a good advice to, at least, try another IDE. However, this can be a challenge since the developer has already created some kind of mental map for the one IDE, and it is quite difficult, but not impossible, to also learn the functions and features provided by another IDE.

If the developer is working alone during the dashboard design and implementation it is actually not a big issue to change the IDE from time to time. However, if the developer is working in a larger project, collaborating with other developers it can be challenging to just take the IDE that one desires. Here, the developer is typically provided an environment with which all others are familiar to avoid ugly side effects during the implementation phase. One powerful but also feature-overloaded tool is GitHub (Section 3.2.4), providing additional functions like a version control working in a common code repository to see the changes and modifications of all developers in the code, to archive those changes, and in the worst case, to rebuild an earlier running version of the code. Those code repositories provide a wealth of additional tools today, to make software development a successful and time-efficient endeavor since software development can cost a lot of money and might include various other cost-intensive resources. Finally, if we work in a more or less isolated fashion to create a very simple dashboard for our own purposes, a simple Jupyter Notebook might be the best option to avoid many of the aforementioned challenges during the implementation phase.

Exercises

- Exercise 6.2.2.1: Try several IDEs to implement a dashboard. Make a table of desired features and briefly explain which IDE is best for your purposes. Which one would you recommend to a newcomer, which one to a professional Python developer?
- Exercise 6.2.2.2: Start a dashboard project in GitHub and get familiar with the functions and features there.

6.2.3 Developers and experience levels

In some situations the designed dashboards, we are planning to implement are already quite complex, meaning the developers need a lot of experience to integrate all the functionality and visual outputs in the right place. For this, we need a profound knowledge of Dash, Python, and Plotly with all its ingredients like Dash core components, Dash HTML components, CSS, and the callback mechanism. Some developers might have experience in programming but come from a different programming language than Python, and hence, they have to adjust to the new situation. However, from the already taught lectures in programming, visualization, and dashboard design [52] we know that the learning curve is not that steep, even for nonexperts or even newcomers in the field. It is a good advice to start with simple dashboards with just a handful of functions and features and extend such an interactive tool step-by-step, with an increasing number of functions and also with a higher complexity level related to the callback mechanisms and the way the visualizations and algorithmic analyses play together. In particular, the linking between visualizations can be a challenging programming task for developers who are nonexperts.

Working in a collaborative way for a larger and more complex project can bring into play even more challenges since each developer might have a different level of experience, stemming from another kind of programming language and programming paradigm. Hence, it is advised to find a suitable consensus before starting with the implementation in order to make the interactive visualization tool in form of a dashboard to a success. After the design phase, the involved developers should discuss the ingredients and who will take the different roles during the implementation phase. This strategy can actually be communicated and controlled by using GitHub for collaborative development. Moreover, version control is helpful to see what the others did and to step back to an earlier version in case a code iteration was not as successful as desired. But still, finding a programming consensus between many developers themselves can be a challenge since not all of them might be open to adjust to a given or new programming situation.

Exercises

- Exercise 6.2.3.1: Discuss the programming languages you are familiar with. What are the benefits and drawbacks of those programming languages?
- Exercise 6.2.3.2: How would you start a collaboration with other developers in order to create a successful tool based on a more or less effortless development phase?

6.2.4 Operating systems

Actually, we consider the most popular operating systems here which are Windows, Linux, and MacOS. Programming in Python works quite smoothly under all operating systems. But still, there are some negative issues we should be aware of. Those are, for example, that some libraries might behave differently on each operating system, hence it is recommended to test the dashboard not only for the available web browser (Section 6.2.6) but even under the available operating systems. Otherwise, the divergence issue can lead to unwanted side effects. Which operating system is best cannot be answered easily. It depends on the camp of developers. One camp is more Windows-related, the other one tends to use Linux. Even others, but less, use MacOS, but still, the recommendation is to not adapt to another operating system but try to get it running under your operating system, even if you think that the software might fail or misbehave under other operating systems.

The whole thing might get tricky if the software is implemented in a collaborative way with various developers, all having different operating systems on their machines. This problem here could be that the code does not really work on one machine or the other since the operating system in use is some kind of mixture of systems. Also, from the installation perspective it can be harder to get the integrated development environments (IDEs) running on MacOS, which we learned from our own experiences in various student courses. However, in the end, we got the IDEs running on each platform, but to be honest it costed some more time in some situations. When using several IDEs and several operating systems, the cross-platform effect can cause serious challenges for the programmer, even more in situations in which third-party tools or libraries are integrated as well. The more ingredients we include in this implementation cocktail, the more bottlenecks, we will typically be confronted with, however, there is always a solution, the only issue here is that it might be a waste of time to get it running in the end.

Exercises

- Exercise 6.2.4.1: Make a literature research on the web to find the positive and negative issues when comparing Windows and Linux operating systems with respect to dashboard design.
- Exercise 6.2.4.2: Compare a Windows and a Linux operating system with respect to the visual appearance and interactive functionality of the same dashboard code. Can you find any differences?

6.2.5 Internet connection and servers

If we plan to provide a web-based dashboard solution, that is, an interactive visualization tool that is accessible from everywhere on earth [61] where we have a stable internet connection and a web browser, we come across further challenges apart from those with respect to the design rules and the standard implementation for a local tool, running only on one's own machine. One big issue can be real-time data that has to be accessed in regular time rates, like every second, every minute, or every hour. This demands for a server that provides fast access to such data in order to keep up with the changing data over time. In particular, if further advanced algorithms run they have to update the data in an algorithmically processed form to provide solutions to tasks at hand, for example, a clustering, grouping, or ordering of a dataset that is changing over time. If the internet connection is unstable or slow with respect to transmitted data our algorithms and our visualizations might run into problems, that is, not showing the least update or not running smoothly over time. It may be noted that the dashboard itself might run on a different server than the data that the dashboard is processing and visually depicting.

This is a suitable scenario, but we have to be aware of the fact that if one of the servers is not running properly, the dashboard itself might suffer. In case the data server is not working, we might come up with a local (not up-to-date) dataset that is shown for the users instead of the real-time data until the data server is back again. If the dashboard server is not working this might be the bigger evil.

From an implementation and resources perspective, we definitely need more knowledge about programming aspects, in particular, web-based programming, requiring to understand client-server architectures. However, Dash, Python, and Plotly are powerful concepts that take away the burden from us in this implementation direction. The Heroku server (Section 3.4.1) was a good alternative until November 28, 2022. After that date, the service was not offered for free anymore but instead a low-cost alternative replaced the originally very user-friendly concept. Consequently, the costs for setting up a server or deploying the dashboard on a server can become a serious issue, in particular, if the dashboard has to run over longer time periods or if the data itself with which the dashboard is working has to be provided on the same server. There is definitely a limit in terms of dataset sizes as well as algorithmic operations that run on such a server. As a recommendation, it can be a good advice to not care about the server issue when designing and implementing a dashboard as a priority aspect, but concentrate on the server aspect later on. If the dashboard is running locally, getting it running remotely on the web is an option for which we can find various solutions.

Exercises

- Exercise 6.2.5.1: What are the typical challenges when building dashboards for a real-time dataset from an internet connection and server perspective?
- Exercise 6.2.5.2: Search for possible server solutions when creating web-based interactive visualization tools for real-time data.

6.2.6 Web browsers

Since dashboards can be regarded as some kind of web pages, we can open them in a standard web browser. There are several of them, all having slightly different visual appearances, hence, it is a wise idea to check the appearance of a dashboard at least on the standard most popular web browsers. Most of the browsers even have a variety of built-in tools and functionality, which can cause troubles with respect to working with an interactive visualization tool in the form of a dashboard. Sometimes, the loading of the built-in tools causes performance issues, hence the slow performance is not caused by the dashboard but actually comes from the browser side which is sometimes hard to locate. These effects might even be blamed on older browser versions, consequently, a good idea is to have running the latest version of a web browser. This also comes with the problem that even if the dashboard ran a few weeks ago, it might show up completely differently today which can be caused by other browser versions. It is a good advice to keep up with the browser versions and to check the dashboard from time to time on the newer versions to understand if the functionality and features are still the same as a time ago. If this is not the case, the dashboard developers might have to adapt the code to get back the old visual appearance, interaction techniques, and algorithmic functions. Popular web browsers are, by the way, Google Chrome, Firefox, Microsoft Edge, Opera, or Safari, just to mention a few.

An extension to the code brings into play modifications in the functionality, as a consequence, it is a good advice to test whether the dashboard is still running in the most popular web browser or if this extension has a bad impact on some of the features. Apart from the features such an extension can also have an impact on the performance, sometimes the extension itself is the bottleneck, for example, when changing from one library to another one with a similar functionality or when actually implementing a new algorithm that has not been tested before. But typically, this issue is caused by the algorithm itself, not by the web browser. The biggest challenge is mostly to locate the cause of the performance issues. Is it coming from the code itself or is it coming from the web browser or even a library that causes trouble when used together with a specific algorithmic or visual feature. A good advice to reduce browser issues can be to clean the cache which might still contain some problematic data. Moreover, the cookies might bring additional challenges into play. Take a closer look at all browser-related aspects in case the dashboard is not showing up properly. Before digging too deep into one browser start the dashboard with several popular browsers to see if it is running at all, or if the code itself might be the problem.

Exercises

- Exercise 6.2.6.1: Check your own dashboard in the most popular web browsers like Mozilla Firefox, Google Chrome, Microsoft Edge, Opera, and Safari. Can you find any differences between the web browsers?
- Exercise 6.2.6.2: Inspect the diagrams in your dashboard and if they are visually depicted differently in each of the aforementioned web browsers.

6.3 Challenges during runtime

We can design and implement the best dashboard ever, but on a piece of paper, everything is fine while running the code in the end can uncover serious problems which we have not been aware of before. Such challenges during runtime can come in a variety of forms including data aspects with respect to the data format, size, or structure, the algorithmic processes [59, 62] with runtime complexities or NP-completeness [102], the visual output with a combination of visual variables that are not suitable to show the entire or a large part of a dataset, and even perceptual issues ranging from color blindness problems, over visual acuity issues, to display limitations asking the question whether a dashboard should run on a small-scale smart phone, a medium-scale laptop or computer display, or a large-scale high-resolution powerwall [210]. All of those aspects also include interaction techniques that might suffer from one or several of those negative issues. In some situations, we cannot even avoid such problems, for example, if the data has a size with which our designed and implemented dashboard cannot keep up. This means we definitely run into data, algorithmic, visual, and perceptual challenges, no matter what we do. Consequently, the data itself has to be filtered or preprocessed in a way to allow a dashboard to efficiently and effectively show it to our users.

In this section, we discuss the challenges with respect to data scalability (Section 6.3.1) focusing on the data format, the structure, and the size. Moreover, we take a look at typical algorithmic issues that can happen when processing and transforming data (Section 6.3.2), for example, when there is no efficient algorithm for solving a problem optimally, but rather heuristically. From a visualization perspective it makes sense to think about the number of data elements that can be visually depicted on the display, that is, visual scalability asks the question whether a dashboard can keep up with visualizing the increasing size of data (Section 6.3.3). Also of interest are challenges related to human perception, for example, taking into account how large our display can be or how many colors can be perceived and distinguished (Section 6.3.4). All of those challenges play a big role during the design and implementation processes of an interactive visualization tool, also in the specific case of a dashboard.

6.3.1 Data scalability

With today's technologies, we are able to measure, record, and store vast amounts of data in a multitude of data formats spread over several files and databases. Such typically heterogeneous data is mostly related to the term big data [24] including data aspects like volume, velocity, veracity, value, variability, and variety. These aspects bring into play various challenges with which an interactive visualization or visual analytics tool has to keep up to be a powerful, efficient, and effective candidate for data analysis, data exploration, and data visualization. The data scalability aspect does not only include the size of the data (as mentioned earlier) but also the rate of change, that is, in a dynamically updated dataset, a real-time dataset, we must be aware of the problem that the data can change at infinitesimally small changing rates, ranging from milliseconds, to seconds, to minutes, to hours, to days, and so on, or even at much smaller rates. This time granularity is oftentimes aggregated into another coarser granularity to let the data analysis in form of algorithms keep up with the incoming data chunks from time to time. However, the question is whether the algorithm is still able to compute the results fast enough, that is, faster than the data is coming in; otherwise, the results might already be outdated.

Another big issue with data scalability is the fact about how many data sources can be combined and how much data has to be stored after such a combination. Moreover, when combining or linking data sources we typically need some kind of unique key with which we can start connecting the data sources in a reliable way. The linking of the data sources cannot happen during runtime since this will always cost valuable resources that are needed elsewhere. In most of the situations, the linking of data sources can be done as a preprocess, that is, before or even during working with the dashboard while the results of such a preprocessing are stored to use them later after the preprocessing is finished. Once the results are computed, and the data are available, we do not need the same preprocessing again, hence the computing time is not wasted again. However, a big problem here is that we typically do not know what and how to preprocess the data. The users can actually request any kind of data transformation and we do not know the behavior of most of our users beforehand.

Exercises

- Exercise 6.3.1.1: What is the biggest dataset that your dashboard can work with? If you do not have your own dashboard, check the dataset size for the dashboard examples in Chapter 5.
- Exercise 6.3.1.2: Discuss the problem for analyzing and visualizing real-time data.

6.3.2 Algorithmic scalability

Algorithms play a crucial role in data analysis and also in visualization. They have an impact on the interactive responsiveness of a visualization tool. The challenge is to do not let the users wait too long for a solution, but, in some cases, a fast solution cannot be computed that easily. It is not an issue of the programming style it is more an issue of the algorithmic problem itself. There are some algorithms that are said to be NP-hard [163] which actually means that an optimal solution cannot be computed in a few steps. We have to wait for a long time to get the optimum, even if we had a machine with a lot of computing power. If the problem instance is increased a little bit, our powerful machine cannot keep up with the little bit bigger problem again. Those algorithmic problems are also called intractable for the computer [102]. Hence, we are typically not interested in an optimum but we more or less try to compute a good but not optimal solution which is generated by a heuristical approach which has a much lower runtime complexity.

Sometimes we cannot judge the runtime of an algorithm in terms of processing steps, for example as a mathematical function f with input n and output $f(n)$. But we can still get an impression about the runtime complexity based on the dataset size as input parameter. The idea here is to execute the program several times for a given dataset size and increase the dataset sizes step-by-step. We can measure the time taken to process the dataset of a certain size for any kind of included algorithm or even the rendering routine for a visualization technique. Finally, we plot the dataset size on the average runtime which gives some kind of mathematical function with a certain shape. This shape of the underlying curve can be used to judge which function the runtime is following. There are several options (maybe with some outliers) but the general curve can uncover the runtime behavior of a linear, quadratic, cubic, or even exponential function. Asking now the question about a still suitable dataset size for which the dashboard is algorithmically scalable can be answered by looking at the y-axis and the corresponding runtime while following the line back to the curve, then reading the dataset size value from the x-axis. But still, a challenge with the performance measure can be that an algorithm will behave differently each time for the same dataset, hence, the only way to create such a runtime plot is by averaging, but again each individual run can differ from the average curve a lot, hence, such a prediction might not be very reliable.

Exercises

- Exercise 6.3.2.1: Read a dataset with your dashboard and measure the time it takes until the data is read and parsed. Increase the dataset size by copying it 2, 3, 4, 5, and 10 times and append the copies. Measure the times for all those dataset sizes and create a line plot for showing the performance of the reading and parsing algorithm.
- Exercise 6.3.2.2: Is there a difference in terms of performances for the diagrams integrated into the dashboards in Chapter 5?

6.3.3 Visual scalability

The number of data elements to be displayed can grow to an immense amount, too many to show all of them at the same time in a nonaggregated fashion. This is actually the challenge, to show as much data as possible but still be able to detect visual patterns and anomalies in the data. Once the data reaches a certain size we cannot simply show all data elements, but we might show them in an aggregated fashion or we could allow filtering techniques to get rid of the irrelevant ones. This comes with the problem that we do not know what to aggregate or how to filter the data since we typically do not know where the most important data elements are located in the dataset or what the aggregation level will be. Hence, we need some interaction techniques [258] that help to rapidly modify our views and the data portions in the display [55]. Such a step-by-step exploration can be helpful but still for really huge data sources, interaction alone cannot help to get rid of the visual scalability issue. Each visualization tool reaches its limits at a certain dataset size, at this stage more advanced algorithms are required to reduce the amount of data to the most needed one, for example, dimensionality reduction techniques [94] project high-dimensional data to a lower dimension with the goal to preserve the structure in the data somehow. Moreover, also clustering approaches can help to derive patterns in the data that we would not detect otherwise. Hence, clustering can also add some benefit to visual scalability, just by restructuring, grouping, and ordering the data.

Visual clutter is the state in which too many data elements are shown or even their disorganization leads to performance issues when solving certain tasks [202]. This effect is happening in most of the situations we have visual scalability issues. Even if a visualization technique is powerful for a small number of elements, it can be useless for a growing number of data elements. Then, we might consider another more visually scalable visualization technique for the same kind of data but in a more scalable fashion. A famous example can be found for graph or network data for which node-link diagrams exist, but those only visually scale for around 20 vertices with a few edges. Matrix-like visualizations are better in this case since they can be scaled down to pixel size, even if they do not allow path-related tasks anymore [106]. Such a situation can be found in many application fields, typically based on a certain data type, like network data as we mentioned before. The idea is to provide a visualization technique from a repertoire of many techniques for the same type of data but one that supports task solutions in data exploration for as many tasks as possible, however, the task with the highest priority should be under the supported tasks in any case.

Exercises

- Exercise 6.3.3.1: Imagine you had a network consisting of your friends and the relations they have with each other. How would you visualize such a dataset, and how visually scalable is your technique?
- Exercise 6.3.3.2: For histograms, we can include really many data values, but at some point, they also reach a limit in terms of visual scalability. What can we do with the shown data values to get a more scalable approach?

6.3.4 Perceptual scalability

Even if the data, algorithmic, and visual scalability issues are not existing, for example, because the data itself is not big and has a clear structure, we might still run into the problem of perceptual scalability. This can happen if we have to deal with a multitude of colors, for categorical data, for example, too many that the visual observer cannot distinguish them anymore to reliably and efficiently solve comparison tasks. Although there is a huge number of different colors, only a few of them can be visually separated, for example, in a scenario in which data elements use similar colors and are visually represented at locations in the display that are far apart [245, 246]. This effect can also be seen in the famous Rubik cube illusion. Color is not the only challenge here, also the size of the display itself can be a problem. If the display is too small we might not be able to read the visual depiction of a dataset, if the display is too large, our visual field is not large enough to see all visual elements in one view. Also, the human observer can suffer from visual deficiencies or color blindness, not being able to distinguish colors or read text in any acceptable font. Hence, wearing glasses or contact lenses can be a solution, but they will not solve all visual deficiency problems for the spectator. In the end, we need an advanced user study [48, 57, 60] to find out which negative perceptual issues exist for each individual person who is using our dashboard.

Also, effects related to the visual memory can be regarded as perceptual issues. For example, we can only remember a limited number of objects in our mind [229]. This is important for comparison tasks if we have to identify visual patterns first, remember them in our short term memory, to compare them with other visual patterns in a visual scene that can be found at a different location in the display. To detect differences between two visual scenes, we typically run into the problem called change blindness [115], that is, the visual observers cannot easily find such differences unless they really pop out from the display like in a preattentive kind of visual depiction. Moreover, if we do not pay attention to a visual scene, typically a dynamic scene, it can be quite hard to later tell an experimenter whether a visual pattern was present or not. Examples for such perceptual effects are demonstrated in the door study or the invisible gorilla [105, 218]. An object or a person is not recognized due to the fact that the attention was paid to something else because a task related to that had to be answered. In visualization this can be a problem for animated diagrams [233] in which we might miss important information because we paid attention to something else.

Exercises

- Exercise 6.3.4.1: Discuss the design of a dashboard with respect to differently large displays, that is, a small-scale smart phone, a medium-scale computer monitor, and a large-scale powerwall display.

- Exercise 6.3.4.2: What would you modify in your standard dashboard design to make it usable by visually impaired people who have issues with visual deficiency, visual acuity, and color blindness?

6.4 Testing Challenges

After the design phase and either during or after the implementation phase, we have to test the created dashboard. This is important to find out whether the functionality and features are available but also if those have performance issues with respect to the integrated algorithms but also with respect to the response time, accuracy, or visual attention behavior of real users. All of those insights can help to detect design and implementation flaws to find possible ways to improve the dashboard. Hence, it might be the better but also more expensive solution to do the testing from time to time and not only in the end after the final product is ready. Testing costs a lot of time and can even lead to a complete redesign and, consequently, a reimplementation of the entire or at least parts of the visualization tool. Testing is challenging since it should include real users as well as software-related parameters and environments [39, 82], for example, in case of a dashboard accessible online we must test the web browsers in use as well as operating systems and the like. Moreover, the users themselves can stem from any part in the world with different cultures, languages, signage, symbols, reading habits, and many more. In some situations, we cannot even work with real data since the data in use is quite small and artificially making it larger is not a real-world situation.

In this section, we will take a look at some aspects to be tested in a dashboard before it can be made available to real users. We discuss online accessibility, that is, how the data can be accessed, processed, and displayed in a remote web-based approach (Section 6.4.1). The runtime performance also stands in focus of testing. A low performance of the algorithms can cause delays in the interaction, and hence, the user-friendliness can suffer from that (Section 6.4.2). Finally, we take into account, the human users with their perceptual and visual abilities when using the dashboard. This brings into play again some challenges with respect to user evaluation, controlled versus uncontrolled, with or without eye tracking, small-scale versus crowdsourcing, or many other user study aspects (Section 6.4.3).

6.4.1 Online accessibility

Testing if users can access our dashboard online is a challenging task since we do not know anything about their operating systems, environments, or web browsers. What we can do is to record user feedback and track their clicking behavior while at the same time storing information about their personal details as well as the system properties they are working in. If we had enough information about many users, we might hypothesize why certain users with a certain system property are not confident with the dashboard while others are. This kind of user evaluation can provide valuable insights about possible negative issues that our online users have. This perspective is on the global dashboard but even locally we might find out if certain components like drop-down menus, sliders, or text fields as well as Plotly diagrams are working based on user behavior, however, this is some kind of uncontrolled study setting since we do not know much about our study participants. A large number of users can, on the other hand, give already some intuition about what might be a problematic feature worth investigating and improving in the future.

Further issues can be the location on earth that might have an impact on the accessibility. Typically, the internet is not that fast everywhere and this can be problematic when large datasets have to be transmitted to show results for a server side exploration for example. The speed of the connection can have an influence on users' behavior data, that is, when we track mouse behavior, for example, the mouse movement might be dependent on the interactive responsiveness of the dashboard, a fact that we actually do not see but what we might request from our users as qualitative feedback. For most of the dashboards, the data that is shown in the dashboard is not stored on the dashboard server but rather on a data server. This is a good idea, but on the other hand, we are dependent on two servers for which reliable connections are required to keep the online accessibility criterion stable. If the data server does not provide the data fast enough, we have to react somehow on this problem by maybe only showing data elements at a more coarse-grained temporal rate. On the other hand, this might lead to missing data elements which is actually not the problem of the dashboard itself but rather of the data server that is not providing the required data chunks fast enough for our algorithmic or visual explorations.

Exercises

- Exercise 6.4.1.1: Test the explained dashboards in Chapter 5 from different locations, for example, from home and from your office at a company.
- Exercise 6.4.1.2: Add a text field as a dash core component in each of the dashboards in Chapter 5 and request feedback from your online users. How can you find insights in such qualitative user feedback.

6.4.2 Runtime performance

As already mentioned earlier, a dashboard can be very simple with only a few functions, but on the other hand, it can be a quite complex system consisting of algorithms and interactive visualizations like in a visual analytics tool that is typically based on the data stemming from a specific application area and on users' tasks at hand. In the most complex scenario, it is hard to judge whether it is scalable or not, that is, arguing about runtime performance can be a challenging task since we do not have clear input and output parameters used in asymptotic runtime functions. This means we have to let run our tool several times for the same dataset and measure the time taken. By increasing the dataset sizes, we can estimate what the runtime performance will be depending on the dataset sizes. This strategy is a good idea but due to the fact that our dashboard is already quite complex containing various functions and features, the measured runtimes will always reflect the total times. Hence, it is a wise idea to test the individual components separately. This means each algorithm has to be tested for the growing dataset sizes to find out where in the code the bottlenecks are located. This is a tedious task, as already mentioned, there are various algorithms in a complex dashboard if this is understood as a visual analytics system. However, this is the only way to understand the runtimes in a real scenario. It may be noted that the best way to explore the runtime performance over dataset sizes is by plotting them in a line chart to see whether there is a linear, quadratic, cubic, or exponential behavior, for example.

Again, the testing is not only dependent on the algorithms themselves. As we have seen in Section 6.4.1, the internet connection might also play a crucial role in such runtimes, that is, how fast an algorithm can access its data to process it. For example, having an unstructured dataset with various data elements and requesting a clustering algorithm that runs server side can compute a clustering solution for us, but we never know whether the runtime is purely based on the algorithm; instead, the biggest part of the runtime can also be caused by transmitting data. Hence, it is a wise idea to first understand the functioning of an algorithm and how and where it is implemented, that is, where it is running: client or server side. In some situations, the dataset is already too large to wait for an algorithm to terminate. In this scenario it is good to work in the opposite direction, that is, reducing the size of the data instead of increasing it, and then computing the runtimes. This can give us a natural limitation for the largest dataset that can be processed, transformed, and analyzed by our dashboard.

Exercises

- Exercise 6.4.2.1: Implement different versions of a sorting algorithm and integrate that into a dashboard. Measure the runtime performances under different circumstances like operating system, web browser, or the fact that the algorithm runs on the server or on the client side.
- Exercise 6.4.2.2: Which options do we have when the runtime of an algorithm integrated into a dashboard is too high, that is, leading to a noninteractively responsive tool? Discuss!

6.4.3 User performance and evaluation

The best idea to test a dashboard for its functionality and features is to ask real users. Each of the users has a different experience, ranging from novices to real experts. Moreover, the users can have a set of properties that hinder them more or less to properly use the dashboard, for example the visual acuity, visual deficiency, color blindness, or other visually or physically impaired issues can occur that all have an impact on the user performance [25]. To measure the usefulness of a dashboard we have a quite long list of points, however each of the measured data has to be evaluated, statistically, algorithmically, or visually to find insights in the user behavior to get an impression about possible design flaws in the dashboard, either with respect to the user interface, to the visualization techniques, to the interactions, or to the algorithmic concepts. Possible metrics under investigation are the following:

- Qualitative feedback
  - Verbal: Spoken words can be a good source for finding the bottlenecks and design flaws in a dashboard. They should be recorded during a study to not disturb the study participant [129].

– Gestures: Gestures can show if a person is confident with a dashboard or not, based on the movements of the fingers, hands, and arms [162].
– Facial expressions: The face is an important means to derive insights from the confidence of a dashboard user. Smiling, laughing, crying, and the like, all of them carry some meaning worth exploring [7].
– Textual feedback: Written words are probably the clearest way to get feedback in a qualitative form [219]; however, they are not that fine-grained as verbal, gesture, or facial expression feedback.

• Quantitative feedback

– Response times: Giving study participants concrete tasks can also be a good strategy to measure and record how long it takes until they come up with an answer. The longer it takes the less clear the task might have been [60].
– Error rates: A similar measure might be the error rates but this time we do not record the time taken but more whether the task was answered correctly, or sometimes even to what extent it was answered correctly, given as some kind of correctness probability.

• Spatio-temporal user behavior

– Eye movements: Recording the movement of the eyes by using an eye tracking device is a powerful idea, but the recorded eye movement data have a spatiotemporal nature [40, 44] which makes a statistical analysis quite difficult. We could even generate derived metrics from this kind of data like saccade lengths/orientations, fixation durations, AOIs, time to first fixation, and many more [87, 123].
– Mouse movements/clicks: Tracking the movements of the computer mouse and additional mouse operations like clicks, drag-and-drop, hover, and the like can be an additional spatiotemporal measure to the eye movements. Mouse data is easier to collect since each user is equipped with one, eye trackers are not that prominent and typically much more expensive.
– Body movements: Another useful measure is given by the body movements, for example, in a virtual environment (VR), immersive analytics, or large-display environment [210] in which users can freely walk around.

- Physiological measures

  - Blood pressure: Blood values or properties can give insights in how stressed a study participant is [136]. However, measuring such values requires a medical assistant and makes the study setup much more complicated and ethically problematic.
  - Pupil dilation: Eye tracking devices can also measure pupil dilations [14] that give insights into a variety of aspects, one of which is how much attention is focused on a certain display area.
  - Galvanic skin response: Another useful measure is the galvanic skin response [131] that might provide insights into further body-related aspects, for example, what the stress level or the sport activity level is.

These are just a few important measurements about user behavior but there are many more. The biggest challenge here is the evaluation, and analysis of all the recorded user data, that is, finding insights in such study data to improve the dashboard design, its implementation, and finally, the usefulness and user-friendliness.

Exercises

- Exercise 6.4.3.1: Ask 20 people to use one of your created dashboards. Give them a concrete task and measure the time taken and the error rate. Ask them for verbal feedback. Which insights can you find in the recorded user study data to improve your dashboard? Are there any design flaws?
- Exercise 6.4.3.2: What are the challenges before, during, or after a user study? Discuss!

7

Conclusion

In this book, we described a combination of concepts to help design and implement dashboards for interactive visualization tools. The book is actually written for bachelor and master students with not much experience in information visualization, visual analytics, interaction design, Python programming, and dashboard implementation. The book is organized in a way to be studied in its completeness, step-by-step, but also as a chapter-wise introduction to one or more concepts. We also added various references to other literature that is related to one or more of the topics in the book. In many cases, we recommend to read further details in the corresponding literature since our book cannot cover all topics and close all gaps in all of the mighty concepts with a focus on visualization, interaction, design, and programming. To repeat the content of each subsection, we provided a few exercises at the end of each subsection. The topic of the exercises always has a strong relation to the subsection in which they can be found. For questions about exercise understanding or their solution, as well as topics from the book, we recommend the reader to send emails to the book authors.

We started the book with introducing and motivating the general idea of using dashboards for interactive visualization for exploratory data analysis, for example. Moreover, we also mentioned the use of algorithms to handle datasets consisting of several data types. A dashboard can be understood as a webpage containing a graphical user interface that is composed of the interface following more or less prominent interface design rules as well as visualization techniques following visual design rules. Only their combination and interplay can create a powerful and interactive visualization tool, together with advanced, efficient, and effective algorithms that are powerful enough to process static or dynamic (even real-time) data with the best user experience possible. Before starting with the implementation phase to get a promising dashboard result, we also have to take into account a prototyping step to create a mockup on which the implementors' programming steps are based.

There are various ways to build an interactive visualization or visual analytics tool. In this book, we describe one possible way to get a solution, without mentioning that this solution is the best one. Python, Dash, and Plotly are powerful concepts to get a dashboard running, but we have to know how those ingredients have to be put together, which is a tedious task for someone who has not much programming experience and maybe also not much visualization experience. We showed how to install the most required tools, and we even gave some insights into the deployment of the running dashboard, that is, uploading the code to a server to make it accessible online, from everywhere on the earth where we have an internet connection and a web browser. For the newcomers we even introduced the programming language Python step-by-step, the advanced programmer can just jump to the next chapter in the book. To tap the full potential of the book, the reader is recommended to study the dashboard examples with hand-drawn mockups, Python code, and a screenshot of the running example, as well as detailed explanations of the Python code. Finally, we conclude the book by looking into challenges and limitations.

References

[1] Moataz Abdelaal, Marcel Hlawatsch, Michael Burch, and Daniel Weiskopf. Clustering for stacked edge splatting. In Fabian Beck, Carsten Dachsbacher, and Filip Sadlo, editors, *Proceedings of 23rd International Symposium on Vision, Modeling, and Visualization, VMV*, pages 127–134. Eurographics Association, 2018.

[2] Alfie Abdul-Rahman, Karl J. Proctor, Brian Duffy, and Min Chen. Repeated measures design in crowdsourcing-based experiments for visualization. In Heidi Lam, Petra Isenberg, Tobias Isenberg, and Michael Sedlmair, editors, *Proceedings of the Fifth Workshop on Beyond Time and Errors: Novel Evaluation Methods for Visualization, BELIV*, pages 95–102. ACM, 2014.

[3] Amir Ahmad and Shehroz S. Khan. Survey of state-of-the-art mixed data clustering algorithms. *IEEE Access*, 7:31883–31902, 2019.

[4] Wolfgang Aigner, Silvia Miksch, Heidrun Schumann, and Christian Tominski. *Visualization of Time-Oriented Data*. Human-Computer Interaction Series. Springer, 2011.

[5] Badr Al-Harbi, Ali Alturki, and Adel Ahmed. An application of measuring aesthetics in visualization. In Yuhua Luo, editor, *Proceedings of the 13th Conference on Cooperative Design, Visualization, and Engineering, CDVE*, volume 9929 of *Lecture Notes in Computer Science*, pages 332–339, 2016.

[6] Aretha Barbosa Alencar, Maria Cristina Ferreira de Oliveira, and Fernando Vieira Paulovich. Seeing beyond reading: a survey on visual text analytics. *WIREs Data Mining and Knowledge Discovery*, 2(6):476–492, 2012.

[7] Abdulrhman Alharbi. Analyzing facial expressions and body gestures through multimodal metaphors: An intelligent e-feedback interface. In Masaaki Kurosu, editor, *Proceedings of the International Conference on Human-Computer Interaction, HCI*, volume 13303 of *Lecture Notes in Computer Science*, pages 291–302. Springer, 2022.

[8] Gennady L. Andrienko, Natalia V. Andrienko, Michael Burch, and Daniel Weiskopf. Visual analytics methodology for eye movement studies. *IEEE Transactions on Visualization and Computer Graphics*, 18(12):2889–2898, 2012.

[9] Daniel Archambault and Helen C. Purchase. The "map" in the mental map: Experimental results in dynamic graph drawing. *International Journal on Human-Computer Studies*, 71(11):1044–1055, 2013.

[10] Daniel W. Archambault and Helen C. Purchase. The mental map and memorability in dynamic graphs. In Helwig Hauser, Stephen G. Kobourov, and Huamin Qu, editors, *Proceedings of the IEEE Pacific Visualization Symposium, PacificVis*, pages 89–96. IEEE Computer Society, 2012.

[11] Noppadol Assavakamhaenghan, Waralee Tanaphantaruk, Ponlakit Suwanworaboon, Morakot Choetkiertikul, and Suppawong Tuarob. Quantifying effectiveness of team recommendation for collaborative software development. *Automated Software Engineering*, 29(2):51, 2022.

[12] Mirjam Augstein and Thomas Neumayr. A human-centered taxonomy of interaction modalities and devices. *Interacting with Computers*, 31(1):27–58, 2019.

[13] Benjamin Bach, Euan Freeman, Alfie Abdul-Rahman, Cagatay Turkay, Saiful Khan, Yulei Fan, and Min Chen. Dashboard design patterns. *IEEE Transactions on Visualization and Computer Graphics*, 29(1):342–352, 2023.

[14] Per Bækgaard, John Paulin Hansen, Katsumi Minakata, and I. Scott MacKenzie. A fitts' law study of pupil dilations in a head-mounted display. In Krzysztof Krejtz and Bonita Sharif, editors, *Proceedings of the 11th ACM Symposium on Eye Tracking Research & Applications, ETRA*, pages 32:1–32:5. ACM, 2019.

[15] Moshe Bar and Maital Neta. Humans prefer curved visual objects. *Psychological Science*, 17(8):645–648, 2006.

[16] Dirk Bäumer, Walter R. Bischofberger, Horst Lichter, and Heinz Züllighoven. User interface prototyping - concepts, tools, and experience. In H. Dieter Rombach, T. S. E. Maibaum, and Marvin V. Zelkowitz, editors, *Proceedings of the 18th International Conference on Software Engineering*, pages 532–541. IEEE Computer Society, 1996.

[17] Fabian Beck. Software feathers - figurative visualization of software metrics. In Robert S. Laramee, Andreas Kerren, and José Braz, editors,

Proceedings of the 5th International Conference on Information Visualization Theory and Applications, IVAPP, pages 5–16. SciTePress, 2014.

[18] Fabian Beck, Michael Burch, Stephan Diehl, and Daniel Weiskopf. A taxonomy and survey of dynamic graph visualization. *Computer Graphics Forum*, 36(1):133–159, 2017.

[19] Arnold Beckmann. Notations for exponentiation. *Theoretical Computer Science*, 288(1):3–19, 2002.

[20] Michael Behrisch, Benjamin Bach, Nathalie Henry Riche, Tobias Schreck, and Jean-Daniel Fekete. Matrix reordering methods for table and network visualization. *Computer Graphics Forum*, 35(3):693–716, 2016.

[21] Jacques Bertin. *Semiology of Graphics: Diagrams, Networks, Maps*. Wisconsin: University of Wisconsin Press, (first published in French in 1967 translated by William J. Berg in 1983), 1967.

[22] Jacques Bertin. *Graphics and Graphic Information Processing*. De Gruyter, Berlin. Translation:William J. Berg, Paul Scott, 1981.

[23] Jacques Bertin. *Semiology of Graphics - Diagrams, Networks, Maps*. ESRI, 2010.

[24] Nikos Bikakis, George Papastefanatos, and Olga Papaemmanouil. Big data exploration, visualization and analytics. *Big Data Research*, 18, 2019.

[25] Tanja Blascheck, Michael Burch, Michael Raschke, and Daniel Weiskopf. Challenges and perspectives in big eye-movement data visual analytics. In *Big Data Visual Analytics, BDVA*, pages 17–24. IEEE, 2015.

[26] Tanja Blascheck and Thomas Ertl. Towards analyzing eye tracking data for evaluating interactive visualization systems. In Heidi Lam, Petra Isenberg, Tobias Isenberg, and Michael Sedlmair, editors, *Proceedings of the Fifth Workshop on Beyond Time and Errors: Novel Evaluation Methods for Visualization, BELIV*, pages 70–77. ACM, 2014.

[27] Tanja Blascheck, Markus John, Kuno Kurzhals, Steffen Koch, and Thomas Ertl. VA^2: A visual analytics approach for evaluating visual analytics applications. *IEEE Transactions on Visualization and Computer Graphics*, 22(1):61–70, 2016.

[28] Marcus D. Bloice and Andreas Holzinger. A tutorial on machine learning and data science tools with python. In Andreas Holzinger, editor, *Machine Learning for Health Informatics - State-of-the-Art*

and Future Challenges, volume 9605 of *Lecture Notes in Computer Science*, pages 435–480. Springer, 2016.

[29] Marina Bloj and Monika Hedrich. Color perception. In Janglin Chen, Wayne Cranton, and Mark Fihn, editors, *Handbook of Visual Display Technology*, pages 171–178. Springer, 2012.

[30] Agnieszka Bojko. Informative or misleading? heatmaps deconstructed. In Julie A. Jacko, editor, *Proceedings of the Conference on Human-Computer Interaction, HCI*, volume 5610 of *Lecture Notes in Computer Science*, pages 30–39. Springer, 2009.

[31] Sergey Bolshchikov, Judith Somekh, Shay Mazor, Niva Wengrowicz, Mordechai Choder, and Dov Dori. Cognition-based visualization of the dynamics of conceptual models: The vivid OPM scene player. *Systems Engineering*, 18(5):431–440, 2015.

[32] David Borland and Russell M. Taylor II. Rainbow color map (still) considered harmful. *IEEE Computer Graphics and Applications*, 27(2):14–17, 2007.

[33] Nadia Boukhelifa, Waldo Cancino Ticona, Anastasia Bezerianos, and Evelyne Lutton. Evolutionary visual exploration: Evaluation with expert users. *Computer Graphics Forum*, 32(3):31–40, 2013.

[34] Jan Lauren Boyles and Eric Meyer. Letting the data speak. *Digital Journalism*, 4(7):944–954, 2016.

[35] Marc H. Brown. Exploring algorithms using balsa-ii. *Computer*, 21(5):14–36, 1988.

[36] Valentin Bruder, Christoph Müller, Steffen Frey, and Thomas Ertl. On evaluating runtime performance of interactive visualizations. *IEEE Transactions on Visualization and Computer Graphics*, 26(9):2848–2862, 2020.

[37] William Bugden and Ayman Diyab Alahmar. The safety and performance of prominent programming languages. *International Journal of Software Engineering and Knowledge Engineering*, 32(5):713–744, 2022.

[38] Michael Burch. The aesthetics of diagrams. In *Proceedings of the 10th Joint Conference on Computer Vision, Imaging and Computer Graphics Theory and Applications, (VISIGRAPP)*. SciTePress, 2015.

[39] Michael Burch. Visualizing software metrics in a software system hierarchy. In George Bebis, Richard Boyle, Bahram Parvin, Darko Koracin, Ioannis T. Pavlidis, Rogério Schmidt Feris, Tim McGraw, Mark Elendt, Regis Kopper, Eric D. Ragan, Zhao Ye, and Gunther H. Weber, editors, *Proceedings of 11th International Symposium on*

Advances in Visual Computing, ISVC, volume 9475 of *Lecture Notes in Computer Science*, pages 733–744. Springer, 2015.

[40] Michael Burch. Identifying similar eye movement patterns with t-sne. In Fabian Beck, Carsten Dachsbacher, and Filip Sadlo, editors, *Proceedings of the 23rd International Symposium on Vision, Modeling, and Visualization, VMV*, pages 111–118. Eurographics Association, 2018.

[41] Michael Burch. Interaction graphs: visual analysis of eye movement data from interactive stimuli. In Krzysztof Krejtz and Bonita Sharif, editors, *Proceedings of the 11th ACM Symposium on Eye Tracking Research & Applications, ETRA*, pages 89:1–89:5. ACM, 2019.

[42] Michael Burch. The importance of requirements engineering for teaching large visualization courses. In *Proceedings of 4th International Workshop on Learning from Other Disciplines for Requirements Engineering, D4RE@RE*, pages 6–10. IEEE, 2020.

[43] Michael Burch. Teaching eye tracking visual analytics in computer and data science bachelor courses. In Andreas Bulling, Anke Huckauf, Eakta Jain, Ralph Radach, and Daniel Weiskopf, editors, *Proceedings of the Symposium on Eye Tracking Research and Applications, ETRA*, pages 17:1–17:9. ACM, 2020.

[44] Michael Burch. *Eye Tracking and Visual Analytics*. River Publishers, 2022.

[45] Michael Burch. How students design visual interfaces for information visualization tools. In Michael Burch, Günter Wallner, and Daniel Limberger, editors, *Proceedings of the 15th International Symposium on Visual Information Communication and Interaction, VINCI*, pages 1:1–1:8. ACM, 2022.

[46] Michael Burch, Gennady L. Andrienko, Natalia V. Andrienko, Markus Höferlin, Michael Raschke, and Daniel Weiskopf. Visual task solution strategies in tree diagrams. In Sheelagh Carpendale, Wei Chen, and Seok-Hee Hong, editors, *Proceedings of IEEE Pacific Visualization Symposium, PacificVis*, pages 169–176. IEEE Computer Society, 2013.

[47] Michael Burch, Weidong Huang, Mathew Wakefield, Helen C. Purchase, Daniel Weiskopf, and Jie Hua. The state of the art in empirical user evaluation of graph visualizations. *IEEE Access*, 9:4173–4198, 2021.

[48] Michael Burch, Natalia Konevtsova, Julian Heinrich, Markus Höferlin, and Daniel Weiskopf. Evaluation of traditional, orthogonal, and radial

tree diagrams by an eye tracking study. *IEEE Transactions on Visualization and Computer Graphics*, 17(12):2440–2448, 2011.

[49] Michael Burch, Andreas Kull, and Daniel Weiskopf. AOI rivers for visualizing dynamic eye gaze frequencies. *Computer Graphics Forum*, 32(3):281–290, 2013.

[50] Michael Burch, Ayush Kumar, and Neil Timmermans. An interactive web-based visual analytics tool for detecting strategic eye movement patterns. In Krzysztof Krejtz and Bonita Sharif, editors, *Proceedings of the 11th ACM Symposium on Eye Tracking Research & Applications, ETRA*, pages 93:1–93:5. ACM, 2019.

[51] Michael Burch, Steffen Lohmann, Daniel Pompe, and Daniel Weiskopf. Prefix tag clouds. In *Proceedings of 17th International Conference on Information Visualisation, IV*, pages 45–50. IEEE Computer Society, 2013.

[52] Michael Burch and Elisabeth Melby. What more than a hundred project groups reveal about teaching visualization. *Journal of Visualization*, 23(5):895–911, 2020.

[53] Michael Burch, Tanja Munz, Fabian Beck, and Daniel Weiskopf. Visualizing work processes in software engineering with developer rivers. In *Proceedings of the 3rd IEEE Working Conference on Software Visualization, VISSOFT*, pages 116–124. IEEE Computer Society, 2015.

[54] Michael Burch, Michael Raschke, Adrian Zeyfang, and Daniel Weiskopf. A scalable visualization for dynamic data in software system hierarchies. In *Proceedings of the IEEE Working Conference on Software Visualization, VISSOFT*, pages 85–93. IEEE, 2017.

[55] Michael Burch and Hansjörg Schmauder. Challenges and perspectives of interacting with hierarchy visualizations on large-scale displays. In Andreas Kerren, Karsten Klein, and Yi-Na Li, editors, *Proceedings of the 11th International Symposium on Visual Information Communication and Interaction, VINCI*, pages 33–40. ACM, 2018.

[56] Michael Burch, Hansjörg Schmauder, Michael Raschke, and Daniel Weiskopf. Saccade plots. In Pernilla Qvarfordt and Dan Witzner Hansen, editors, *Proceedings of the Symposium on Eye Tracking Research and Applications, ETRA*, pages 307–310. ACM, 2014.

[57] Michael Burch, Hansjörg Schmauder, and Daniel Weiskopf. Indented pixel tree browser for exploring huge hierarchies. In *Proceedings of the 7th International Symposium on Advances in Visual Computing, ISVC,*

volume 6938 of *Lecture Notes in Computer Science*, pages 301–312. Springer, 2011.

[58] Michael Burch, Julian Strotzer, and Daniel Weiskopf. Visual analysis of source code similarities. In Ebad Banissi et al., editor, *Proceedings of the 19th International Conference on Information Visualisation, IV*, pages 21–27. IEEE Computer Society, 2015.

[59] Michael Burch, Huub van de Wetering, Günter Wallner, Freek Rooks, and Olof Morra. Exploring the dynamics of graph algorithms. *Journal of Visualization*, 2022.

[60] Michael Burch, Corinna Vehlow, Natalia Konevtsova, and Daniel Weiskopf. Evaluating partially drawn links for directed graph edges. In Marc J. van Kreveld and Bettina Speckmann, editors, *Proceedings of the 19th International Symposium on Graph Drawing, GD*, volume 7034 of *Lecture Notes in Computer Science*, pages 226–237. Springer, 2011.

[61] Michael Burch, Adrian Vramulet, Alex Thieme, Alina Vorobiova, Denis Shehu, Mara Miulescu, Mehrdad Farsadyar, and Tar van Krieken. Vizwick: a multiperspective view of hierarchical data. In Michael Burch, Michel A. Westenberg, Quang Vinh Nguyen, and Ying Zhao, editors, *Proceedings of the 13th International Symposium on Visual Information Communication and Interaction, VINCI*, pages 23:1–23:5. ACM, 2020.

[62] Michael Burch, Günter Wallner, Huub van de Wetering, Freek Rooks, and Olof Morra. Visual analysis of graph algorithm dynamics. In Karsten Klein, Michael Burch, Daniel Limberger, and Matthias Trapp, editors, *Proceedings of the 14th International Symposium on Visual Information Communication and Interaction, VINCI*, pages 16:1–16:5. ACM, 2021.

[63] Michael Burch, Günter Wallner, Huub van de Wetering, Shahrukh Tufail, Linda Zandt-Sloot, Stasius Gladkis, Minji Hong, and Carlo Lepelaars. Famsearch: Visual analysis of genealogical data. In George Bebis, Vassilis Athitsos, Tong Yan, Manfred Lau, Frederick Li, Conglei Shi, Xiaoru Yuan, Christos Mousas, and Gerd Bruder, editors, *Proceedings of 16th International Symposium on Advances in Visual Computing, ISVC*, volume 13018 of *Lecture Notes in Computer Science*, pages 374–385. Springer, 2021.

[64] Michael Burch and Daniel Weiskopf. A flip-book of edge-splatted small multiples for visualizing dynamic graphs. In Tomasz Bednarz,

Weidong Huang, Quang Vinh Nguyen, and Yingcai Wu, editors, *Proceedings of the 7th International Symposium on Visual Information Communication and Interaction, VINCI*, page 29.

[65] Michael Burch and Daniel Weiskopf. Visualizing dynamic quantitative data in hierarchies - timeedgetrees: Attaching dynamic weights to tree edges. In Gabriela Csurka, Martin Kraus, and José Braz, editors, *Proceedings of the International Conference on Imaging Theory and Applications and International Conference on Information Visualization Theory and Applications*, pages 177–186. SciTePress, 2011.

[66] Wolfram Büttner and Helmut Simonis. Embedding boolean expressions into logic programming. *Journal of Symbolic Computation*, 4(2):191–205, 1987.

[67] Bram C. M. Cappers, Paulus N. Meessen, Sandro Etalle, and Jarke J. van Wijk. Eventpad: Rapid malware analysis and reverse engineering using visual analytics. In Diane Staheli, Celeste Lyn Paul, Jörn Kohlhammer, Daniel M. Best, Stoney Trent, Nicolas Prigent, Robert Gove, and Graig Sauer, editors, *Proceedings of IEEE Symposium on Visualization for Cyber Security, VizSec*, pages 1–8. IEEE, 2018.

[68] Mónica A. Carreño-León, Jesús Andrés Sandoval-Bringas, Teresita de Jesús Álvarez Robles, Rafael Cosio-Castro, Italia Estrada Cota, and Alejandro Leyva Carrillo. Designing a tangible user interface for braille teaching. In Constantine Stephanidis, Margherita Antona, Qin Gao, and Jia Zhou, editors, *Proceedings of the 22nd HCI International Conference - Late Breaking Papers: Universal Access and Inclusive Design*, volume 12426 of *Lecture Notes in Computer Science*, pages 197–207. Springer, 2020.

[69] Marco A. Casanova. A theory of data dependencies over relational expressions. *International Journal of Parallel Programming*, 12(3):151–191, 1983.

[70] Carl Chapman and Kathryn T. Stolee. Exploring regular expression usage and context in python. In Andreas Zeller and Abhik Roychoudhury, editors, *Proceedings of the 25th International Symposium on Software Testing and Analysis, ISSTA*, pages 282–293. ACM, 2016.

[71] Colombe Chappey, A. Danckaert, Philippe Dessen, and Serge A. Hazout. MASH: an interactive program for multiple alignment and consensus sequence construction for biological sequences. *Computer Applications in the Biosciences*, 7(2):195–202, 1991.

[72] Herman Chernoff. Chernoff faces. In Miodrag Lovric, editor, *International Encyclopedia of Statistical Science*, pages 243–244. Springer, 2011.

[73] William S. Cleveland and Robert McGill. An experiment in graphical perception. *International Journal of Man-Machine Studies*, 25(5):491–501, 1986.

[74] Johanne Cohen, Fedor V. Fomin, Pinar Heggernes, Dieter Kratsch, and Gregory Kucherov. Optimal linear arrangement of interval graphs. In Rastislav Kralovic and Pawel Urzyczyn, editors, *Proceedings of the 31st International Symposium on Mathematical Foundations of Computer Science, MFCS*, volume 4162 of *Lecture Notes in Computer Science*, pages 267–279. Springer, 2006.

[75] Alberto Corvò, Marc A. van Driel, and Michel A. Westenberg. Pathova: A visual analytics tool for pathology diagnosis and reporting. In *Proceedings of IEEE Workshop on Visual Analytics in Healthcare, VAHC*, pages 77–83. IEEE, 2017.

[76] Alberto Corvò, Michel A. Westenberg, Reinhold Wimberger-Friedl, Stephan Fromme, Michel M. R. Peeters, Marc A. van Driel, and Jarke J. van Wijk. Visual analytics in digital pathology: Challenges and opportunities. In Barbora Kozlíková and Renata Georgia Raidou, editors, *Proceedings of the Eurographics Workshop on Visual Computing for Biology and Medicine, VCBM*, pages 129–143. Eurographics Association, 2019.

[77] Adrien Coyette, Suzanne Kieffer, and Jean Vanderdonckt. Multi-fidelity prototyping of user interfaces. In Maria Cecília Calani Baranauskas, Philippe A. Palanque, Julio Abascal, and Simone Diniz Junqueira Barbosa, editors, *Proceedings of the International Conference on Human-Computer Interaction, INTERACT*, volume 4662 of *Lecture Notes in Computer Science*, pages 150–164. Springer, 2007.

[78] Qingguang Cui, Matthew O. Ward, and Elke A. Rundensteiner. Enhancing scatterplot matrices for data with ordering or spatial attributes. In Robert F. Erbacher, Jonathan C. Roberts, Matti T. Gröhn, and Katy Börner, editors, *Proceedings of the Conference on Visualization and Data Analysis, VDA*, volume 6060 of *SPIE Proceedings*, page 60600R. SPIE, 2006.

[79] Andrea Cuttone, Sune Lehmann, and Jakob Eg Larsen. Geoplotlib: a python toolbox for visualizing geographical data. *CoRR*, abs/1608.01933, 2016.

[80] Sarah D'Angelo and Bertrand Schneider. Shared gaze visualizations in collaborative interactions: Past, present and future. *Interacting with Computers*, 33(2):115–133, 2021.

[81] Patrik Danielsson, Tom Postema, and Hussan Munir. Heroku-based innovative platform for web-based deployment in product development at axis. *IEEE Access*, 9:10805–10819, 2021.

[82] Stephan Diehl. *Software Visualization - Visualizing the Structure, Behaviour, and Evolution of Software*. Springer, 2007.

[83] Stephan Diehl, Fabian Beck, and Michael Burch. Uncovering strengths and weaknesses of radial visualizations—an empirical approach. *IEEE Transactions on Visualization and Computer Graphics*, 16(6):935–942, 2010.

[84] Stephan Diehl and Carsten Görg. Graphs, they are changing. In Stephen G. Kobourov and Michael T. Goodrich, editors, *Proceedings of the 10th International Symposium on Graph Drawing, GD*, volume 2528 of *Lecture Notes in Computer Science*, pages 23–30. Springer, 2002.

[85] Thomas Ditzinger. Optical illusions: Examples for nonlinear dynamics in perception. In Raoul Huys and Viktor K. Jirsa, editors, *Nonlinear Dynamics in Human Behavior*, volume 328 of *Studies in Computational Intelligence*, pages 179–191. 2011.

[86] Andrew T. Duchowski. *Eye Tracking Methodology - Theory and Practice, Third Edition*. Springer, 2017.

[87] Andrew T. Duchowski, Eric Medlin, Nathan Cournia, Anand K. Gramopadhye, Brian J. Melloy, and Santosh Nair. 3d eye movement analysis for VR visual inspection training. In Andrew T. Duchowski, Roel Vertegaal, and John W. Senders, editors, *Proceedings of the Eye Tracking Research & Application Symposium, ETRA*, pages 103–110. ACM, 2002.

[88] Alireza Ebrahimi. VPCL: A visual language for teaching and learning programming. (A picture is worth a thousand words). *Journal of Visual Languages and Computing*, 3(3):299–317, 1992.

[89] Alistair D. N. Edwards. The design of auditory interfaces for visually disabled users. In J. J. O'Hare, editor, *Proceedings of the SIGCHI Conference on Human Factors in Computing Systems, CHI*, pages 83–88. ACM, 1988.

[90] Raku Egawa and Takashi Ijiri. Multi-window web browser with history tree visualization for virtual reality environment. In Jeffrey Nichols, Ranjitha Kumar, and Michael Nebeling, editors, *Proceedings of the*

Adjunct Publication of the 34th Annual ACM Symposium on User Interface Software and Technology, Virtual Event, UIST, pages 32–34. ACM, 2021.

[91] Stephen G. Eick, Joseph L. Steffen, and Eric E. Sumner Jr. Seesoft-a tool for visualizing line oriented software statistics. *IEEE Transactions on Software Engineering*, 18(11):957–968, 1992.

[92] Albert Einstein. *Die Grundlage der allgemeinen Relativitätstheorie. In: Das Relativitätsprinzip. Fortschritte der Mathematischen Wissenschaften in Monographien*. Vieweg+Teubner Verlag, Wiesbaden, 1923.

[93] Geoffrey P. Ellis and Alan J. Dix. An explorative analysis of user evaluation studies in information visualisation. In Enrico Bertini, Catherine Plaisant, and Giuseppe Santucci, editors, *Proceedings of the AVI Workshop on BEyond time and errors: novel evaluation methods for information visualization, BELIV*, pages 1–7. ACM Press, 2006.

[94] Mateus Espadoto, Rafael Messias Martins, Andreas Kerren, Nina S. T. Hirata, and Alexandru C. Telea. Toward a quantitative survey of dimension reduction techniques. *IEEE Transactions on Visualization and Computer Graphics*, 27(3):2153–2173, 2021.

[95] Jean-Daniel Fekete, Jarke J. van Wijk, John T. Stasko, and Chris North. The value of information visualization. In Andreas Kerren, John T. Stasko, Jean-Daniel Fekete, and Chris North, editors, *Information Visualization - Human-Centered Issues and Perspectives*, volume 4950 of *Lecture Notes in Computer Science*, pages 1–18. Springer, 2008.

[96] Amanda Coelho Figliolia, Frode Eika Sandnes, and Fausto Orsi Medola. Experiences using three app prototyping tools with different levels of fidelity from a product design student's perspective. In Tien-Chi Huang, Ting-Ting Wu, João Barroso, Frode Eika Sandnes, Paulo Martins, and Yueh-Min Huang, editors, *Proceedings of the 3rd International Conference on Innovative Technologies and Learning, ICITL*, volume 12555 of *Lecture Notes in Computer Science*, pages 557–566. Springer, 2020.

[97] Charles N. Fischer. On parsing and compiling arithmetic expressions on vector computers. *ACM Transactions on Programming Languages and Systems*, 2(2):203–224, 1980.

[98] Johann Christoph Freytag, Raghu Ramakrishnan, and Rakesh Agrawal. Data mining: The next generation. *it - Information Technology*, 47(5):308–312, 2005.

[99] Johannes Fuchs, Dominik Jäckle, Niklas Weiler, and Tobias Schreck. Leaf glyph - visualizing multi-dimensional data with environmental cues. In José Braz, Andreas Kerren, and Lars Linsen, editors, *Proceedings of the 6th International Conference on Information Visualization Theory and Applications, IVAPP*, pages 195–206. SciTePress, 2015.

[100] Katarína Furmanová, Samuel Gratzl, Holger Stitz, Thomas Zichner, Miroslava Jaresová, Alexander Lex, and Marc Streit. Taggle: Combining overview and details in tabular data visualizations. *Information Visualization*, 19(2), 2020.

[101] Daniel Fürstenau, Flavio Morelli, Kristina Meindl, Matthias Schulte-Althoff, and Jochen Rabe. A social citizen dashboard for participatory urban planning in berlin: Prototype and evaluation. In *Proceedings of the 54th Hawaii International Conference on System Sciences, HICSS*, pages 1–10. ScholarSpace, 2021.

[102] Michael R. Garey and David S. Johnson. *Computers and Intractability: A Guide to the Theory of NP-Completeness*. W. H. Freeman, 1979.

[103] Fengpei Ge and Yonghong Yan. Deep neural network based wake-up-word speech recognition with two-stage detection. In *Proceedings of the IEEE International Conference on Acoustics, Speech and Signal Processing, ICASSP*, pages 2761–2765. IEEE, 2017.

[104] Narain H. Gehani. *Data Types for Very High Level Programming Languages*. PhD thesis, Cornell University, USA, 1975.

[105] Helene Gelderblom and Leanne Menge. The invisible gorilla revisited: using eye tracking to investigate inattentional blindness in interface design. In Tiziana Catarci, Kent L. Norman, and Massimo Mecella, editors, *Proceedings of the International Conference on Advanced Visual Interfaces, AVI*, pages 39:1–39:9. ACM, 2018.

[106] Mohammad Ghoniem, Jean-Daniel Fekete, and Philippe Castagliola. On the readability of graphs using node-link and matrix-based representations: a controlled experiment and statistical analysis. *Information Visualization*, 4(2):114–135, 2005.

[107] Tiago Gonçalves, Ana Paula Afonso, and Bruno Martins. Visualization techniques of trajectory data: Challenges and limitations. In Stephan Mäs, Lars Bernard, and Hardy Pundt, editors, *Proceedings of the 2nd AGILE PhD School*, volume 1136 of *CEUR Workshop Proceedings*. CEUR-WS.org, 2013.

[108] Saul Gorn. Code extension in ASCII. *Communications of the ACM*, 9(10):758–762, 1966.

[109] Lars Grammel. *User interfaces supporting information visualization novices in visualization construction*. PhD thesis, University of Victoria, Canada, 2012.

[110] Daniel Graziotin, Xiaofeng Wang, and Pekka Abrahamsson. Software developers, moods, emotions, and performance. *IEEE Software*, 31(4):24–27, 2014.

[111] Martin Greilich, Michael Burch, and Stephan Diehl. Visualizing the evolution of compound digraphs with timearctrees. *Computer Graphics Forum*, 28(3):975–982, 2009.

[112] David Gries and Gary Levin. Computing fibonacci numbers (and similarly defined functions) in log time. *Information Processing Letters*, 11(2):68–69, 1980.

[113] Irène Guessarian and José Meseguer. On the axiomatization of "if-then-else". *SIAM Journal on Computing*, 16(2):332–357, 1987.

[114] Jens Gulden. Recommendations for data visualizations based on gestalt patterns. In Gang Li and Yale Yu, editors, *Proceedings of the 4th International Conference on Enterprise Systems, ES*, pages 168–177. IEEE Computer Society, 2016.

[115] Christopher G. Healey and James T. Enns. Attention and visual memory in visualization and computer graphics. *IEEE Transactions on Visualization and Computer Graphics*, 18(7):1170–1188, 2012.

[116] Julian Heinrich. *Visualization techniques for parallel coordinates*. PhD thesis, University of Stuttgart, 2013.

[117] Julian Heinrich and Daniel Weiskopf. State of the art of parallel coordinates. In Mateu Sbert and László Szirmay-Kalos, editors, *Proceedings of 34th Annual Conference of the European Association for Computer Graphics, Eurographics - State of the Art Reports*, pages 95–116. Eurographics Association, 2013.

[118] Nathalie Henry and Jean-Daniel Fekete. Matlink: Enhanced matrix visualization for analyzing social networks. In Maria Cecília Calani Baranauskas, Philippe A. Palanque, Julio Abascal, and Simone Diniz Junqueira Barbosa, editors, *Proceedings of the International Conference on Human-Computer Interaction - INTERACT*, volume 4663 of *Lecture Notes in Computer Science*, pages 288–302. Springer, 2007.

[119] Nathalie Henry, Jean-Daniel Fekete, and Michael J. McGuffin. Nodetrix: a hybrid visualization of social networks. *IEEE Transactions on Visualization and Computer Graphics*, 13(6):1302–1309, 2007.

[120] Gregor Herda and Robert McNabb. Python for smarter cities: Comparison of python libraries for static and interactive visualisations of large vector data. *CoRR*, abs/2202.13105, 2022.

[121] Marcel Hlawatsch, Michael Burch, and Daniel Weiskopf. Visual adjacency lists for dynamic graphs. *IEEE Transactions on Visualization and Computer Graphics*, 20(11):1590–1603, 2014.

[122] Heike Hofmann and Marie Vendettuoli. Common angle plots as perception-true visualizations of categorical associations. *IEEE Transactions on Visualization and Computer Graphics*, 19(12):2297–2305, 2013.

[123] Kenneth Holmqvist. *Eye tracking: a comprehensive guide to methods and measures*. Oxford University Press, 2011.

[124] Danny Holten. Hierarchical edge bundles: Visualization of adjacency relations in hierarchical data. *IEEE Transactions on Visualization and Computer Graphics*, 12(5):741–748, 2006.

[125] Danny Holten, Petra Isenberg, Jarke J. van Wijk, and Jean-Daniel Fekete. An extended evaluation of the readability of tapered, animated, and textured directed-edge representations in node-link graphs. In Giuseppe Di Battista, Jean-Daniel Fekete, and Huamin Qu, editors, *Proceedings of the IEEE Pacific Visualization Symposium, PacificVis*, pages 195–202. IEEE Computer Society, 2011.

[126] Danny Holten and Jarke J. van Wijk. Force-directed edge bundling for graph visualization. *Computer Graphics Forum*, 28(3):983–990, 2009.

[127] Chen Hong. Design of human-computer interaction interface considering user friendliness. *International Journal of Reasoning-based Intelligent Systems*, 9(3/4):162–169, 2017.

[128] Tom Horak, Philip Berger, Heidrun Schumann, Raimund Dachselt, and Christian Tominski. Responsive matrix cells: A focus+context approach for exploring and editing multivariate graphs. *IEEE Transactions on Visualization and Computer Graphics*, 27(2):1644–1654, 2021.

[129] Derek Hwang, Vardhan Agarwal, Yuzi Lyu, Divyam Rana, Satya Ganesh Susarla, and Adalbert Gerald Soosai Raj. A qualitative analysis of lecture videos and student feedback on static code examples and live coding: A case study. In Claudia Szabo and Judy Sheard, editors, *Proceedings of the 23rd Australasian Computing Education Conference, ACE*, pages 147–157. ACM, 2021.

[130] Alfred Inselberg and Bernard Dimsdale. Parallel coordinates: A tool for visualizing multi-dimensional geometry. In Arie E. Kaufman,

editor, *Proceedings of 1st IEEE Visualization Conference, IEEE Vis,* pages 361–378. IEEE Computer Society Press, 1990.

[131] Atiqul Islam, Jinshuai Ma, Tom Gedeon, Md. Zakir Hossain, and Ying-Hsang Liu. Measuring user responses to driving simulators: A galvanic skin response based study. In *Proceedings of the IEEE International Conference on Artificial Intelligence and Virtual Reality, AIVR,* pages 33–40. IEEE, 2019.

[132] Wolfgang Jeltsch. *Strongly typed and efficient functional reactive programming.* PhD thesis, Brandenburg University of Technology, 2011.

[133] Markus John, Eduard Marbach, Steffen Lohmann, Florian Heimerl, and Thomas Ertl. Multicloud: Interactive word cloud visualization for the analysis of multiple texts. In Christopher Batty and Derek Reilly, editors, *Proceedings of the 44th Graphics Interface Conference,* pages 34–41. ACM, 2018.

[134] Toon Jouck and Benoît Depaire. Ptandloggenerator: A generator for artificial event data. In Leonardo Azevedo and Cristina Cabanillas, editors, *Proceedings of the BPM Demo Track Co-located with the 14th International Conference on Business Process Management BPM,* volume 1789 of *CEUR Workshop Proceedings,* pages 23–27. CEUR-WS.org, 2016.

[135] Byeongdo Kang. An integrated software development environment for web applications. In Walter Dosch, Roger Y. Lee, and Chisu Wu, editors, *Proceedings of the 2nd International Conference on Software Engineering Research, Management and Applications, SERA,* volume 3647 of *Lecture Notes in Computer Science,* pages 138–155. Springer, 2004.

[136] Ya-Ling Kao, Yu-Kuang Chen, and Jai-Tsung Hong. The efficacy of heart spectrum blood pressure monitor: A study of bus drivers. In *IEEE International Conference on Consumer Electronics-Taiwan, ICCE-TW,* pages 1–2. IEEE, 2021.

[137] Mohammed Kayed and Ahmed A. Elngar. Nestmsa: a new multiple sequence alignment algorithm. *The Journal of Supercomputing,* 76(11):9168–9188, 2020.

[138] Mandy Keck and Lars Engeln. Sparkle glyphs: A glyph design for the analysis of temporal multivariate audio features. In Paolo Bottoni and Emanuele Panizzi, editors, *Proceedings of the International Conference on Advanced Visual Interfaces, AVI,* pages 66:1–66:3. ACM, 2022.

[139] Daniel A. Keim. Solving problems with visual analytics: Challenges and applications. In *Proceedings of Machine Learning and Knowledge Discovery in Databases - European Conference*, pages 5–6, 2012.

[140] Daniel A. Keim. Solving problems with visual analytics: The role of visualization and analytics in exploring big data. In Volker Markl, Gunter Saake, Kai-Uwe Sattler, Gregor Hackenbroich, Bernhard Mitschang, Theo Härder, and Veit Köppen, editors, *Datenbanksysteme für Business, Technologie und Web (BTW), 15. Fachtagung des GI-Fachbereichs "Datenbanken und Informationssysteme" (DBIS), 11.-15.3.2013 in Magdeburg, Germany. Proceedings*, volume P-214 of *LNI*, pages 17–18. GI, 2013.

[141] Daniel A. Keim, Gennady L. Andrienko, Jean-Daniel Fekete, Carsten Görg, Jörn Kohlhammer, and Guy Melançon. Visual analytics: Definition, process, and challenges. In Andreas Kerren, John T. Stasko, Jean-Daniel Fekete, and Chris North, editors, *Information Visualization - Human-Centered Issues and Perspectives*, volume 4950 of *Lecture Notes in Computer Science*, pages 154–175. Springer, 2008.

[142] Daniel A. Keim, Peter Bak, and Matthias Schäfer. Dense pixel displays. In Ling Liu and M. Tamer Özsu, editors, *Encyclopedia of Database Systems, Second Edition*. Springer, 2018.

[143] Daniel A. Keim, Florian Mansmann, Jörn Schneidewind, Jim Thomas, and Hartmut Ziegler. Visual analytics: Scope and challenges. In Simeon J. Simoff, Michael H. Böhlen, and Arturas Mazeika, editors, *Visual Data Mining - Theory, Techniques and Tools for Visual Analytics*, volume 4404 of *Lecture Notes in Computer Science*, pages 76–90. Springer, 2008.

[144] Daniel A. Keim, Florian Mansmann, Jörn Schneidewind, and Hartmut Ziegler. Challenges in visual data analysis. In *Proceedings of 10th International Conference on Information Visualisation, IV*, pages 9–16. IEEE Computer Society, 2006.

[145] Saiful Khan, Phong Hai Nguyen, Alfie Abdul-Rahman, Benjamin Bach, Min Chen, Euan Freeman, and Cagatay Turkay. Propagating visual designs to numerous plots and dashboards. *IEEE Transactions on Visualization and Computer Graphics*, 28(1):86–95, 2022.

[146] Karsten Klein, Sabrina Jaeger, Jörg Melzheimer, Bettina Wachter, Heribert Hofer, Artur Baltabayev, and Falk Schreiber. Visual analytics of sensor movement data for cheetah behaviour analysis. *Journal of Visualization*, 24(4):807–825, 2021.

[147] Kurt Koffka. *Principles of Gestalt Psychology*. New York: Harcourt, Brace, 1935.

[148] Jun Kogure, Noboru Kunihiro, and Hirosuke Yamamoto. On the hardness of subset sum problem from different intervals. *IEICE Transactions on Fundamentals of Electronics, Communications and Computer Science*, 95-A(5):903–908, 2012.

[149] Tobias Kohn. *Teaching Python Programming to Novices: Addressing Misconceptions and Creating a Development Environment*. PhD thesis, ETH Zurich, Zürich, Switzerland, 2017.

[150] Joseph Kotlarek, Oh-Hyun Kwon, Kwan-Liu Ma, Peter Eades, Andreas Kerren, Karsten Klein, and Falk Schreiber. A study of mental maps in immersive network visualization. In *Proceedings of the IEEE Pacific Visualization Symposium, PacificVis*, pages 1–10. IEEE, 2020.

[151] Kuno Kurzhals, Michael Burch, Tanja Blascheck, Gennady Andrienko, Natalia Andrienko, and Daniel Weiskopf. A task-based view on the visual analysis of eye-tracking data. In Michael Burch, Lewis Chuang, Brian Fisher, Albrecht Schmidt, and Daniel Weiskopf, editors, *Eye Tracking and Visualization*, pages 3–22. Springer International Publishing, 2017.

[152] Kuno Kurzhals, Brian D. Fisher, Michael Burch, and Daniel Weiskopf. Evaluating visual analytics with eye tracking. In Heidi Lam, Petra Isenberg, Tobias Isenberg, and Michael Sedlmair, editors, *Proceedings of the Fifth Workshop on Beyond Time and Errors: Novel Evaluation Methods for Visualization, BELIV*, pages 61–69. ACM, 2014.

[153] Kuno Kurzhals, Brian D. Fisher, Michael Burch, and Daniel Weiskopf. Eye tracking evaluation of visual analytics. *Information Visualization*, 15(4):340–358, 2016.

[154] Kuno Kurzhals, Florian Heimerl, and Daniel Weiskopf. ISeeCube: visual analysis of gaze data for video. In Pernilla Qvarfordt and Dan Witzner Hansen, editors, *Proceedings of Symposium on Eye Tracking Research and Applications, ETRA*, pages 43–50. ACM, 2014.

[155] Kuno Kurzhals, Marcel Hlawatsch, Florian Heimerl, Michael Burch, Thomas Ertl, and Daniel Weiskopf. Gaze stripes: Image-based visualization of eye tracking data. *IEEE Transactions on Visualization and Computer Graphics*, 22(1):1005–1014, 2016.

[156] Florian Lachner, Mai-Anh Nguyen, and Andreas Butz. Culturally sensitive user interface design: a case study with German and Vietnamese users. In Heike Winschiers-Theophilus, Izak van Zyl, Naska Goagoses, Dharm Singh Jat, Elefelious G. Belay, Rita Orji,

Anicia Peters, Med Salim Bouhlel, and Nobert Jere, editors, *Proceedings of the Second African Conference for Human Computer Interaction: Thriving Communities, AfriCHI*, pages 1:1–1:12. ACM, 2018.

[157] Fabrizio Lamberti, Federico Manuri, and Andrea Sanna. Multivariate visualization using scatterplots. In Newton Lee, editor, *Encyclopedia of Computer Graphics and Games*. Springer, 2019.

[158] Ricardo Langner, Ulrike Kister, and Raimund Dachselt. Multiple coordinated views at large displays for multiple users: Empirical findings on user behavior, movements, and distances. *IEEE Transactions on Visualization and Computer Graphics*, 25(1):608–618, 2019.

[159] Janusz W. Laski. On readability of programs with loops. *ACM SIGPLAN Notices*, 14(11):73–83, 1979.

[160] Daewon Lee. Nezzle: an interactive and programmable visualization of biological networks in python. *Bioinformatics*, 38(12):3310–3311, 2022.

[161] Meng-Tse Lee, Fong-Ci Lin, Szu-Ta Chen, Wan-Ting Hsu, Samuel Lin, Tzer-Shyong Chen, Feipei Lai, and Chien-Chang Lee. Web-based dashboard for the interactive visualization and analysis of national risk-standardized mortality rates of sepsis in the US. *Journal of Medical Systems*, 44(2):54, 2020.

[162] Grégoire Lefebvre, Emmanuelle Boyer, and Sophie Zijp-Rouzier. Coupling gestures with tactile feedback: a comparative user study. In Lone Malmborg and Thomas Pederson, editors, *Proceedings of the Nordic Conference on Human-Computer Interaction, NordiCHI*, pages 380–387. ACM, 2012.

[163] Wenjun Li, Yang Ding, Yongjie Yang, R. Simon Sherratt, Jong Hyuk Park, and Jin Wang. Parameterized algorithms of fundamental np-hard problems: a survey. *Human-centric Computing and Information Sciences*, 10:29, 2020.

[164] Xiao-Hui Li, Caleb Chen Cao, Yuhan Shi, Wei Bai, Han Gao, Luyu Qiu, Cong Wang, Yuanyuan Gao, Shenjia Zhang, Xun Xue, and Lei Chen. A survey of data-driven and knowledge-aware explainable AI. *IEEE Transactions on Knowledge and Data Engineering*, 34(1):29–49, 2022.

[165] Lars Lischke. *Interacting with large high-resolution display workplaces*. PhD thesis, University of Stuttgart, Germany, 2018.

[166] Lars Lischke, Sven Mayer, Andreas Preikschat, Markus Schweizer, Ba Vu, Pawel W. Wozniak, and Niels Henze. Understanding large display environments: Contextual inquiry in a control room. In Regan L. Mandryk, Mark Hancock, Mark Perry, and Anna L. Cox, editors, *Extended Abstracts of the 2018 CHI Conference on Human Factors in Computing Systems, CHI*. ACM, 2018.

[167] Jon Loelinger and Matthew MacCullogh. *Version Control with Git - Powerful Tools and Techniques for Collaborative Software Development: Covers GitHub, Second Edition*. O'Reilly, 2012.

[168] María T. López, Antonio Fernández-Caballero, Miguel Angel Fernández, and Ana E. Delgado García. Sensitivity from short-term memory vs. stability from long-term memory in visual attention method. In José Mira and José R. Álvarez, editors, *Proceedings of the Conference on Artificial Intelligence and Knowledge Engineering Applications: A Bioinspired Approach: First International Work-Conference on the Interplay Between Natural and Artificial Computation, IWINAC*, volume 3562 of *Lecture Notes in Computer Science*, pages 448–458. Springer, 2005.

[169] Steven J. Lynden and Waran Taveekarn. Semi-automated augmentation of pandas dataframes. In Ying Tan and Yuhui Shi, editors, *Proceedings of the 4th International Conference on Data Mining and Big Data, DMBD*, volume 1071 of *Communications in Computer and Information Science*, pages 70–79. Springer, 2019.

[170] Jock D. Mackinlay. Automating the design of graphical presentations of relational information. *ACM Transactions on Graphics, TOG*, 5(2):110–141, 1986.

[171] Soujanya Mantravadi, Andreas Dyrøy Jansson, and Charles Møller. User-friendly MES interfaces: Recommendations for an ai-based chatbot assistance in industry 4.0 shop floors. In Ngoc Thanh Nguyen, Kietikul Jearanaitanakij, Ali Selamat, Bogdan Trawinski, and Suphamit Chittayasothorn, editors, *Proceedings of the 12th Asian Conference on Intelligent Information and Database Systems - 12th Asian Conference, ACIIDS*, volume 12034 of *Lecture Notes in Computer Science*, pages 189–201. Springer, 2020.

[172] Greice C. Mariano, Veda Adnani, Iman Kewalramani, Bo Wang, Matthew J. Roorda, Jeremy Bowes, and Sara Diamond. Designing a dashboard visualization tool for urban planners to assess the completeness of streets. In Sakae Yamamoto and Hirohiko Mori, editors, *Proceedings of the 22nd International Conference on Human*

Interface and the Management of Information, HIMI, volume 12184 of *Lecture Notes in Computer Science*, pages 85–103. Springer, 2020.

[173] Kim Marriott, Falk Schreiber, Tim Dwyer, Karsten Klein, Nathalie Henry Riche, Takayuki Itoh, Wolfgang Stuerzlinger, and Bruce H. Thomas, editors. *Immersive Analytics*, volume 11190 of *Lecture Notes in Computer Science*. Springer, 2018.

[174] Curtis E. Martin, J. O. Keller, Steven K. Rogers, and Matthew Kabrisky. Color blindness and a color human visual system model. *IEEE Transactions on Systems, Man, and Cybernetics Part A*, 30(4):494–500, 2000.

[175] Rod McBeth. A generalization of ackermann's function. *Mathematical Logic Quarterly*, 26(32-33):509–516, 1980.

[176] Craig S. Miller, Amber Settle, and John Lalor. Learning object-oriented programming in python: Towards an inventory of difficulties and testing pitfalls. In Amber Settle, Terry Steinbach, and Deborah Boisvert, editors, *Proceedings of the 16th Annual Conference on Information Technology Education, SIGITE*, pages 59–64. ACM, 2015.

[177] Kenneth Moreland. A survey of visualization pipelines. *IEEE Transactions on Visualization and Computer Graphics*, 19(3):367–378, 2013.

[178] Tamara Munzner. *Process and Pitfalls in Writing Information Visualization Research Papers*, pages 134–153. Springer Berlin Heidelberg, Berlin, Heidelberg, 2008.

[179] Tamara Munzner. *Visualization Analysis and Design*. A.K. Peters visualization series. A K Peters, 2014.

[180] Kawa Nazemi and Jörn Kohlhammer. Visual variables in adaptive visualizations. In Shlomo Berkovsky, Eelco Herder, Pasquale Lops, and Olga C. Santos, editors, *Late-Breaking Results, Project Papers and Workshop Proceedings of the 21st Conference on User Modeling, Adaptation, and Personalization*, volume 997 of *CEUR Workshop Proceedings*. CEUR-WS.org, 2013.

[181] Lucy T. Nowell, Elizabeth G. Hetzler, and Ted Tanasse. Change blindness in information visualization: A case study. In Keith Andrews, Steven F. Roth, and Pak Chung Wong, editors, *Proceedings of IEEE Symposium on Information Visualization (INFOVIS)*, pages 15–22. IEEE Computer Society, 2001.

[182] Paul W. Oman, Curtis R. Cook, and Murthi Nanja. Effects of programming experience in debugging semantic errors. *Journal of Systems and Software*, 9(3):197–207, 1989.

[183] Fatih Baha Omeroglu and Yueqing Li. Effects of background music on visual short-term memory: A preliminary study. In Don Harris and Wen-Chin Li, editors, *Proceedings of the 19th International Conference on Engineering Psychology and Cognitive Ergonomics, EPCE*, volume 13307 of *Lecture Notes in Computer Science*, pages 85–96. Springer, 2022.

[184] Jorge Piazentin Ono, Juliana Freire, Cláudio T. Silva, João Comba, and Kelly P. Gaither. Interactive data visualization in jupyter notebooks. *Computing in Science and Engineering*, 23(2):99–106, 2021.

[185] Elias Pampalk, Andreas Rauber, and Dieter Merkl. Using smoothed data histograms for cluster visualization in self-organizing maps. In José R. Dorronsoro, editor, *Proceedings of International Conference on Artificial Neural Networks, ICANN*, volume 2415 of *Lecture Notes in Computer Science*, pages 871–876. Springer, 2002.

[186] Deok Gun Park, Mohamed Suhail, Minsheng Zheng, Cody Dunne, Eric D. Ragan, and Niklas Elmqvist. Storyfacets: A design study on storytelling with visualizations for collaborative data analysis. *Information Visualization*, 21(1):3–16, 2022.

[187] Hima Patel, Shanmukha C. Guttula, Ruhi Sharma Mittal, Naresh Manwani, Laure Berti-Équille, and Abhijit Manatkar. Advances in exploratory data analysis, visualisation and quality for data centric AI systems. In Aidong Zhang and Huzefa Rangwala, editors, *Proceedings of the 28th ACM SIGKDD Conference on Knowledge Discovery and Data Mining*, pages 4814–4815. ACM, 2022.

[188] Lawrence C. Paulson. Ackermann's function is not primitive recursive. *Archive of Formal Proofs*, 2022, 2022.

[189] Catherine Plaisant and Ben Shneiderman. Scheduling home control devices: Design issues and usability evaluation of four touchscreen interfaces. *International Journal of Man-Machine Studies*, 36(3):375–393, 1992.

[190] Helen C. Purchase. Effective information visualisation: a study of graph drawing aesthetics and algorithms. *Interacting with Computers*, 13(2):147–162, 2000.

[191] Helen C. Purchase. Metrics for graph drawing aesthetics. *Journal of Visual Languages and Computing*, 13(5):501–516, 2002.

[192] Helen C. Purchase, Robert F. Cohen, and Murray I. James. Validating graph drawing aesthetics. In *Proceedings of the Symposium on Graph Drawing*, pages 435–446, 1995.

[193] Aung Pyae and Paul Scifleet. Investigating the role of user's english language proficiency in using a voice user interface: A case of google home smart speaker. In Regan L. Mandryk, Stephen A. Brewster, Mark Hancock, Geraldine Fitzpatrick, Anna L. Cox, Vassilis Kostakos, and Mark Perry, editors, *Proceedings of the extended abstracts of the CHI Conference on Human Factors in Computing Systems*. ACM, 2019.

[194] Aaron J. Quigley and Peter Eades. FADE: graph drawing, clustering, and visual abstraction. In Joe Marks, editor, *Proceedings of 8th International Symposium on Graph Drawing, GD*, volume 1984 of *Lecture Notes in Computer Science*, pages 197–210. Springer, 2000.

[195] Ramana Rao and Stuart K. Card. The table lens: merging graphical and symbolic representations in an interactive focus+context visualization for tabular information. In Catherine Plaisant, editor, *Proceedings of the Conference on Human Factors in Computing Systems, CHI*, page 222. ACM, 1994.

[196] Edward M. Reingold and John S. Tilford. Tidier drawings of trees. *IEEE Transactions on Software Engineering*, 7(2):223–228, 1981.

[197] Donghao Ren, Xin Zhang, Zhenhuang Wang, Jing Li, and Xiaoru Yuan. Weiboevents: A crowd sourcing weibo visual analytic system. In Issei Fujishiro, Ulrik Brandes, Hans Hagen, and Shigeo Takahashi, editors, *Proceedings of the IEEE Pacific Visualization Symposium, PacificVis*, pages 330–334. IEEE Computer Society, 2014.

[198] Long Ren and Yun Chen. Influence of color perception on consumer behavior. In Fiona Fui-Hoon Nah and Bo Sophia Xiao, editors, *Proceedings of 5th International Conference on HCI in Business, Government, and Organizations, HCIBGO*, volume 10923 of *Lecture Notes in Computer Science*, pages 413–421. Springer, 2018.

[199] Theresa-Marie Rhyne. Color matters for digital media & visualization. In *SIGGRAPH: Special Interest Group on Computer Graphics and Interactive Techniques Conference, Courses, Virtual Event*, pages 12:1–12:92. ACM, 2021.

[200] Jonathan C. Roberts. Guest editor's introduction: special issue on coordinated and multiple views in exploratory visualization. *Information Visualization*, 2(4):199–200, 2003.

[201] Douglas Rolim, Jorge Silva, Thaís Batista, and Everton Cavalcante. Web-based development and visualization dashboards for smart city applications. In Mária Bieliková, Tommi Mikkonen, and Cesare Pautasso, editors, *Proceedings of tthe 20th International Conference on*

Web Engineering, ICWE, volume 12128 of *Lecture Notes in Computer Science*, pages 337–344. Springer, 2020.

[202] Ruth Rosenholtz, Yuanzhen Li, Jonathan Mansfield, and Zhenlan Jin. Feature congestion: a measure of display clutter. In Gerrit C. van der Veer and Carolyn Gale, editors, *Proceedings of the Conference on Human Factors in Computing Systems, CHI*, pages 761–770. ACM, 2005.

[203] Matt Rounds, Chris Lucas, and Frank Keller. Inattentional blindness in visual search. In Ashok K. Goel, Colleen M. Seifert, and Christian Freksa, editors, *Proceedings of the 41th Annual Meeting of the Cognitive Science Society, CogSci*, pages 2688–2694. cognitivesciencesociety.org, 2019.

[204] Stuart H. Rubin, Thouraya Bouabana-Tebibel, Yasmin Hoadjli, and Zahira Ghalem. Reusing the np-hard traveling-salesman problem to demonstrate that p~np (invited paper). In *Proceedings of the 17th IEEE International Conference on Information Reuse and Integration, IRI*, pages 574–581. IEEE Computer Society, 2016.

[205] Dominik Sacha. *Knowledge Generation in Visual Analytics: Integrating Human and Machine Intelligence for Exploration of Big Data*. PhD thesis, University of Konstanz, Germany, 2018.

[206] Seref Sagiroglu and Duygu Sinanc. Big data: A review. In Geoffrey Charles Fox and Waleed W. Smari, editors, *Proceedings of International Conference on Collaboration Technologies and Systems, CTS*, pages 42–47. IEEE, 2013.

[207] William B. Sanders. Learning OOP with weakly typed web programming languages: adding concrete strategies to a PHP strategy design pattern. In William R. Cook, Siobhán Clarke, and Martin C. Rinard, editors, *Proceedings of the Companion to the 25th Annual ACM SIGPLAN Conference on Object-Oriented Programming, Systems, Languages, and Applications, OOPSLA*, pages 189–192. ACM, 2010.

[208] Masataka Sassa and Ikuo Nakata. Time-optimal short-circuit evaluation of boolean expressions. *Information Processing Letters*, 29(1):43–51, 1988.

[209] Makoto Sato and Yasuharu Koike. Playing rubik's cube in mixed reality. In Ryohei Nakatsu and Jun'ichi Hoshino, editors, *Proceedings of First International Workshop on Entertainment Computing: Technologies and Applications, IFIP*, volume 240 of *IFIP Conference Proceedings*, pages 415–422. Kluwer, 2002.

[210] Hansjörg Schmauder, Michael Burch, Christoph Müller, and Daniel Weiskopf. Distributed visual analytics on large-scale high-resolution displays. In *Proceedings of the Symposium on Big Data Visual Analytics, BDVA*, pages 33–40. IEEE, 2015.

[211] Hans-Jörg Schulz. Treevis.net: A tree visualization reference. *IEEE Computer Graphics and Applications*, 31(6):11–15, 2011.

[212] Hans-Jörg Schulz, Steffen Hadlak, and Heidrun Schumann. The design space of implicit hierarchy visualization: A survey. *IEEE Transactions on Visualization and Computer Graphics*, 17(4):393–411, 2011.

[213] Raquel Sebastião, João Gama, and Teresa Mendonça. Comparing data distribution using fading histograms. In Torsten Schaub, Gerhard Friedrich, and Barry O'Sullivan, editors, *Proceedings of the 21st European Conference on Artificial Intelligence, ECAI and Including Prestigious Applications of Intelligent Systems, PAIS*, volume 263 of *Frontiers in Artificial Intelligence and Applications*, pages 1095–1096. IOS Press, 2014.

[214] Michael Sedlmair, Petra Isenberg, Dominikus Baur, and Andreas Butz. Information visualization evaluation in large companies: Challenges, experiences and recommendations. *Information Visualization*, 10(3):248–266, 2011.

[215] Ben Shneiderman. Tree visualization with tree-maps: 2-d space-filling approach. *ACM Transactions on Graphics*, 11(1):92–99, 1992.

[216] Ben Shneiderman. The eyes have it: A task by data type taxonomy for information visualizations. In *Proceedings of the IEEE Symposium on Visual Languages*, pages 336–343. IEEE Computer Society, 1996.

[217] Ben Shneiderman, Catherine Plaisant, Maxine Cohen, Steven Jacobs, and Niklas Elmqvist. *Designing the User Interface - Strategies for Effective Human-Computer Interaction, 6th Edition*. Pearson, 2016.

[218] Daniel J. Simons and Christopher F. Chabris. Gorillas in our midst: Sustained inattentional blindness for dynamic events. *Perception*, 28(9):1059–1074, 1999.

[219] Ashok Sivaji, Søren Nielsen, and Torkil Clemmensen. A textual feedback tool for empowering participants in usability and UX evaluations. *International Journal of Human-Computer Interaction*, 33(5):357–370, 2017.

[220] Samuel Thomas Smith, James Michael Hogan, Xin-Yi Chua, Margot Brereton, Daniel M. Johnson, and Markus Rittenbruch. Iterative design

and evaluation of regulatory network visualisation at scale. In *Proceedings of the 13th IEEE International Conference on e-Science*, pages 354–363. IEEE Computer Society, 2017.

[221] Laura South, David Saffo, Olga Vitek, Cody Dunne, and Michelle A. Borkin. Effective use of likert scales in visualization evaluations: A systematic review. *Computer Graphics Forum*, 41(3):43–55, 2022.

[222] Robert Spence. *Information Visualization: Design for Interaction.* Pearson/Prentice Hall, 2 edition, 2007.

[223] Leonhard F. Spiegelberg, Rahul Yesantharao, Malte Schwarzkopf, and Tim Kraska. Tuplex: Data science in python at native code speed. In Guoliang Li, Zhanhuai Li, Stratos Idreos, and Divesh Srivastava, editors, *Proceedings of the International Conference on Management of Data, Virtual Event, SIGMOD*, pages 1718–1731. ACM, 2021.

[224] John T. Stasko, Richard Catrambone, Mark Guzdial, and Kevin McDonald. An evaluation of space-filling information visualizations for depicting hierarchical structures. *International Journal of Human Computer Studies*, 53(5):663–694, 2000.

[225] Stuart G. Stubblebine. *Regular expression pocket reference - regular expressions for Perl, Ruby, PHP, Python, C, Java, and .NET (2. ed.).* O'Reilly, 2007.

[226] Yasuhiro Sugiyama. A highly extensible graphical user interface in a software development environment. In Michael J. Smith, Gavriel Salvendy, and Richard J. Koubek, editors, *Proceedings of the 7th International Conference on Human-Computer Interaction, (HCI International)*, pages 327–330. Elsevier, 1997.

[227] Matús Sulír and Jaroslav Porubän. Source code documentation generation using program execution. *Information*, 8(4):148, 2017.

[228] Erxin Sun, Zongjuan Chen, Sixing Li, and Xiaoxiao Li. Real-time data visualization of intelligent networked vehicles. In *Proceedings of the International Conference on Computing, Networks and Internet of Things*, pages 180–184. ACM, 2020.

[229] Anne Treisman. Preattentive processing in vision. *Computer Vision, Graphics, and Image Processing*, 31(2):156–177, 1985.

[230] Lesley Trenner. How to win friends and influence people: definitions of user-friendliness in interactive computer systems. *Journal of Information Science*, 13(2):99–107, 1987.

[231] Eduard Tudoreanu. Designing effective program visualization tools for reducing user's cognitive effort. In Stephan Diehl, John T. Stasko,

and Stephen N. Spencer, editors, *Proceedings of ACM Symposium on Software Visualization*, pages 105–114. ACM, 2003.

[232] Edward Rolf Tufte. *The visual display of quantitative information.* Graphics Press, 1992.

[233] Barbara Tversky, Julie Bauer Morrison, and Mireille Bétrancourt. Animation: can it facilitate? *International Journal of Human Computer Studies*, 57(4):247–262, 2002.

[234] Franck van Breugel. *Comparative metric semantics of programming languages - nondeterminism and recursion.* Progress in theoretical computer science. Birkhäuser, 1998.

[235] Laurens van der Maaten and Geoffrey Hinton. Visualizing high-dimensional data using t-SNE. *Journal of Machine Learning Research*, 9:2579–2605, 2008.

[236] Guido van Rossum. Scripting the web with python. *World Wide Web Journal*, 2:97–120, 1997.

[237] Jarke J. van Wijk. The value of visualization. In *Proceedings of 16th IEEE Visualization Conference, IEEE*, pages 79–86. IEEE Computer Society, 2005.

[238] Corinna Vehlow, Fabian Beck, and Daniel Weiskopf. Visualizing group structures in graphs: A survey. *Computer Graphics Forum*, 36(6):201–225, 2017.

[239] Boris M. Velichkovsky, Andreas Sprenger, and Pieter Unema. Towards gaze-mediated interaction: Collecting solutions of the "midas touch problem". In Steve Howard, Judy Hammond, and Gitte Lindgaard, editors, *Proceedings of the International Conference on Human-Computer Interaction, INTERACT*, volume 96, pages 509–516. Chapman & Hall, 1997.

[240] Spyros Vosinakis and George Anastassakis. Touch your own device! A covid-safe alternative to multi-touch interactions with public touchscreens. In *Proceedings of the 1st International Conference of the ACM Greek SIGCHI Chapter*, pages 14:1–14:6. ACM, 2021.

[241] Marion Walton, Vera Vukovic, and Gary Marsden. 'visual literacy' as challenge to the internationalisation of interfaces: a study of south african student web users. In Loren G. Terveen and Dennis R. Wixon, editors, *Proceedings of the extended abstracts of the Conference on Human Factors in Computing Systems, CHI*, pages 530–531. ACM, 2002.

[242] Yunzhe Wang, George Baciu, and Chenhui Li. Smooth animation of structure evolution in time-varying graphs with pattern matching. In

Koji Koyamada and Puripant Ruchikachorn, editors, *Proceedings of the Symposium on Visualization, SIGGRAPH ASIA*, pages 12:1–12:8. ACM, 2017.

[243] Matthew O. Ward. Linking and brushing. In Ling Liu and M. Tamer Özsu, editors, *Encyclopedia of Database Systems, Second Edition*. Springer, 2018.

[244] Colin Ware. Perception & data visualization: The foundations of experimental semiotics. In Wayne A. Davis, Kellogg S. Booth, and Alain Fournier, editors, *Proceedings of the Graphics Interface Conference*, pages 92–98. Canadian Human-Computer Communications Society, 1998.

[245] Colin Ware. *Information Visualization: Perception for Design*. Morgan Kaufmann, 2004.

[246] Colin Ware. *Visual Thinking: for Design*. Morgan Kaufmann Series in Interactive Technologies, Paperback, 2008.

[247] Ross T. Whitaker and Ingrid Hotz. Transformations, mappings, and data summaries. In Min Chen, Helwig Hauser, Penny Rheingans, and Gerik Scheuermann, editors, *Foundations of Data Visualization*, pages 121–157. Springer, 2020.

[248] Roland Wiese, Markus Eiglsperger, and Michael Kaufmann. yFiles: Visualization and automatic layout of graphs. In Petra Mutzel, Michael Jünger, and Sebastian Leipert, editors, *Proceedings of 9th International Symposium on Graph Drawing, GD*, volume 2265 of *Lecture Notes in Computer Science*, pages 453–454. Springer, 2001.

[249] Rand R. Wilcox. Robust multivariate regression when there is heteroscedasticity. *Communications in Statistics - Simulation and Computation*, 38(1):1–13, 2009.

[250] Christoph Wimmer, Alex Untertrifaller, and Thomas Grechenig. SketchingInterfaces: A tool for automatically generating high-fidelity user interface mockups from hand-drawn sketches. In Naseem Ahmadpour, Tuck Wah Leong, Bernd Ploderer, Callum Parker, Sarah Webber, Diego Muñoz, Lian Loke, and Martin Tomitsch, editors, *Proceedings of the 32nd Australian Conference on Human-Computer-Interaction, OzCHI*, pages 538–545. ACM, 2020.

[251] Pak Chung Wong, Han-Wei Shen, Christopher R. Johnson, Chaomei Chen, and Robert B. Ross. The top 10 challenges in extreme-scale visual analytics. *IEEE Computer Graphics and Applications*, 32(4):63–67, 2012.

[252] Pak Chung Wong and Jim Thomas. Visual analytics. *IEEE Computer Graphics and Applications*, 24(5):20–21, 2004.

[253] Liwei Wu, Fei Li, Youhua Wu, and Tao Zheng. GGF: A graph-based method for programming language syntax error correction. In *Proceedings of the 28th International Conference on Program Comprehension, ICPC*, pages 139–148. ACM, 2020.

[254] Yiqun Xie, Shashi Shekhar, and Yan Li. Statistically-robust clustering techniques for mapping spatial hotspots: A survey. *ACM Computing Surveys*, 55(2):36:1–36:38, 2023.

[255] Sophia Yang, Marc Skov Madsen, and James A. Bednar. Holoviz: Visualization and interactive dashboards in python. In Aidong Zhang and Huzefa Rangwala, editors, *Proceedings of the 28th ACM SIGKDD Conference on Knowledge Discovery and Data Mining, KDD*, pages 4846–4847. ACM, 2022.

[256] Alfred L. Yarbus. *Eye Movements and Vision*. Springer, 1967.

[257] Yucong Chris Ye, Franz Sauer, Kwan-Liu Ma, Aditya Konduri, and Jacqueline Chen. A user-centered design study in scientific visualization targeting domain experts. *IEEE Transactions on Visualization and Computer Graphics*, 26(6):2192–2203, 2020.

[258] Ji Soo Yi, Youn ah Kang, John T. Stasko, and Julie A. Jacko. Toward a deeper understanding of the role of interaction in information visualization. *IEEE Transaction on Visualization and Computer Graphics*, 13(6):1224–1231, 2007.

[259] Qi Zhang. Medical data and mathematically modeled implicit surface real-rime visualization in web browsers. *International Journal of Image and Graphics*, 22(4):2250027:1–2250027:29, 2022.

[260] Zuyao Zhang and Yuan Zhu. Research on users' and designers' product color perception. In Yongchuan Tang and Jonathan Lawry, editors, *Proceedings of the Second International Symposium on Computational Intelligence and Design, ISCID*, pages 264–267. IEEE Computer Society, 2009.

Index

About the Authors

Michael Burch studied computer science and mathematics at the Saarland University in Saarbrücken, Germany. He received his PhD from the University of Trier in 2010 in the fields of information visualization and visual analytics. After 8 years of having been a PostDoc in the Visualization Research Center (VISUS) in Stuttgart, he moved to the Eindhoven University of Technology (TU/e) as an assistant professor for visual analytics. From October 2020 he has been working as a lecturer in visualization at the University of Applied Sciences in Chur, Switzerland. Michael Burch is on many international program committees and has published more than 190 conference papers and journal articles in the field of visualization. His main interests are in information visualization, visual analytics, eye tracking, and data science.

Marco Schmid studied Natural Resource Science (with specialization in Renewable Resources and Sustainable Energy) at the School of Life Sciences and Facility Management (ZHAW) in Zurich, Switzerland. During his study he worked as a scientific research assistant at the Institute of Applied Simulation at ZHAW. Then he worked for 3 years in a start-up company focused on machine learning and predictive models before he moved to the University of Applied Sciences in Chur, Switzerland in 2019 where he works as a scientific researcher. His main fields of interest are data science and software development.